Living the High Life in Minsk

Living the High Life in Minsk

Russian Energy Rents, Domestic Populism and Belarus' Impending Crisis

Margarita M. Balmaceda

Budapest – New York

Published in 2014 by
Central European University Press
An imprint of the Central European University Limited Liability Company
Nádor utca 11, H-1051 Budapest, Hungary
Tel: +36-1-327-3138 or 327-3000
Fax: +36-1-327-3183
E-mail: ceupress@ceu.hu
Website: www.ceupress.com
224 West 57th Street, New York NY 10019, USA
Tel: +1-212-547-6932
Fax: +1-646-557-2416
E-mail: martin.greenwald@opensocietyfoundations.org

ISBN 978-615-5225-19-2 cloth
ISBN 978-963-386-703-7 paperback

Library of Congress Cataloging-in-Publication Data

Balmaceda, Margarita Mercedes, 1965-
Living the high life in Minsk : Russian energy rents, domestic populism and Belarus' impending crisis / Margarita M. Balmaceda.
pages ; cm
Includes bibliographical references and index.
ISBN 978-6155225192 (hardbound)
1. Belarus--Relations--Russia (Federation) 2. Russia (Federation)--Relations--Belarus. 3. Energy policy--Political aspects--Belarus. 4. Petroleum industry and trade--Political aspects--Belarus. 5. Petroleum industry and trade--Political aspects--Russia (Federation) 6. Belarus--Politics and government--1991- I. Title.

DK507.69.R8B35 2012
303.48'2478047--dc23

2012019690

Table of Contents

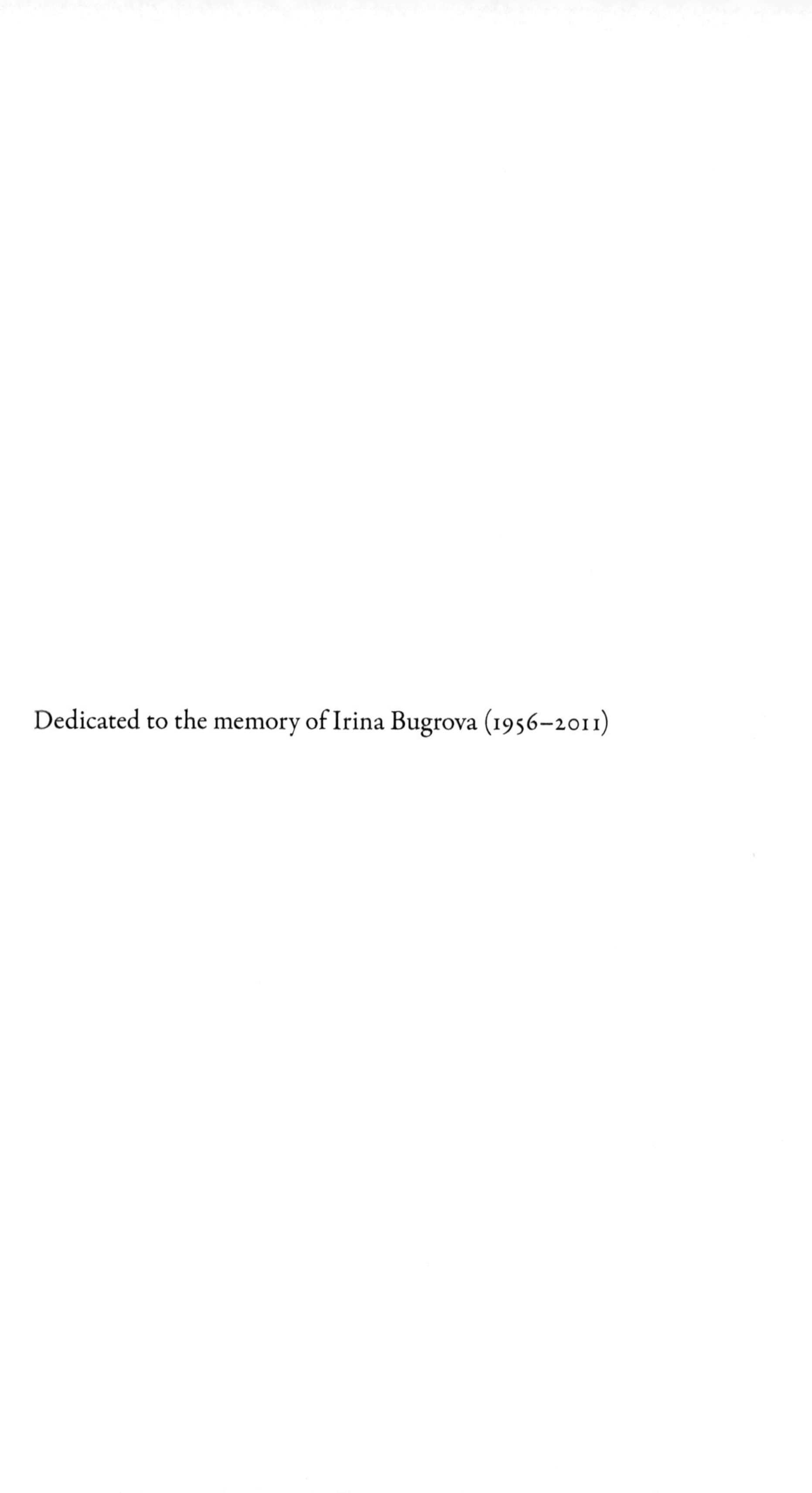

Dedicated to the memory of Irina Bugrova (1956–2011)

List of Tables, Graphs and Figures

Preface and Acknowledgements

Sometimes fate brings us unexpected and undeserved gifts that come to enrich our life path for many years to come. Such has been the case of Belarus for me. The long road from my first visit to the country as a Fulbright lecturer at the Belarusian State University in 1997 to the completion of this manuscript has been a challenging but, above all, an enormously enriching one. To try to make sense of the less transparent sector of the economy in the least open country in Europe, with what on some long work evenings seemed like the most contradictory statistics in the world, proved a truly trying challenge. If I was to any degree successful in this endeavor, it was thanks to the generosity and professionalism of many Belarusian colleagues, and to countless discussions in the course of nearly 20 visits to Belarus since 1997. I am privileged to have been able to go on this path, to have had the chance to accompany the last 16 years of Belarus' complex history, and in the process, to be able to count on the support of many institutions beyond Belarus as well, among others, the Fulbright Commission of the U.S. Department of Education, the Smith-Richardson Foundation, the German Belarusian Society, the Alexander von Humboldt Foundation, the Marie Curie Program of the European Commission, and Seton Hall University, Harvard University, and the University of Helsinki. The very beginning of this path, in 1996, was marked by two individuals who, through Belarus, have had a lasting impact on my life: my late colleague Hugh Hinton, who—always supportive of younger colleagues—insistently pointed to the Belarus vacancy announced at the Fulbright desk at the 1996 meeting of the AAASS in Boston, and Muriel Joffe, who was standing behind that desk and, as the main person responsible for Fulbright's Belarus program, made it possible for this dream to become a reality. The last revisions of the manuscript were completed in the reflective quietness of the Alfried Krupp Wissenschaftskolleg in Greifswald, Germany—

just at the end point of the new Nord Stream Gas Pipeline—where a Senior Fellowship gave me the tranquility to reflect on Belarus and its path.

Irina Tochitskaya, Alyaksandr Chubrik, Valeria Kostiugova, Elena Rakova and many other Belarusian colleagues provided important perspectives through their longstanding work on energy issues. That institutions such as the *Institut Privatizatsii i Menedzhmenta* and the Belarusian Institute of Strategic Studies (BISS) exist in Belarus is no less than a miracle, and one that has greatly added to my knowledge and insight. Vital Silitski's work on Belarusian social contracts and as scientific director of BISS remains essential for anyone seeking to understand Belarus seriously, and his untimely passing in June 2011 is a deep blow to us all. Elena Gapova of the European Humanities University and my colleagues at the Faculty of International Relations of the Belarusian State University helped me gain a deeper understanding of Belarus during my work there as a Fulbright Fellow in 1997 and 1999.

Special thanks to Alexei Pikulik of the European Humanities University in Vilnius, Elena Rakova of the European Commission Delegation in Minsk, and Leonid Zlotnikov of Invila Institute in Minsk for their thorough review of an earlier version of the whole manuscript. Each of them, from their own perspectives in political science, energy economics, and economic policy, respectively, contributed invaluable insights and helped catch serious and less-serious mistakes of fact and interpretation. Responsibility for any errors remains my own. Srinivas Ghandi generously agreed to read and comment on the whole manuscript through the eyes of a non-Eastern Europe, non-energy specialized political scientist.

I am especially indebted to Leonid Zlotnikov, whose own work on the Belarusian economy has not failed to inspire me since our first meeting in 1998. That I quickly grew to love Belarus—and, perhaps, slowly came to understand it—is due in no small measure to him, not only to memorable discussions around his dinner table over the years, but, in no less measure, to many hours spent poring over Excel tables at his computer. Through *Belorusyi Rynok* and through the radio waves, Tatsyana Manenok never ceased to fuel my interest, and greatly helped me gain a more nuanced understanding of Belarusian energy issues. From the pages of *Narodnaya Volia, Belorusskaya Delovaya Gazeta*, and *Ezhednevnik*, Sviatlana Kalinkina and Vadim Sekhovich provided invaluable insights. While I am indebted to these and many other Belarusian friends and colleagues for sharing their knowledge and research insights, I am first and foremost thankful for their unwavering optimism and life strength through thick and thin. Nobody embodied these qualities more sincerely than Irina Bugrova, political scientist, regional NGO organizer and dear friend, who passed away in December 2011. Her memory is very much alive through the inspiration of her optimism, intellectual honesty, high standards, and civic engagement.

Minsk's Internationale Bildungs- und Begegnungsstätte "Johannes Rau" (IBB) has provided an unfailingly warm welcome over the years and was the center of countless discussions reflected in this book. Its director from 2006 to 2011, Astrid Sahm, has inspired my work on Belarus since our first meeting in Minsk in 1997, through three summers of joint work at the University of Mannheim in Germany in 2001–2003, and countless visits to the IBB since then. Sabine Fischer, Head of the Eastern Europe and Eurasia Research Group at the Stiftung Wissenschaft und Politik in Berlin, provided invaluable insights on Belarus and countless other projects, and was always ready to share both her friendship and her expertise.

I am also indebted to my colleagues from the Belarus Department of the *Deutsche Welle*, especially to Vladimir Dorokhov. The Belarusian service of *Radio Svaboda* has been an invaluable research source for many years now, and the familiar voices of analysts Yurii Drakhokhrust and Valer Karbalevich over the radio waves and through *Belsat TV* made the Belarusian language a part of my daily life. Sadly, since December 19, 2010, this vocabulary has been augmented by words and phrases many of us hoped would never be needed in Belarus again: "*pjeratrus,*" "*aryshty i dopyty w KDB,*" "*1937 god*" ("home searches by the police," "arrests and interrogations by the KGB," and "year 1937").

Last but not least, this book would not have been possible without the continued work of colleagues in many countries who, despite tremendous odds, have kept Belarus present in Western discourse and academic debates: among others Alexandra Goujon, Grigory Ioffe, Elena Korosteleva, Robert Levgold, Rainer Lindner, David Marples, Astrid Sahm, Andrew Wilson, Curt Woolhiser, and Jan Zaprudnik. I am thankful to Linda Kunos and Virág Illés of the Central European University Press for their support of the project from the very beginning, and for their help with small and large technical and substantive issues.

In the United States, I remain indebted to my academic home, the School of Diplomacy and International Relations at Seton Hall University. Deans Amb. John Menzies and Andrea Bartoli, Associate Dean Courtney Smith, Chairs Assefaw Bariagaber and Benjamin Goldfrank, and School Secretary Susan Malcolm deserve special thanks for their encouragement and steadfast support of my work. At Harvard University, I thank the Harvard Ukrainian Research Institute (HURI) and the Davis Center for Russian and Eurasian Studies for many years of inspiring joint work and for their support in the organization of a major conference on Belarus in 1999, where many of the themes developed in this book started to take shape. Halyna Hryn and Marika Whaley of HURI, as well as Mary Ann Szporluk, a longstanding member of the broader HURI family, provided invaluable help during the final stages of the preparation of the manuscript. At the Davis Center, the Workshop on Post-Communist Politics and Economics, in which I have participated regularly since 2004, deserves my strongest recognition as a unique venue for in-depth academic discussion of ongoing work.

My family—starting with my parents Eudoro Balmaceda and Margarita Sastre de Balmaceda—and loved ones remain the basis without which this book would not have been possible. Our life conversation with economist and gender studies institution-builder Maren Jochimsen started almost at the same time as Belarus came into my life, and it was in many ways these conversations, and the desire to tell her about my experiences in Belarus, that helped shape—and, once again, reshape—my understanding of the country. Marianne Sághy's visit to Minsk in December 1997 helped me to see the country in a new light. And, as her fresh-from-Budapest suitcase full of oranges and grapefruits burst open on my Minsk kitchen table, I was reminded that, indeed, oranges are not the only fruit.

A Note on Statistical Sources, Translations and Transliteration

Energy research on the former USSR presents serious data and statistical challenges. In particular, preparing time series and comparative tables remains a difficult endeavor: most Belarusian publications give only current snapshot information, while international sources (the most exhaustive being the International Energy Agency (IEA), International Monetary Fund (IMF), World Bank, and US Department of Energy) normally have a three-year delay and often use different base years and measuring units. While conversions to common units have been carefully performed, there is a small margin of error possible, as some of the "original" units may have been themselves arrived at through conversion from another measuring unit. For coherence and comparability purposes, international (mainly IEA and IMF) sources have been used whenever possible. However, IEA and IMF data, itself derived from local data, is not immune to the above problems and may not be fully coherent from one publication or table to another. Official Belarusian data presents serious challenges due to significant gaps in publicly accessible information and to the frequent co-existence of different (in some cases, contradictory) data on a single item by two or more state sources. The advice of Elena Rakova and Leonid Zlotnikov, born of their many years of experience working with Belarusian statistical sources, has been invaluable in terms of helping me make sense of this data and presenting the reader with as clear and objective a picture as possible. Their work and example also shows how it is indeed possible to conduct serious research using official Belarusian sources, while keeping a critical perspective on them.

Transliteration of Russian and Belarusian-language materials was done using the ISO 9 transliteration standard using the translit.cc software, which simplifies reverse transliteration. Exceptions include the following. For the few words which for which there is a standard English-language usage (personal names, among others), this has been used instead. Names of companies and, to the extent available, public figures are spelled as presented in their official English-language websites. Other names were transliterated without diacritical marks. Many Belarusian citizens regularly use both the Russian and Belarusian versions of their names; I present the second spelling in parenthesis following the first use of the name. I have done my best to refer to them using the most common usage, but errors are unavoidable. In bibliographical references, their names are transliterated in accordance with spelling in the original source. In keeping with their most common usage in Belarus, place names are provided in their Russian variant. Unless otherwise noted, all translations from Russian, Belarusian and German are by the author. Website information is correct as of the time the item was accessed; please note that many non-governmental publications in Belarus are forced to change web-addresses frequently.

Abbreviations

bbl/d	barrels per day
b	billion
bcm	billion cubic meters (gas)
m	million
Mt	million tons (oil)
tcm	thousand cubic meters (gas)
m	million
BLR	Belarusian rouble
US$	US dollar (in tables)
$	US dollar (in main text)

1

Introduction

Radio reporter: *"Babusia, what has been the biggest change in the country, in your village, since Belarus became an independent state 15 years ago?"*
Elderly lady: *"Mmm ... I cannot think of any changes ... Oh, yes! Piped-in gas came to my village and to my house."*[1]

The period from December 2010 to December 2011 could not have brought a starker contrast to the economic situation of ordinary Belarusians and their perceptions of their economic well-being. By the end of December 2010, Aleksander Lukashenka commemorated sixteen and a half years in power, and was celebrating another 80-percent victory in presidential elections which, by all accounts, were far from free and fair. The short-lived election campaign, with unprecedented levels of media access for opposition candidates, suddenly came to an end. On the very night of the elections, with heavy-handed repression of those protesting against the voting manipulation, and the arrest of five presidential candidates and of hundreds of other participants, the world was at a loose end as to what to do.

If in December of 2010, despite the political repression, most common citizens were still riding in the wave of the expansionist economic policies implemented by Lukashenka in the period just preceding the elections, by December 2011, after a year of over 100 percent inflation and nearly 300 percent devaluation of the Belarusian rouble (BLR), their personal economic situation had changed sharply. And nothing was so much at the basis of this, of the highs and lows of the Lukashenka regime, than his manipulation of energy policy to manage relations, not only with his main patron, Russia, but also with the domestic nomenklatura and the Belarusian electorate.

1 Heard on a RFE/RL program for Belarus (Radio Svaboda), February 2007.

Since 1994, neither sticks nor carrots from the West had seemed to produce any lasting improvements concerning the movement to democracy. Until 2010, despite a decrease in his level of popular support—from an estimated real pro-Lukashenka vote of 63.6 percent in the March 2006 elections to 51.1 percent in December 2010[2]—Lukashenka remained firmly in power, having surpassed the other electoral candidates. He achieved this, if not cleanly and "elegantly," and by no means with the officially announced 79.7 percent support in the December 2010 elections, then at least by a plurality of votes.[3] All of this occurred while the country was suffering from the effects of the world economic crisis (which reduced Belarus' GDP growth from 10.2 percent in 2008 to 0.2 percent in 2009), and going through unprecedented external pressure in the form of increased energy prices from Russia and an anti-Lukashenka public-relations campaign openly orchestrated from Moscow. In the short term, and despite a 13-point drop in estimated real electoral support between 2006 and 2010, none of these problems seemed able to chip away at Lukashenka's power. In fact, as we look back at the 1994–2011 period, we see a remarkable level of stability in Lukashenka's power, despite significant ups and downs in external economic conditions and relations with Russia and Western states.

This is at first glance surprising, given the fact that since the late-1990s, both foreign observers and domestic analysts critical of the regime have warned about the imminent collapse of Lukashenka's power. The arguments for this often-predicted collapse have been many: Lukashenka's lack of support from the old nomenklatura (in the mid 1990s); the reduction and expected withdrawal of support from Moscow (in the late 2000s); or, simply, the collapse of the Belarusian economy and the wave of popular dissatisfaction that would ensue. Arguments for the collapse of the Belarusian economy, too, were many: the exhaustion of the country's productive basis (in the late 1990s); an increase in gas prices (2007); cyclical waves of economic confrontation with and import restrictions from Russia; and the sharp reduction of rents from oil trade with Russia following a 2006–2007 "oil war" with Rus-

2 Source: *Novosti NISEPI*, No. 2 (40), April 2006, 3, Table 1 (for 2006), available at: www.iiseps.org/bullet.html; and (for 2011) Table 16 in the report of the December 21–31, 2010 national poll, available at: http://www.iiseps.org/data10-431.html (both accessed May 26, 2011). Official results gave Lukashenka 83% support in the 2006 presidential elections.

3 Given the margin of error in the exit polls conducted by NISEPI, it is impossible to know whether Lukashenka received more than 50% of the vote in the first round of the 2010 elections; the Belarusian Constitution prescribes a second round if none of the candidates receives over 50% of the votes. One can only guess what the result of such a second round would have been in December 2010.

sia over control of these rents[4] and subsequent worsening of relations (2007–2010). Yet none of these scenarios came to pass in the short term. None of the above scenarios about Lukashenka's loss of power came to be realized either.

This book is an attempt to understand the role of energy relations, policies, and discourses in the maintenance of this power. The central empirical question it seeks to answer is, what has been the role of energy policies in the maintenance of Aleksander Lukashenka's power in Belarus? In the process of doing so, the book also sheds new light on important issues for understanding Belarus' political development and, more generally, sources of stability and instability in post-Soviet authoritarian states and authoritarian states as a whole.

Research on Energy and Stability in Belarus: the Broader Theoretical and Academic Context

Previous analyses of sources of political stability in Lukashenka's Belarus

Lukashenka's longevity in power is part of the wider issue of authoritarian resilience (i.e., what factors or combination of factors help explain the longevity of authoritarian regimes). Looking at this phenomenon in a worldwide perspective, authors have paid attention to external factors, such as access to external (often oil) rents;[5] pressure from the external economic environment given a state's mode of integration into the international economy;[6] policies of major world actors towards the regime; and perceptions of external threat. Other authors have focused on more domestic-related factors such as level of state coercion and cohesiveness of the coercive apparatus,[7] inclusion of key social groups with the help of political institutions such as a one-

4 As will be discussed in Chapter 5, in late 2006 Russia decided, effective January 1, 2007, to eliminate oil export tax preferences for Belarus, and to substantially increase its share of export duties charged on oil products refined in Belarus from Russian oil. On January 8, 2007 Russia's pipeline monopoly Transneft shut off supplies to the Druzhba oil pipeline entirely, briefly interrupting oil supplies to Belarus, Poland and other points west, the first time that Russian (or Soviet) oil supplies to EU consumer countries had been interrupted.

5 See Morrison, "Oil, Nontax Revenue."

6 Karl, *The Paradox of Plenty.*

7 Way, "Authoritarian State Building."

party system[8] and cooptation, economic growth,[9] the stability of state spending towards key social groups,[10] and the economic incentives for the defection of members of the ruling circle to the opposition.[11]

In seeking to understand the reasons behind Lukashenka's longevity in power, observers have focused on factors such as the use of pre-emptive soft[12] or, especially, hard repression and control over Belarusian society;[13] ideological control;[14] his control of the *nomenklatura* through blackmail and repression; encouraging citizens' economic dependence on the state;[15] his charisma and the use of populist and demagogic tactics to create a direct link with the electorate;[16] the weakness of the democratic opposition; the inability of nationalism as a strong social and political force to galvanize an anti-Lukashenka opposition;[17] a Soviet-era paternalistic social contract between the state and the population that has continued to find acceptance from the Belarusian public;[18] a state with relatively strong capacities and "an effective, top-down system of accounting and control";[19] and last but not least, economic support from Moscow.

It is, of, course, likely that the source of stability lies in a combination of these factors, and that this combination itself has evolved throughout Lukashenka's rule, from one relying mostly on his charisma, to one increasingly based on individual citizens' perception of their short and medium-term economic interests,[20] to, following the 2011 economic crisis, one based on a renewed wave of repression.

8 See Smith, "Life of the Party"; Geddes, "What Do We Know"; Brownlee, *Authoritarianism*; and Magaloni, "Credible Power-Sharing."

9 Przeworski and Limong, "Modernization."

10 Richer, "The Political Economy."

11 Radnitz, "The Color of Money."

12 Balmaceda, "Understanding Repression."

13 Silitski, "Preempting Democracy."

14 Leshchenko, "The National Ideology." Such control is carried out through the overwhelmingly state-controlled media, pro-Lukashenka youth organizations, and other "ideological education" measures at educational institutions and workplaces (such as the government-controlled Belarusian Republican Youth Movement).

15 Throughout the whole post-independence period, the private sector share of Belarus' GDP remained at a very low level, slowly increasing from 20% to 30% of GDP from 1997 to 2010, while in neighboring countries it had reached 65–75% by the mid 2000s. Data from EBRD, *Transition Report*.

16 Korosteleva, "Is Belarus a Demagogical." Belarus is perhaps a unique example in Europe of a presidential regime without an evident power or party political base other than the president himself. Marples, "Color Revolutions," 355.

17 Eke and Kuzio, "Sultanism."

18 Karbalevich, *Aleksandr Lukashenko*; and Haiduk and Chubrik, "Specifikaciâ ponâtiâ."

19 Fritz, *State-building*, 224.

20 See Haiduk, "Social Contract," 8. Haiduk et al. discuss Lukashenka's social contract as a continuation of the "Masheraw social contract" (under charismatic long-time leader of Soviet Belarus Piotr Masheraw in the 1970s), when the country saw an unprecedented growth in urbanization and living standards. Haiduk et al., "Editor's Foreword," 6.

Seen in this context, this book's unique contribution lies in its attempt to make sense of the connections between external and internal sources of regime legitimacy in Belarus. In other words, the book goes beyond arguing that it was simply external support and the existence of energy subsidies from Russia that accounted for stability in Lukashenka's regime. Rather, it argues that it was not only the existence of these external rents, but the *way* these were used domestically which helps explain the longevity of the Lukashenka regime.

While some authors (Karbalevich, Haiduk, et al.) have focused on the role of populist economic policies in the maintenance of Lukashenka's power, little work has been done in terms of analyzing the role of energy policies. Similarly, previous research has concentrated on external forces (i.e., the importance of energy subsidies from Russia), but less on the domestic sources and effects of Lukashenka's energy policies,[21] and the way in which Russian energy subsidies are brought into play domestically.

Previous analyses of energy and politics in Belarus

Independent research institutes in Belarus regularly publish analyses of energy-related issues; their focus, however, has been mainly on the economic aspects of the question.[22] The only English-language book published to date on Belarusian–Russian energy relations (Yafimava's *Post-Soviet Russian–Belarussian Relationships: The Role of Gas Transit Pipelines*) focuses solely on gas and does not address domestic political factors. My 2006 study on *Belarus: oil, gas, transit pipelines and Russian foreign energy policy*[23] focused mainly on the external aspects of the question. Most other Western research has concentrated on nuclear power issues in the country, and particularly on the 1986 Chernobyl disaster.[24] Belarusian energy issues have also been covered in more general studies on energy and the environment in the region.[25]

21 One partial exception is Pikulik, "Comparative Pathways," which analyzes the role of external rents on the evolution of economic and political institutions.

22 Here the main player has been the Research Center of the *Institut Privatizatsii i Menedzhmenta* (hereafter IPM), which regularly publishes working papers and policy briefs on energy-related issues, often in coauthorship with German partners, and also covers energy issues in its yearly *Monitoring Infrastrukturi Belarusi*. In addition, since 2006, the Belarusian Institute of Strategic Studies (BISS) has occasionally been publishing short research reports on energy-related issues.

23 Balmaceda, *Belarus: oil, gas.*

24 See for example Marples and Young, *Nuclear Energy*; and Marples, "The Energy Dilemma."

25 See for example Cherp et al., *Environment and Security*; and Bergasse et al., "CIS role for the EU" and "Strategies and policy," 172–258.

Approach and focus of the book

This book explores the issue of authoritarian stability and instability in Belarus by analyzing the role of energy and energy policies in the management of Lukashenka's relationship with three main constituencies: Russian actors, the Belarusian *nomenklatura*, and the Belarusian electorate. The focus on these three (sets of) actors is warranted by the fact that each has been crucial in the maintenance of Lukashenka's power. Energy issues (and, in particular, the flow of energy-related rents) provide a unique prism through which to look at each of these relationships. While these relationships have been three main pillars of stability for the Lukashenka regime since 1994, each of them also carries within it potential sources of pressure for change.

This book makes two central arguments: the first focusing on relations with external actors; the second on domestic relations.

Relations with external actors: energy, power, and the social construction of the Belarusian–Russian relationship

Since the January 2007 Russian-Belarusian disputes on the division of oil rents that led to the first ever interruption of Russian (or Soviet) oil supplies to EU consumer countries,[26] energy issues in Belarus have reached Western headlines and elicited Western interest mainly through the issue of Belarus' role in the transit of Russian oil and gas to Western Europe. Before that, the issue, if at all, entered analysts' field of interest mainly through the issue of Russian energy subsidies to Belarus. While these questions are important, key issues essential for their understanding remained outside Western attention. Among these, most crucial was Aleksander Lukashenka's use of energy policies, bargaining and rhetoric to pursue dual goals vis-à-vis Russian actors: to seek to increase political and (especially) economic support from Russia, while seeking to keep at bay any actual Russian economic presence in Belarus that could come to challenge his own hold on power. (As will be discussed below, the sale of the national gas transit company Beltransgaz in 2011, acquiesced to under extreme conditions, does not invalidate these goals.)

As will be discussed at length throughout the book, the advantages accruing from Belarus' special energy relationship with Russia undoubtedly con-

26 See Footnote 4. The issue is further discussed in Chapter 5.

stituted an important source of stability for the regime. Yet the question remains: how was Lukashenka able to maintain such level of support from Russia, given its apparently limited bargaining power vis-à-vis its much more powerful partner? How can we use various theories of domestic and international bargaining to better understand Belarus' energy negotiations with Russia and Lukashenka's ability, despite his country's weakness, to assert his goals with Moscow in a short-term perspective? At a more theoretical level, this is related to the question of how weak states can bargain with more powerful ones. More specifically, how are states that depend largely on aid or preferential treatment from more powerful partners able to navigate and manipulate these relationships to their own benefit?[27]

As early as 1971, authors such as Keohane were paying attention to the diplomatic and security behaviors small states may use to gain leverage vis-à-vis larger and more powerful partners.[28] While Keohane focused mostly on strategic behaviors, such as balancing and bandwagoning, by the smaller ally in the context of broader Cold War relationships, Harrison argues that both in the cases of the Soviet and the Western Cold War alliances the larger partner's fear of the domino effects of a (weaker) ally's leaving the alliance gave the weaker partners increased bargaining power in the relationship.[29] A clear implication of Harrison's argument is that the weaker state's power in this situation derives largely from its ability to adversely affect the prestige of the larger state.

Authors such as Carney have looked at this question from the perspective of the factors that go into an asymmetrical, patron-client relationship, including affinity between the parties and the "intangible goods" the patron may accrue from a strong alliance (or, in some cases, the perception of such) with the client, goods such as "ideological convergence," "international solidarity," and "strategic advantage," in addition to increased international prestige.[30] The implicit role of reputational and prestige issues in both Harrison's and Carney's argument forms a bridge between these perspectives and a constructivist one.

---

27 We use the term "weak states" (sometimes also covered by the literature on "small states") to denote states with a comparatively weak bargaining position vis-à-vis neighboring states or allies, not in the sense of internally weak states in danger of disintegration or civil war.

28 Keohane, "The Big Influence." For a discussion of the various methods used by small states to leverage effectively, see also Cooper and Shaw, *The Diplomacies of Small States*.

29 See Harrison, *Driving the Soviets up the Wall*, 3.

30 Carney, "International Patron-Client," 48–51, making reference to Shoemaker and Spanier, *Patron-client*, 18–19.

Constructivist insights on the broad "needs" states have (in their words, "pre-given" national interests) going above and beyond strategic interests can further add to our understanding of the intangible goods a weaker state such as Belarus may provide to a stronger ally or "patron," such as Russia. Wendt's inclusion of "collective self-esteem" (alongside "physical survival," "autonomy," and "economic well-being") as a central "pre-given" national interest adds a further dimension to the patronal state goals discussed above, opening the door to including goals related to the weaker client state's ability to help fulfill the other state's collective self-esteem needs.[31]

But, how does the importance of a weak state (as an ally for example) in terms of fulfilling the more powerful state's "collective self-esteem" needs become clear? In many cases, this may happen spontaneously. In other cases, politicians in the weaker state may emphasize this connection in the hope of gaining additional advantages in the relationship. They may do so, for example, by means of what Putman calls "reverberation" through key actors in the other (possibly more powerful) state—a reverberation intended to create an environment for negotiating outcomes favored by the other (possibly weaker) state by increasing the domestic win-set in the other state's bargaining options so as to increase the chances of it coinciding with the win-set of the other (possibly weaker) state's leader.[32]

More specifically, there are situations where the leader of the weaker partner state may "raise the cost of no-agreement to key constituents on the other side, thus rendering even unfavorable agreements relatively more attractive."[33] This, it could be argued, is exactly what, at different times and under different circumstances, weaker partners such as East Germany (with the USSR), Austria (with the US and its Western allies), Taiwan, Israel and Pakistan (with the US) have pursued vis-à-vis their more powerful partners.[34] In particular, the weaker parties have been able to manipulate the relationship by arguing to key constituencies in the partner state that without its support, the whole system may fall apart, with serious consequences, especially in situa-

31 Wendt, *Social Theory*, 236.

32 See Putman, "Diplomacy and Domestic Politics." For an expansion of the concept and application to the case of Anwar Sadat's negotiation strategy with Israel in the late 1970s, see Stein, "The Political Economy." While Putman does not refer specifically to weak and strong partners, the framework lends itself easily to the analysis of relations between weaker and more powerful partners, such as between Belarus and Russia.

33 Moravcsik, "Introduction," 29.

34 On Austria, see Bischof, *Austria in the First Cold War*. On the GDR, see Harrison, *Driving the Soviets up the Wall*.

tions where dangerous regional rivals—or countries perceived as dangerous regional rivals—are concerned.

These perspectives help us gain a deeper insight into two important issues: how Lukashenka was able to achieve his policy preferences despite Belarus' relative weakness; and how Belarus was able to maintain relatively high levels of support from Russia despite worsening relations. The answer, we hypothesize, lies in two areas, each of which is explored in this book.

First, we cannot look at the preferential energy treatment received by Belarus as simply dictated by Russia as a unified external actor. Rather, it makes sense to look at the interests and value-added chains of various actors within Russia, and at the way they will involve various sets of local actors. Some of these actors included, in addition to the Kremlin, other political forces in Russia, the military leadership, oil companies and traders, oil transit regulator Transneft, gas monopolist Gazprom, and regional politicians and policy-makers. While their interests coincided at times, this coincidence cannot be taken for granted.

Second, it is necessary to look at the energy relationship in the context of the broader Russian-Belarusian relationship, a relationship in which Belarus was not only a recipient, but also a provider of tangible (such as military facilities) and intangible goods. As we will see throughout this book, the Belarusian leadership pursued a double strategy: appealing to Belarus' strategic value by reminding Russia of what strategic situation ("NATO at Russia's footsteps") might ensue would that alliance no longer be in place, and appealing to Russia's "collective self esteem" as translated by specific actors within Russia.

Relations with domestic actors

The second main argument of the book concerns the role of energy policies, energy relations with Russia, and discourses around them in the management of relations with domestic actors in Belarus.

The literature on natural resources and political development has looked at the impact of energy-related rents in the stability of authoritarian regimes. In general terms, this literature has argued that an *abundance* of (exportable) energy resources (and the resulting abundance of export revenue) makes a state prone to a number of problems which may hinder democratic governance. As these rents make it possible for the state to access significant resources without needing to tax its population, the state evolves from a "production" to an "allocation" stance, weakening crucial links with its citizens, as well as governance.[35] While this literature is not directly applicable to the case of energy-poor Belarus, one element—the focus on *easily accessible, external rents*—may help us gain additional insights into the Belarusian case.

While energy-poor itself, due to a variety of reasons, Belarus has been able to enjoy both price subsidies (mainly in the gas area) and the trickle-down effect of Russian energy rents (mainly in oil). How significant was this rent? Table 1 provides a comparative sense of gas-related rents for the period 2001–2006, in comparison with Ukraine and Lithuania.

In addition to these gas-related rents, the World Bank estimated that in the mid-2000s, profits related to especially advantageous oil import prices constituted around three percent of Belarus' GDP. In addition, during 2007–2009, export duties on oil products provided between 3.63 and 5.78 percent of the country's GDP, equivalent to 9–16 percent of budget revenues.[36]

While the potential revenue streams discussed above are not resource rents in the sense usually used in the literature, there is a connection in the sense that these are large, external, and easily-accessible rents. From that perspective, the resource rents literature's argument about the governance and representation problems that are likely to come together with a situation of access to significant external resources without needing to tax a state's population is relevant to the Belarusian case as well. Here the focus on *easily accessible, external* rents is crucial.[37]

35 See Beblawy and Luciani, *The Rentier State, vol.* 2. See also Chaudhry, *The Price of Wealth*; and Vandewalle, *Libya since Independence.*

36 Manenok, "Valûtnye donory slabeût." In 2007, 2008, and 2009, export duties on oil products amounted to 4.2%, 5.78%, and 3.63% of Belarus' GDP respectively, equivalent to 9-16% of the budget. (Calculated by Leonid Zlotnikov on the basis of *Projekt Budgeta Respubliki Belarus'.*) As will be discussed in Chapters 3 and 5 below, this was not the case prior to 2007, when income from export duties on oil products amounted to around 1% of the budget.

37 These rents, however, do not perforce need to be associated with the energy sector. In a separate publication, I discuss the concept of "rent-seeking swamps" to denote areas of economic activity where opportunities for large-scale rent seeking are easily available. In addition to energy trade-related rents as an easy (in fact, "too easy") source of external rents for the economy, other cases of "rent-seeking swamps" discussed in the literature include those related to gambling in Macao (where the overwhelming role of (legal) gambling in the economy created enormous rent-seeking opportunities which ended up creating a context that "offers too much to sectional interests to allow an independent anti-corruption agency to be fully independent or effective"), and possibly, the case of the Philippines (income from US military bases and from "preferential access for Philippine products in American markets"). The sudden influx of large and illegal drug-trade revenue to Bolivia in the early 1980s presents another possible example. What seems to be common to these situations is something Babanin and Dubrovskyi directed attention to when seeking to understand the sources of what they call "pseudo Dutch Disease": the fact that these rents distort incentives and crowd out value-adding activity, leading to imbalances and structural deterioration. (Babanin et al., *Ukraine: The Lost Decade*, 29 (Footnote 10)). See Balmaceda, "Some Thoughts on," Lo, "Bureaucratic Corruption"; Doig and McIvor, "Corruption and its control"; Hutchcroft, "Booty Capitalism"; Johnston, "The Political Consequences." For a detailed discussion, see Balmaceda, *The Politics of Energy*

TABLE 1.1
BELARUS' POTENTIAL RENT POOLS IN THE GAS AREA IN COMPARATIVE PERSPECTIVE, 2001–2006, IN US$

	Belarus	Ukraine	Lithuania
Gas Transit fees	1.25 b	9.73 b	17.9 m
Gas price differentials	13.79 b	20.09 b	937.64 m
Total	15.04 b	29.82 b	0.955 b
Population in 2005	9.8 m	47.1 m	3.4 m
Per-capita value of potential rent pools in the gas area	1534	633	280

Sources:
Data for transit income: Belarus (Rakova, "Ènergetičeskij sektor Belarusi," 8); Lithuania (Janeliunas and Molis, "Energy Security," 22); Ukraine (Pirani, *Ukraine's Gas Sector*, 83, Table 6.5).
Price differentials are calculated on the basis of the difference between gas prices paid to Gazprom and European prices for 2001–2006. For ease of comparability, for "European Prices" we use the same prices used in Rakova, (ibid.) based on Gazprom data. Data for Ukraine from price data in Table 4.4 in Balmaceda, *The Politics of Energy Dependency*, and import volumes from Russia of assumed 23 billion cubic meters/year for 2001–2005 (IEA, *Ukraine Energy*, 178) and 56.9 ("cocktail" of Russian and Central Asian gas) (Pirani, ibid., 28).
Data for Belarus from Rakova (ibid.)
Prices for Lithuania calculated on the basis of, for 2001–2004, an average price of $102.25, noted in International Atomic Energy Agency, *Energy supply options*, 78; and the 2005–2006 prices noted in Balmaceda, *The Politics of Energy Dependency*.

The main argument of this book concerning domestic politics is that it was not only the influx of energy rents and subsidies that was crucial for Lukashenka's hold on power, but the way he dealt with these. In this sense, the argument is in line with a new strand in the literature on resource rents and authoritarianism, which has pointed out the need to look further than the existence of rents itself, and focus on the ways in which resources interact with domestic political structures to lead to various outcomes.[38] Some recent research also analyzes the effect of external energy rents on populist regimes, such as that of Hugo Chávez in Venezuela.[39] In the case of Belarus, income from energy-related exports (mainly refined oil products) was, at over 25 per-

Dependency, Chapter 1. Other authors have focused on similar phenomena through the concept of non-tax revenues. On the political impact of non-tax revenue, see Morrison, "Nontax Revenue."

38 See Jones Luong and Weinthal, "Rethinking the Resource Curse"; Smith, *Hard Times in the Lands of Plenty*; and Dunning, *Crude Democracy*.

39 On oil revenues, social spending, regime type and (indirectly) populism in Venezuela, see Corrales, "Oil and Regime Change"; and Dunning, "Endogenous Oil Rents."

cent of exports for most of the 2000s, the largest source of foreign revenue during the period under consideration in this book. The closely related chemical industry accounted for an additional 25 percent of exports.[40]

Belarus' Cycle of Rents

One useful way to look at the further impact of energy rents and subsidies (see below for definitions) is by focusing on the ways these rents are *extracted*, *distributed*, and *reincorporated* into the political system, i.e., by looking at Belarus' particular *cycle of rents*.[41] The first element of the cycle of rents concerns the *sources of extraction* of energy-related rents. Here the main issues concern the relative size of these (potential) rents, as well as their source ("internal" or "external"). By "internal" rents, we mean those accrued mainly from domestic users or the state budget; "external" rents refer to those originating from outside sources. In the case of Belarus, these external rents included those accrued through preferential prices received from the main supplier; preferential tax and duty regimes also affecting the export of refined products using imported crude oil; preferential intra-corporate arrangements; transit revenue; and the arbitrage gains able to be made from the differences between import, domestic and export prices for energy.[42]

The second element of the model concerns the patterns of energy rents *distribution*. This concerns first and foremost the type of actors participating most actively in the accrual of these rents. Are these mainly individuals or corporations, or the state budget as a whole? This also concerns the formal or informal mechanisms and institutions by which the distribution of these rents is regulated, including mechanisms involving the trans-border distribution (and sharing) of rents, in particular with actors from supplier countries.

The third element of the model concerns the *reincorporation* (or "recycling") of these energy rents into the political system. This dynamic goes above and beyond the issue of *who* is benefiting from these rents, and into issues such as what kinds of institutions and patterns are strengthened or weakened as a result of specific actors' accrual of these rents (and interest in continuing

40 Sekhovich, "1991–2006. Itogi."

41 For a detailed discussion of this perspective, see Balmaceda, *The Politics of Energy Dependency*.

42 Arbitrage refers to the possibility of making a profit out of manipulating price differentials for the same good between various markets or within sectors of the same market.

to accrue them). The reincorporation of energy rents into the political system concerns the impact of these rents on policy-making, especially energy policy-making,[43] on the popularity of the incumbent and, ultimately, the development of the political system more broadly.

In the case of Belarus, this cycle of rent distribution and re-incorporation has most directly affected Lukashenka's relationship with two domestic groupings: the country's elite, and the electorate.

Energy, power, and Lukashenka's relationship with the Belarusian elite

It would be impossible for Aleksander Lukashenka to remain in power without the implicit or explicit support of the Belarusian elite. By "elite," we mean here first and foremost the new *nomenklatura*—officials appointed by Lukashenka himself—but also remnants of the old Soviet *nomenklatura*, large-scale businessmen, and others who have risen through the ranks of the military and other bureaucratic organizations. While most analysts' (both Western and Belarusian) emphasis on Lukashenka's power would lead to an assumption of his unbridled power over the country's elite, there has been little written specifically on the more nuanced aspects of this relationship;[44] this includes the degree of mutual reliance between them, as well as the role of corruption-related rents in the relationship (discussed in Chapter 4). This is also an area where an examination of energy-related issues can provide important insights.

Energy, power, and Lukashenka's relationship with the Belarusian electorate[45]

While Lukashenka is often referred to as "Europe's last dictator," nuanced analyses of Belarusian politics have taken account of the real degree of popular support he enjoyed for most of the period between 1994 and 2011 and possibly beyond.[46] At a socio-political and social psychological level, this degree

43 By "impact on elections" we also mean impact on the overall popularity of the incumbent.

44 For an exception, see Silitski, "The Tsar and his Boyars."

45 The word "electorate" is used here in a broad sense, not simply to denote voters in free elections, but in the sense of those on whose tacit or explicit support Lukashenka has relied in order to maintain power. More generally, electoral politics in Belarus were only one part of a broader game including important doses of "administrative resources," direct political control by the executive and, when deemed necessary, sheer repression.

46 See Ioffe, "Understanding Belarus: Economy," and ibid., "Understanding Belarus."

of popular support may be explained by his ability to offer simple answers to the complex questions facing the country, and by the way in which he reflects the majority population's dominant political culture.[47] On the economic side, his ability to delay painful reforms and their attendant social costs (and at the same time, to provide steadily rising wages and living standards for most of this period) has contributed significantly to his popularity and, importantly, has helped legitimize his administration. (Whether any of these strategies would be sustainable over the long term is a separate question.)

This book explores three important aspects of this issue: First, how Lukashenka's policies vis-à-vis Russia have helped to improve living standards through a continued subsidization of the economy via an important stream of energy-related rents. Second, how domestic-oriented energy policies have also contributed to the maintenance of the economic model. Third, how, at times of crisis in the Russian subsidization model, Lukashenka's rhetoric on energy issues helped to limit dissatisfaction with his policies and, on the contrary, allowed him to use the situation and the opposition's response to it to seek to disqualify it in the eyes of the population.

Main concepts used in the book

This book uses a set of closely related concepts to describe monetary relationships in the energy area: concepts such as "subsidies," "energy rents," "rent seeking," "rents of energy dependency," and "corruption." Although related, in the benefit of conceptual clarity some definitions are in order.

By *subsidies* we refer to a monetary or easily monetizable grant from one government to another government.

Energy rents are, for working purposes, defined as similar to energy-related profits. Further, we define "macro-level rents" as the subsidy effect experienced by the whole economy, and "micro-level rents" as the concrete benefits received by specific economic groups or individuals, regardless of the means by which these rents are actually extracted.[48]

Rent-seeking refers to the attempt by an individual or entity to obtain unjustifiably high profits, often through the illegal or semi-legal manipula-

47 See Eke and Kuzio, "Sultanism;" Ioffe, "Understanding Belarus: Belarusian Identity;" and Ioffe and Yarashevich, "Debating Belarus." See also comments by Sheremet, *Pratskii akzent.*

48 On macro- and micro-level rents, see Babanin et al., *Ukraine: The Lost Decade,* 12.

tion of the economic environment (including lobbying, bribery, or the use of privileged information).

By *corruption* we understand the use of public office for private gain, with a further differentiation between corruption for a one-time-deal private gain and the "capture" of the state by specific interests in order to push forth their preferences in the form of laws and regulations advantageous to them.[49]

By *rents of energy dependency* we refer to whatever unearned benefits an economic group within a country (or, for that matter, a regime or a country as a whole) may receive from the continuation of energy dependency relationships, especially with longstanding partners, in this case Russia. Such rents of dependency can take a variety of forms: from the subsidy effect experienced by a whole economy to the concrete benefits received by specific economic groups. That large profits can be made in the energy sector may seem obvious in the case of an energy-rich country such as Russia, but counterintuitive in situations of energy import dependency. The apparent paradox of energy rents in a situation of energy dependency can be explained by the fact that in many post-Soviet transition countries the energy import, distribution and re-export business has been a center of corruption activities. At an even more basic level, significant arbitrage gains (i.e., profits related to the possibility of manipulating price differentials for the same good between various markets or within sectors of the same market) were made when Russia found itself inclined to sell energy to these states at lower-than-market prices, and differences between domestic, "near abroad" and export prices continued to be significant. While energy-related arbitrage rents are hardly a monopoly of post-Soviet states, the specific combination of a lack of strong economic institutions after the demise of the USSR and Russia's continued strategic, political, economic, and cultural interest in other post-Soviet states in turn contributed to the maintenance of multiple-pricing schemes for energy, which have created additional arbitrage and rent-seeking opportunities.

Understanding rents of energy dependency and how the economic gains (and losses) from energy trade and transit will be distributed domestically is central for understanding politics and policy-making in energy-dependent post-Soviet states such as Belarus. The various means by which these rents can be extracted or created, and how the associated profits or losses will be distributed domestically, can have a direct effect on the content of energy

49 On state capture as distinct from corruption, see Hellman et al., "Seize the State, Seize the Day."

policies favored by specific groups, and on their ability to turn these into implemented policies. This will thus affect the actual management of energy dependency.

Broader contribution of the book

Contribution to understanding politics in Belarus

Our traditional understanding of politics in Lukashenka's Belarus has been based on two assumptions. First, on the assumption of Lukashenka's almost complete control over the country's political system (his so-called power vertical) and, second, on the assumption of the Belarusian state's overwhelming control over the economy. With its detailed look at the intermingling of political and economic relationships in Belarus' energy sector, this book contributes to a new perspective on these two issues, revealing a much more complex and multi-dimensional system of domestic relationships.

In doing so, this book can make an important contribution to our understanding of three areas of Belarusian politics. First, by providing a more nuanced understanding of the sources of stability and change within the regime. Second, by providing a more accurate picture of relations between President Lukashenka and the Belarusian *nomenklatura*, often mentioned as an important potential source of political change in the country.[50] Third, by helping us understand the *modus operandi* behind Lukashenka's international relationships with and beyond Russia.

Contribution to understanding the behavior of energy transit states

Looking at the way Lukashenka, the leader of an energy-poor transit state, has been able to extract concessions from Russia also forces us to rethink many of the tenets of classical energy bargaining literature. This literature (best known for the concepts of "transit monopoly versus supply monopoly" and "obsolescing bargain") notes as main elements of bargaining counter-power issues such as

50 Such hopes were especially high in 2001 when Mikhail Marynich (former minister of Foreign Economic Relations who switched to the opposition) attempted to run in the presidential elections held that year. After failing to collect sufficient signatures to be registered as a candidate, he was charged and convicted of stealing charges. He remained in prison until 2006.

ownership and physical control over concrete pipelines.[51] Discussions of "obsolescing bargains" focus, for example, on how the bargaining power between a foreign producer state and a politically independent transit state evolves with time, affecting the stability of the "initial bargain." The post-Soviet cases, however, force us to rethink this model, which does not take into account a specific circumstance uniquely affecting these states: the fact that today's transit and exporting states were the same state at the time the transit infrastructure was built, affecting the nature of the initial "bargain" and creating the conditions for serious changes in actors' expectations after the dissolution of the common central state. In addition, the case of Belarus alerts us as to the importance of other, less tangible elements, such as the political bargaining between two states.

Contribution to policy-making

Understanding the sources of stability and change in Lukashenka's regime, as well as the complex dynamics of its relationship with Russian actors and the legacies of its "energy-political model," is essential for the development of proactive and workable Western policies vis-à-vis Belarus. In the short term, an improved understanding of the sources of stability and change in Belarus will facilitate nimbler Western policies. Looking at the medium and long term, an understanding of the legacies and path dependencies created in the first 20 years of Belarusian independence is also crucial for understanding the challenges the country is likely to face in the post-energy rents era—with or without Lukashenka.

Organization of the book

This book is composed of seven chapters. Chapter 1 sets the scene by presenting the most important issues and questions analyzed by the book, and placing them in the context of previous research on authoritarian resilience and bargaining between unequally powerful partners. Chapter 2 presents a brief background of Belarus' historical trajectory between Russia and

51 On the "obsolescing bargain" between transit states and energy suppliers and how the relative bargaining power between both evolves, see Vernon, *Sovereignty at Bay* and Omonbude, "The Transit Oil and Gas Pipeline."

the West, and of Belarus' energy and political setting at the time of Aleksander Lukashenka's coming to power in 1994. Chapter 3 introduces Belarus' "energy-political model" by analyzing the dynamics of the Russian–Belarusian energy relationship in the "high years" of 1994–2004; the means by which Lukashenka was able to capture high energy rents from this relationship; and the role played by these rents as a source of political legitimacy vis-à-vis the Belarusian public. Chapter 4 looks at the role played by the sharing of energy rents between Lukashenka and members of the Belarusian *nomenklatura* in his complex relationship with this important constituency, and at its effects on the domestic system of power. Chapter 5 analyses how the Belarussian "energy-political model" was able to continue functioning, in modified form, even under the pressure of worsened relations with Russia during the "low years" of 2004–2009; and how the new dynamics of energy-related rents and their internal distribution have affected relationships with the *nomenklatura* and the Belarusian electorate. Chapter 6 analyzes the role of energy rents in the dramatic turnaround from the economic euphoria preceding the December 2010 elections, to the country's unprecedented economic crisis and collapse of Lukashenka's preferred mode of relations with Russia a year later. Chapter 7 presents a balance of 20 years of independent Belarusian energy policies, and the impact of Lukashenka's model of energy politics for the country's future development and relations with Russia and the West.

2

Belarus: Between Russia and the West and at the Very Core of the Soviet System

In order to understand the way Belarus was incorporated into the Soviet Union, as well as the way its population approached the changes that came with independence in 1991, it is essential to consider the development of Belarus' unique historical position between Russia and the West. But any attempt to characterize Belarus' existence as a borderland between Russia and the West is perforce inadequate: a realistic assessment would put Belarus and the development of a Belarusian national consciousness at the crossroads, not only between Russia and the West, but between multiple historical and nation/state-building projects: the multi-ethnic Polish-Lithuanian Commonwealth, Russian imperial, and Soviet. At different moments in the region's history, these entities interrelated in a variety of ways: through wars and conquests; cooptation; and competition. In this chapter, we address these issues by looking at the development of the lands which formed the territory of modern Belarus between the 14th century and their full incorporation into the Russian Empire in the late 18th century. We look at the factors supporting or hindering the development of specifically Belarusian elites during the Tsarist period, at the ways in which the republic became functionally and economically integrated into the USSR, and at the effects this had on the sources of regime legitimacy, stability, and change, during the Soviet period.

FROM THE 14TH CENTURY TO 1917

When making reference to the territory of modern Belarus between the 14th century and 1917, it is tempting to call these territories "Belarus," projecting the country's current identity further back in time. Yet to do so would be misleading: for most of this period, there was simply no administratively unified Belarus. Nationally minded Belarusians, instead, have largely had to look for their roots during this period through connections with larger political entities in the region. For many of them, the connection with the Grand Duchy of Lithuania (GDL, together with the Crown Kingdom of Poland a constituent part of the Polish-Lithuanian Commonwealth, 1569–1795) became an important cornerstone of Belarusian identity, to the point of providing the "foundational myth" for much of Belarusian nationalist historiography.[1] Indeed, most of the territories of modern Belarus shared a close connection with the GDL and the Commonwealth, which came to fill some of the political void left by the disintegration of Kievan Rus (Mongol sacking of Kyiv (Kiev) in 1240), quickly became "the prominent power in Eastern Europe," and stretched, at its height, from the Baltic to the Black Sea,[2] encompassing a variety of peoples, languages and religions, including, in addition to Lithuanians and Poles, large numbers of Orthodox Slavs, Jews, Roma and Tatars. The area's population was also multi-confessional, with, by 1781, c. 70 percent Uniates (Greek Catholics), c. 15–20 percent Roman Catholic, c. 6 percent Orthodox, and a number of Moslem Tatars.[3] Mirroring Belarus' geographical location between Russia and the West, the Uniate faith shared by the majority, Wilson argues, provided them with "the halfway house their identity needed—a way of being between Russia and Poland."[4]

Yet during this period, the territories of modern Belarus were not immune to the violent decimation of its population. The war between the Polish–Lithuanian Commonwealth and Muscovy in the mid-17th century (1654–67) had tragic consequences for these territories, which, according to some estimates, lost over half of their inhabitants (by one account, 72 percent).[5] A century later, the partitions of 1772, 1793, and 1795 (often collectively referred to

1 Wilson, *Belarus,* 19.
2 Ibid.,18.
3 Ibid.,55–56.
4 Ibid., 56.
5 Kotljiarchuk, cited in ibid., 45.

as the Polish Partitions), by which Russia, Germany and Austria divided the Commonwealth, would also have severe effects for Belarus.

UNDER THE TSARIST EMPIRE: TERRITORIES, ELITES, RELIGION

The Partitions had a decisive effect on the Belarusian territories, which were incorporated almost in their entirety by the Russian Empire, not as a single unit but as separate individual *gubernii*. A series of restrictions and regulations on religion and education imposed by the new rulers would also have important consequences in terms of the ability of a nationally minded elite to form in Belarus and engage in fruitful dialogue with other groups of the population. Concerning religion, the possibility for the majority Uniate church to become the basis of a national culture was dealt a strong blow when it was banned in most of the Russian Empire in 1839 and mass (often forced) conversions to the official Orthodox faith followed. (While the Ukrainian Uniate Church faced similar limitations, a culturally significant area—Habsburg Galicia—had remained outside the Russian Empire, and served, Piedmont-like, as a cultural magnet; in the case of Belarus, there was little alternative to the restrictions imposed by the Tsarist regime.) These restrictions contributed to a situation where proto-nationalist elites became increasingly identified with the Catholic faith (and, by implication, Poland), a problematic proposition considering the social and economic abyss and lack of trust between the Polish-speaking nobility and Belarusian peasants, the latter part of the 70 percent Orthodox population compared to a mere 15 percent of Roman Catholics.[6] The landed gentry remained largely Catholic and Polish, with peasantry and common folk largely associated with the Orthodox faith; Catholicism's increasing association with the Polish landowners deepened the rift with the peasantry and common folk. This hindered the development of an elite that would be both well-educated and have strong ties to the majority of the population.

On the educational front, the closing of one of the region's major cultural centers, Vilnius University in 1831 (as a Tsarist response to the Polish Uprising of 1830–31), deprived the would-be Belarusian elite of a focal point, and also of educational possibilities outside the specifically Russian realm.

6 Latyshonak and Miranovich, *Historyia Belarusi,* 123, cited in Wilson, *Belarus*, 65.

However, to the extent that Vilnius could at any point become a focal point for Belarusian nationalism, this was a contradictory process, as the city was also claimed by Poland and was the seat of the much stronger Lithuanian national movement. The university was allowed to reopen only in 1919, but by that time the loss of Vilnius—then a much more important cultural center than Minsk—to Poland in 1917 as a result of the myriad confrontations in the region (including the First World War and the Polish–Soviet War of 1919–21) also hampered the development of an elite which could be closely associated with a Belarusian national identity. This was compounded by several factors: Belarus' economic backwardness and low literacy levels; its piecemeal mode of incorporation into the Russian Empire; the predominance of local identities (the so-called *tuteishyia*); the lack of large Belarusian-speaking urban centers (to the extent that these existed, they were largely Polish and Jewish in culture[7]); and the lack of a single, central city able to act as uncontested cultural focus.[8] Indeed, most scholars agree that a strong national movement only started to develop in Belarus in the early 20th century, later than in other Central and Eastern European countries.

The early Soviet period: factors supporting and hindering the development of national-oriented elites

By the time of the 1917 Revolution, much of the territory now known as Belarus was under German (and, later, Polish) control, and the events of the next two years would be determined by troop movements on the ground more than by state-building projects. One of these, however, although ultimately unviable, found fertile ground during these years: the Belarusian People's Republic, established in March 1918. Even though it lasted only a few months and never had full control over its claimed territory, it remained an important inspiration for later nation- and state-building projects. Partially overlapping

7 Despite the heavy-handed tactics imposed by the Tsarist regime, the area remained not only multi-religious, but also multi-lingual and multi-cultural. In 1897, linguistic Belarusians were an absolute majority only in the Minsk and Mahilev *gubernii*, and there were significant Jewish (the only minority with a consistent presence of over 10% in each *guberniia*), Polish, Ukrainian, Lithuanian, Latvian and Russian minorities.

8 As noted by Wilson, this role was fulfilled, at different times from the 10th to the 20th centuries, by Polotsk (Polatsk), Navahrudak, Smolensk, Vilnius, and Minsk. See Wilson, *Belarus*, 11.

in time, the Bolshevik project for the creation of a joint Lithuanian Belarusian Republic (Lit-Bel) based on Lithuania and a small rump Belarus (the Western parts not ceded to Russia) failed to gain support in Belarus, and ceased to exist in August 1919.

As shown by the Lit-Bel concept, the idea of a Belarus as a separate member of a Bolshevik federation was not conceptually developed at this time; Belarus' separate status after 1919 was more the result of Vladimir Lenin's tactical and instrumental thinking and *realpolitik* than of an appreciation for Belarusian identity and autonomy. Regardless of its original motivation, the establishment of a separate Byelorussian Soviet Socialist Republic (BSSR, established in July 1920, and re-established in December 1922 with the creation of the Union of Soviet Socialist Republics) would have important consequences. As a result of boundary revisions in 1921, 1924, and 1926, the size of the first Belarusian entity within the Bolshevik/Soviet federation trebled. With the regaining in 1939 (as a result of the Nazi–Soviet Non-Aggression Pact) of territories that had come under Polish control in 1921–39, most ethnic Belarusian territories came to be united in the BSSR.[9] Similarly, Belarusification—part of the larger Soviet "nativization" campaign of the 1920s[10]—resulted in the promotion of the Belarusian language and a Belarusian cultural elite. (Indeed, much of the development of a Belarusian national literature would take place under the Soviet period, making the Belarusian national project harder to disentangle from the building-of-Soviet Belarus project.) Thus, it could be argued that in many ways the BSSR fulfilled (albeit under close control from Moscow) the dream of creating if not a Belarusian national state, then at least a specifically Belarusian administrative unit, complete with its own institutions, in the form of the BSSR. Yet there was a high price to be paid: the Belarusian cultural elite, with its roots in the pre-Soviet period, was nearly eradicated as a result of Stalinist repression. Most notable was the execution, in the night of October 29, 1937 and following days, of over 100 Belarusian intellectuals in Minsk. To these need to be added the large numbers—between 50,000 and 250,000 according to most estimates—murdered by the Stalinist forces in the Kurapaty forest between 1937 and 1940.

9 In addition, a large area of territory West of Grodno was under temporary Soviet (Byelorussian SSR) control between 1939–1941.

10 See Martin, *The Affirmative Action Empire.*

The Second World War: Destruction, Reconstruction, and Integration

The Second World War and the German occupation of 1941–44 brought a new wave of destruction. Although estimates vary, it is clear that no other European country lost as high a percentage of its population to the Nazis as Belarus did, with deaths amounting to more than a quarter of the population. If those who were forced to move are added, then Belarus lost nearly half of its population during the war.[11] At least 500,000 Jews were killed during the Nazi occupation,[12] completely altering Belarus' multi-cultural landscape. A short-lived puppet quasi-state (the Belarusian Central Council, 1943–44) was set up during the Nazi occupation, a historical fact that would later be used as a major reputational weapon against nationalist-leaning groups the Lukashenka regime wanted to discredit.

The sheer tragedy of the wartime destruction created a dramatic backdrop for Belarus' striking post-war reconstruction effort. With its population ravaged by the war and its industry in shambles, Belarus was rebuilt with the help of citizens from across the USSR, many of whom settled in the republic. Taken together, the brutality of the Nazi occupation, the strength of the partisan movement, and rapid economic growth, created strong roots for Soviet legitimacy in post-war Belarus. A broad expansion of educational opportunities, especially in technical fields, was associated with this growth. The use of the Russian language also increased significantly during the Soviet period. Yet, in the context of the rapid industrialization and urbanization taking place after 1945, Russification was perceived by many not so much as an instrument of national oppression, but as necessary for individual economic and educational advancement and rising living standards. This was an important factor hindering the growth of a more specifically ethnic Belarusian identity into a political movement able to find wide support among the population.[13]

Belarus in the Soviet Union: development, integration, and legitimization

Belarus was an exception to broader trends affecting the region's development even before Lukashenka's coming to power in 1994. During the Soviet period,

11 Snyder, *Bloodlands*, 251.

12 Ibid., 350.

13 See also Ioffe, *Understanding Belarus*, 1–36.

Belarus was considered a special case, if only in the sense of how well the Soviet system seemed to work there, and how little underground opposition to the regime existed. With high levels of industrialization and a highly educated population whose living standards rose steadily after 1945, Belarus was referred to by many as "the most perfectly Soviet" of the republics within the USSR. As noted by Ioffe, the growth of Belarus' industrial output between 1917 and 1986 far exceeded the Soviet average.[14] Belarus was, indeed, one of the Soviet republics most closely integrated into the Soviet division of labor, and most dependent on its smooth functioning for its economic well-being.

Belarus in the Soviet Union: electrification, gasification, and the development of an energy-intensive economy

Belarus' post-war reconstruction and Soviet-style economic boom was characterized by the steady expansion of residential energy services, as well as of an energy-intensive economy.[15] It was also during this period that Belarus developed, not only as an energy-intensive economy, but as an especially gas-intensive one. Between 1985 and 1990, the net use of natural gas increased by nearly 70 percent: from 8.7 to 14.7 bcm/year,[16] a trend related to gasification (the expansion of piped-in gas supplies to end users throughout the country) and to the increased share of gas (instead of other fuels such as heavy oil) used in electricity generation. However, at this time, the Belarusian economy was still focusing on relatively advanced production processes—at least in comparison to its Soviet neighbors—and the role of energy-intensive production in its economy and exports was not the specific characteristic of its economy that it would later become (by the mid 2000s, some 80 percent of Belarus' exports would comprise highly energy-intensive products).[17]

Another important legacy of the Soviet period was the development of an energy infrastructure highly dependent on the rest of the Union for inputs and markets, and, in fact, barely viable outside of this larger system. Belarus

14 Ioffe, "Understanding Belarus: Economy," 86–87. On Belarus as "a major Soviet success story," see ibid., 85–89.

15 The impact of gasification on the rural residential sector remained limited, however: despite a significant increase in gasification, by 1993 traditional fuels such as firewood still played a significant role (an 88% share) in rural areas and lower income (a 76% share) households. World Bank, "Belarus Energy Sector 1995," 10.

16 Ibid., 42.

17 Zlotnikov, personal communication, February 15, 2011. In the mid-2000s, the overall resource-intensity (including energy intensity) of Belarus' products was four or five times higher than in highly-developed countries. Zlotnikov, "Žestkaa posadka," 9.

inherited large and relatively modern oil refineries, originally built as part of a Union-wide system but which, after the break-up of the USSR, became part of the energy infrastructure of a much smaller, independent country. These refineries could only work profitably as part of a larger market which could guarantee regular and inexpensive crude oil supplies, as well as access to markets throughout the former USSR. This (and, more generally, the existence of an excess of installed energy generation and processing infrastructure) was part of a broader process also affecting a number of other post-Soviet republics, especially those, such as Ukraine and the Baltic republics, located in the vicinity of highly populated areas of the Russian Federation.

Chernobyl: Soviet energy culture under stress

An important element of Belarus' Soviet legacy as regards energy is associated with nuclear power and the Chernobyl nuclear disaster of 1986. Although the country never had a nuclear power plant, it took part in the Soviet nuclear power system through electricity imports from the Ignalina and Chernobyl plants in neighboring Lithuania and Ukraine, respectively. Plans for the building of a nuclear power plant on Belarusian territory were underway by 1986. Yet nowhere did the Soviet promise of the "peaceful atom" become as irreparably broken as in Belarus. With the Chernobyl plant located just 12 kilometers from its border in Ukraine, the April 26, 1986 disaster took its heaviest toll on Belarus, with around 70 percent of the radioactive fallout descending there. Eighty percent of Belarus was exposed to dangerous levels of radioactivity in the days following the explosion, and over a fifth of its territory was contaminated by the accident.[18]

Politically and socially, the accident had a significant impact, acting as a catalyst for mobilization against the regime and for the development of a nationally inspired agenda.[19] As more and more information came to light about the extent of the official cover-up of the disaster and its consequences, popular distrust soared.[20] In addition to the "culture of irresponsibility" toward

18 Marples, "The Political Consequences," 57; and United Nations in Belarus, "Chernobyl," available at http://un.by/en/chernobyl/20years/chmaintx.html (accessed May 14, 2011).

19 Marples, in a view echoed by other scholars as well, argues that "public anger about the secrecy surrounding Chernobyl and its impact on Belarus" was an important impulse for the establishment of the Belarusian Popular Front in 1988. Marples, "The Political Consequences," 58. On the broader social and political impact of the Chernobyl disaster on Belarus and its neighboring states, see Sahm, *Transformation im Schatten von Tschernobyl* and Dawson, *Eco-nationalism*.

20 Marples, "The Political Consequences," 59.

the environment and human safety which pervaded the Soviet system,[21] the disaster and its poor management was clearly attributed to the over-centralization of the Soviet energy system, eager to implement top-down policies, with little regard to local needs. Thus, it is not surprising that, from the outset, protests against the management of the disaster "became attacks on the centre [Moscow]."[22] As the Soviet center disappeared, popular discontent on the issue became increasingly associated with the opposition, and starting in 1995, was targeted against President Lukashenka's administration, with the largest public demonstrations against the regime taking place yearly on April 26, the anniversary of the disaster.[23] If these demonstrations remained relatively small (undoubtedly also as a result of the general wave of repression in Belarus), until 2006 the country avoided the turnaround observed in Ukraine (and, especially, Lithuania) during this period, where popular sentiment against nuclear power quickly turned after independence and nuclear generation facilities came to be embraced as a guarantee against energy pressure from Russia. [24]

Energy and Belarus' Independence

Belarus' differences vis-à-vis other post-Soviet states such Ukraine and Lithuania, already visible in the Soviet period, became increasingly evident during the *perestroika* period. The relative weakness of Belarusian national identity, together with the determination of its entrenched communist elite, prevented the growth of a broad-based nationalist independence movement as happened in neighboring Lithuania, for example. Instead, the opposition Belarusian Popular Front remained limited to a relatively small group of intellectuals, and the new Belarusian state was established by those same communist leaders who had opposed independence only a year earlier.

Belarus attained independence in 1991 in a state of deep dependence on Russia. In addition to the cultural factors discussed above, this dependence had a real economic basis. This had to do both with Belarus' high level of integration into largely Russia-centered, USSR-wide economic processes (being the "assembly plant of the USSR"), and with its more direct dependence on

21 See Beissinger, "Chernobyl and the Culture," 17ff.
22 Marples, "The Political Consequences," 60.
23 Ibid., 63–64.
24 See Sabonis-Chafee, "Power Politics," 33; and Dawson, *Eco-nationalism*, 34–63.

Russia, its main trading partner.[25] Exactly because of this dependence on the Soviet Union *as a system*, Belarus was especially hard hit by the disintegration of the USSR, something that would come to have very important economic and political implications in the post-independence period.[26]

With the break-up of the USSR, and the end of centralized Union-level procurement of goods produced in Belarus (particularly military equipment and consumer durables such as TVs and refrigerators), demand for Belarus' exports collapsed, while the cost of imported raw materials, especially energy, increased sharply. With a yearly inflation level of 2,000 percent, and a GDP decline of some 10 percent in 1992, a devalued national currency (the Belarusian rouble) in circulation alongside the old Soviet rouble, a rise in non-cash barter transactions and major liquidity problems, and a drastic fall in real wages (which by 1995 had fallen to 56 percent of their 1990 level), the background was set for a major wave of public discontent.[27]

These issues also affected the Belarusian energy landscape. The growing impact of Belarus' dependency on Russia in the first post-independence years was exemplified by the fact that, although in 1991 fuels and electricity represented around 18 percent of Belarus' total imports from the rest of the Soviet Union (mainly Russia), by 1993 this share had reached some 60 percent.[28] Additionally, although in 1990 Belarus was dependent on imports (almost exclusively from Russia) for around 87 percent of its energy, by 1993, dependence on Russian energy had risen to over 97 percent, with small electricity imports from Lithuania, Latvia, and Ukraine—representing less than 3 percent of Belarus' Total Primary Energy Supply (TPES)—the country's sole non-Russian source of imported energy.[29]

In the absence of clear trade agreements in the immediate post-independence period, the burden of energy imports became an increasingly onerous one. In 1992, Belarus had to spend 25 percent of its GDP on energy imports.[30] The situation in the gas sector, where prices increased quickly to near-world

25 In 1992, 42% of Belarus' exports went to Russia, and 54% of its imports came from there. Interstate Statistical Commission of the Commonwealth of Independent States, *Official Statistics of the Countries of the Commonwealth of Independent States*, cited in Abdelal, "Interpreting Interdependence."

26 In November 1994, Lukashenka ascribed Belarus' crises as being the result of, in equal parts, the break of economic ties resulting from the Soviet dissolution and of the fall of discipline. *Belorusskii Rynok* 1996 No. 4, cited in Karbalevich, *Aleksandr Lukashenko*, 441.

27 See World Bank, "Belarus Energy Sector 1995." Data on real wages from Gotovskij, "Ekonomičeskoe razvitie," 9.

28 See World Bank, "Belarus Energy Sector 1995."

29 See ibid., i, 27.

30 Sahm and Westphal, "Power and the Yamal."

levels, was especially dim. Together with the change from old to new roubles in Russia, this led to a severe payments crisis, the rapid devaluation of the Belarusian currency, and a 66 percent reduction in Russian gas supplies by August 1993.[31] (Full deliveries were restated after Belarus' payment arrears were converted into long-term debt.) By December 1993, a new fuel-delivery crisis emerged, as Belarus' inability to keep up with increased gas prices led to a decrease in gas deliveries.[32]

Problems in the gas area were compounded by new ones in the oil area. With a refining capacity many times larger than the quantity of oil that the country could produce, Belarusian refineries depended on access to larger, (former-) Soviet Union-wide markets, which could guarantee regular crude-oil supplies and access to larger marketing chains. As a refinery's profitability depends directly on the degree to which its production capacity is utilized, the virtual dissolution of the former Union-wide supply chain, and the end of stable oil supplies from Russia in the early 1990s, led to the virtual paralysis of the sector.[33] Oil supplies from Russia decreased abruptly, by nearly half, between 1990 and 1992.[34] By 1993, gasoline rationing had become common;[35] supplies only stabilized—at a lower level—with the signing of a clearing (barter) agreement in 1993, which allowed Belarus to pay oil prices of $40–50/t for Russian imports, while world oil prices hovered around $120–130.[36]

31 In 1993, natural gas was not included in the clearing agreement between Belarus and Russia, with the result that most of Belarus' 16.3 bcm gas imports (with the exception of about 2 bcm received in lieu of gas transit) had to be paid in cash (in Russian roubles) based on the price applied by Russia for exports to CIS states. Although this price remained low throughout the first five months of the year (US$ 15–20/tcm), it started to increase rapidly in June 1993 and reached US$74, close to European prices, by December of that year. The replacement of old roubles in Russia and the imposition of strict credit limits by the Russian Central Bank on Belarus' correspondent account led to a payment crisis for Belarus in the summer of 1993. Due to the trade imbalance, the National Bank of Belarus could not convert the Belarussian rouble holdings of Beltransgaz (the enterprise importing gas) to Russian roubles. In order to make at least minimal payments, Beltransgaz purchased Russian roubles on the open market, pushing down the value of the Belarussian rouble. Faced with an impending collapse of the domestic currency as a result of this practice, the government discouraged this practice, payments for gas virtually stopped, and gas deliveries from Russia dropped to one third of their normal level in August of 1994. World Bank, "Belarus Energy Sector 1995," 50–51.

32 Ibid., 50–51.

33 In addition to political reasons, in the case of Belarus the main reason for unstable supplies were payment arrears.

34 Russian oil supplies fell from 38 to 20 Mt/yr between 1990 and 1992. 1990 figures from Hermann Clement, *Die Energiewirtschaft der GUS*, 55, cited in Sahm and Westphal, "Power and the Yamal," 270–301, here 72.

35 Zagorskaya et al., *Belarus. 1991–2006*, 146.

36 This first large-scale barter agreement called for the importation of 11.4 Mt (out of total supplies of 16 Mt) in exchange for Belarusian goods such as tractors, refrigerators, and butter. Despite the implicit advantage such agreements provided Belarus, in 1993 the agreement was fulfilled only to 60%. "Belarus Energy Sector 1995," 25–26.

The coincidence of the December 1993 crisis with a planned reduction in oil supplies and a period of unusually cold weather brought the energy question to the front of the political agenda, adding to ongoing debates about the country's future political direction and relations with Russia. These debates were vigorous and open in the immediate post-independence period. The first head of state, Stanislau Shushkevich, prioritized the establishment of Belarusian sovereignty vis-à-vis Russia and the development of constructive relationships with international institutions. However, the government and political elites were split between those who wanted neutrality for the country and those who favored close ties with Russia. As the July 1994 elections approached and the crisis deepened, the power of those favoring close relations with Russia strengthened. Infighting over language policy,[37] together with popular frustration over failed economic reform, growing corruption, and income differentiation, led to a strong protest vote against incumbent Premier Vyacheslaw Kebich, and to the election of the populist Aleksander Lukashenka.[38] Lukashenka, on the basis of his background as a low-level Soviet Communist Party functionary far removed from the upper echelons of the Soviet *nomenklatura*, and running on an anti-corruption and anti-Soviet *nomenklatura* platform, was able to successfully position himself as an alternative to both representatives of this elite establishment (such as Kebich),[39] and nationalist politicians (such as Zianon Pazniak). Reflecting broad popular fears, Lukashenka's policies sought to counter the effects of the breakup of the USSR by stopping painful economic reforms, and by promising to build a strong relationship with Russia. Simultaneously, he started to create an increasingly centralized system of personal control over policy decisions, gradually easing out and gaining power over the Soviet-legacy *nomenklatura*, by no means a foregone conclusion at the time of his arrival to the presidency in July 1994. In analyzing this process, we should not overlook the additional element of Lukashenka's personal characteristics, in particular his rhetorical and political skills.[40]

37 Belarus had been heavily russified during the Soviet period and many resisted what they saw as the forced reintroduction of the Belarusian language in education and administration.

38 On the growth of income differentiation between 1991 and 1995, see Zlotnikov, "Possibilities for the Development," 126.

39 On Lukashenka and the "late Soviet" establishment, see Lindner, "The Lukashenka Phenomenon," in Balmaceda et al., *Independent Belarus*, 80–81. Writes Marples: "the public saw him (Lukashenka) as outside the post-Soviet hierarchy, as untainted by the various scandals and failures that had pervaded the government over the previous three years, including Chernobyl." Marples, "The Political Consequences," 64.

40 For a comparison with early 1990s Belarusian leaders lacking such "skills" see Way, "Deer in Headlights."

It was at this moment that the aftershocks of the Soviet dissolution started to become increasingly influential in policy-making. In terms of economic policy, this was reflected in attempts to counter the disintegration of the Soviet system by limiting or preventing economic reform. Politically, this meant popular support for those politicians, such as Lukashenka, who sought to "counter" this disintegration by seeking to build strong ties with Russia. These tendencies both contributed to Lukashenka's election as president in July 1994, and largely influenced his subsequent policies. It is here, in 1994, that our analysis starts.

3

The "High Years": Energy and Russian-Belarusian Relations, 1994–2004

Having looked at Belarus' economic, energy and political situation at the time of Aleksander Lukashenka's coming to power in 1994, this chapter examines his use of energy policies and politics during the first ten years of his presidency, which largely coincided with the "high years" wherein Russia extended preferential energy trade conditions to Belarus, 1994–2004. The year 2004 is chosen as end-point for this period, as it saw the first large-scale suspension of Gazprom gas supplies to Belarus, as well as the end of Russian domestic prices for gas supplies.[1]

This chapter introduces the Belarusian "energy-political model" by analyzing the dynamics of the Russian-Belarusian energy relationship in the "high" years of 1994–2004, the means with which Lukashenka was able to capture high energy rents from this relationship, and the roles played by these rents as a source of political legitimacy vis-à-vis the Belarusian public. The first part of this chapter discusses the political and social background of the first energy measures taken by the Lukashenka regime. The second part analyzes the main features of Belarus' external management of its energy dependency during this period. The third part focuses on the country's domestic management of this energy dependency. The fourth part analyzes the main types of rent that Belarus accrued from this management. The final part outlines the basic contours of the Belarus "energy-political model" which took shape during this period.

---

1 While a case can be made to ascribe the end of the "high years" period to the January 2007 confrontation leading to the cutoff in oil supplies to Belarus that made headlines around the world, 2004 is a more appropriate cut-off point because of it signifying the start of open energy confrontations with Russia.

The Setting

As discussed in Chapter 2, Aleksander Lukashenka came to power at a time of great economic hardship for Belarus. For the population as a whole, coming out of the crisis was a priority, and good relations with Russia were seen to be central to this. In this sense, Lukashenka's attitude towards Russia reflected the widespread feeling of both the population and the country's main economic players. For these players, such as managers of energy-inefficient factories depending on inexpensive energy, finding a way to keep energy bills under control was crucial. This is shown clearly by the fact that, with the exception of the Belarusian Popular Front, none of the main players in the 1994 elections had advocated an economic distancing from Russia. Rather, the contest resembled a "surreal contest between [PM Viacheslav] Kebitch and Lukashenka to prove how much more pro-Eurasian and pro-Russian than the other each was."[2]

At this time, most members of the Belarusian elites lacked a strong sense of Belarusian cultural and economic sovereignty. Having been a central part of the Soviet division of labor, Belarus' economic elite lacked a clear sense of the country's economic interests as being separate from Russia's, a trend that would change only gradually after 1994. (The question remains as to why the Belarusian economic elite had a more limited sense of national economic interests than was the case in neighboring Ukraine.[3]) Although this process of differentiation of national economic interests from Russia's ultimately did take place, it was not until nearly a decade later, and under a more direct role of the president and not necessarily the economic groups themselves.

Despite all the ups and downs in the relationship with Russia, and despite Lukashenka's deep distrust of specific Russian actors, the president did little until 2004 to alter the status quo of dependency on Russian energy. In fact, few conscious, official moves towards energy self-sufficiency and towards an independent conceptualization of energy security were made before 2004. Until that time, the country explicitly advocated a joint energy balance with Russia, and energy dependency was not seen as a problem; indeed, gas sup-

2 Abdelal, "Interpreting Interdependence," 113.

3 Abdelal and other constructivist-inspired authors have stressed the impact of national identity issues on the way post-Soviet states and their elites have conceptualized their economic interests and developed economic and trade relations with Russia. See Abdelal, *National Purpose*. On the Ukrainian case, see also Puglise, "Clashing Agendas?" Other explanations include the deep integration of Belarusian economic actors in the Soviet division of labor.

plies from Russia increased significantly during the period. Although in 1990 (i.e., before the decline in economic activity which immediately followed the dissolution of the USSR) Belarus imported 14.1 bcm of gas, by 2006 this had increased to 21 bcm despite the decline in population.[4]

Despite the fact that the 2001 Concept of National Security had noted the problem that Belarus was receiving 99.9 percent of its energy imports from a single supplier,[5] and although in 2002 a political declaration by Aleksander Lukashenka (in the wake of a gas-related confrontation in December of that year) had called for the need to "immediately work out energy supply alternatives," such apprehension towards an excessive reliance on Russia was not reflected in energy policy documents for several years to come.[6] Analysis of an exhaustive database of energy-related legislation (including government decrees, *ukase*, and resolutions) covering the years 2002–2008[7] reveals that if in 2004, official documents were calling for 25 percent of heat and electricity generation to come from local or alternative energy sources by 2012,[8] the concept of geographical energy diversification as a national policy goal was not mentioned until 2007.[9] For most of this period, dependency on Russia was seen not as a threat, but as an opportunity.[10] This was in sharp contrast with the first two post-independence years, when the shock of rapidly increasing energy prices prompted discussions with international institutions about a change in the energy mix away from those energy sources that could only be imported, such as gas, and towards domestically available sources such as wood. Yet such plans were quickly shelved after a beneficial *modus operandi* was found with Russia after 1994.[11]

4 1990 figures from Clement, *Die Energiewirtschaft der GUS*, 55, cited in Sahm and Westphal, "Power and the Yamal," 272.

5 Text of the document is available at: http://www.mod.mil.by/koncep.html (accessed November 11, 2008).

6 Lukashenka quote from Manenok, "Gaz kak instrument."

7 The Energosoft database can be accessed at: http://energosoft.info/news2004.html.

8 Postanovlenie Soveta Ministrov Respubliki Belarus', № 1680, 30 December 2004, available at: http://laws.newsby.org/documents/sovetm/pos05/sovmin05822/index.htm (accessed March 12, 2012), and *Gosudarstvennaâ kompleksnaâ programma modernizacii.*

9 In the *Direktiva # 3 Prezidenta Respubliki Belarus'* from 14 June 2007. Available at: http://www.government.by/ru/directive-3/ (accessed May 26, 2011).

10 This seemed to be very much in tune with popular beliefs: as late as 2004, in the immediate aftermath of the 2004 conflict involving the suspension of gas deliveries to Belarus, only 13.9% of those polled in a national sample argued the best way to solve it would be by means of Belarus finding alternative sources of energy, as to not depend on Russia. See *Novosti NISEPI* 1/31, 11.

11 The share of alternative energy sources such as wood in Belarus' energy mix increased very modestly, from 2.8% in 1993 to 4.65% in 2009. 2009 data from Rakova, "Analiz ènergetičeskoj," 3–4. See also World Bank, "Belarus Energy Sector 1995."

External management of energy dependency, 1994–2004

The context

Belarus' management of its energy dependency during this period was strongly shaped by President Lukashenka's views and preferences. This was made possible by his growing control over policy-making, both as an individual ruler and through his Presidential Administration, an institution he consciously and consistently built up as a parallel, fully unaccountable center of power starting in 1994, and which, since the approval of a corresponding measure in a 1996 referendum, enjoyed the use of an undisclosed budget outside the control of parliament or other representative bodies. In all policy areas, important decisions came to be concentrated in the Presidential Administration. Undoubtedly, lobbying among various groups existed, yet it took place within the confines of the Presidential Administration and in a non-transparent manner, rather than as part of an open policy-making process. Three additional factors made it virtually impossible for a transparent energy policy-making process to take place: the lack of an independent energy regulatory organ (such as existed in all EU and most post-Soviet states);[12] the direct dependency of high-level policy-makers on Lukashenka; and the lack of any real policy-making power by nominal representative institutions such as the National Assembly. Despite Lukashenka's virtual monopolization of energy policy, the blame for failed policies, however, was passed on to the Council of Ministers, which *de facto* only had control of lower-level, day-to-day operational decisions.[13] Existing evidence points to delays in important policy decisions—for example, during important negotiations with Russia—until a decision had been made by the president.[14]

This concentration of energy policy-making power in the hands of the president, in turn, opened the door for the politicization of external energy

---

12 As of 2011, independent (or at least formally independent) energy regulatory organs existed in every post-Soviet state with the exception of Belarus. Energy Regulators Regional Association.

13 Romanchuk has argued that, while all significant policy decisions were made at the level of the Presidential Administration, "the liability for faults and the results of these decisions lies with the Council of Ministers." Romanchuk, "The Belarusian Republic," 11.

14 For example, during April 2004 negotiations on gas supplies from Russia, despite the country being on the verge of a cut-off in supplies, Lukashenka delayed a resolution of the case by giving the high-level negotiators sent to Moscow little real power to sign agreements. See Blokhin, Russia's ambassador to Belarus, in Manenok, "Prem'ery ne dogovorilis'."

relationships. Lukashenka's ability to politicize the relationship with Russian energy actors, in turn, was related to his domestic monopolization of power (i.e., to the absence of independent actors in the country with sufficient power and connections to offer Russian energy players their own, parallel rent-seeking strategies and business proposals, as was the case in Ukraine for example). This is not invalidated by the fact that, at times, the Belarusian opposition received indirect support from Moscow, as in the case of the July 2010 Russian media campaigns against Lukashenka. The fact remains, however, that opposition leaders lacked control of energy policy levers that could be used in the rent-seeking and value-added chains of Russian energy players.

The essential elements of Lukashenka's management of energy dependence in the 1994–2004 period were: externally, his attempt to deal with energy relations with Russia at an almost exclusively political level, in order to extract as much rent as possible; internally, an approach which concentrated on seeking to make the most of available domestic rents as well. We discuss each of these aspects in this and the next section of the chapter.

Belarus and asymmetrical interdependence

Belarus' energy policy during this period took place within the context of the country's asymmetrical interdependence vis-à-vis Russia. Depending on foreign sources for some 86 percent of its energy supply for most of the post-independence period, Belarus was—and continues to be—one of the most energy-dependent countries of the former Soviet Union, surpassed only by Moldova. Belarus can cover none of its gas needs, and less than 10 percent of its oil needs.[15] This dependence was made worse by Belarus' limited oil-storage facilities and a lack of underground gas-storage facilities, making it largely unable to tap into underground reserves to withstand a stoppage of supplies.[16]

15 Belarus produces around 8% of its oil needs domestically (24% if one does not count as "domestic use" oil refined for export; see Table 5.5); this domestically produced oil is usually earmarked for export. Production has remained relatively stable since 1996, with a slight downward trend (from 1.86Mt in 1996 to 1.76 in 2007). Belarus also possesses some brown coal reserves (in 2008 estimated at 0.5 b tons), but these are located at great depths, making their exploitation difficult and expensive. See *Eurasian Chemical Market*, January 30, 2008.

16 As of 2006, Belarus' two underground gas storage facilities had a total capacity of some 660 million cubic meters, a small fraction of the recommended 6.6 bcm (30% of current yearly gas consumption). Manenok, "Tol'ko po rynočnoj stoimosti." Belarus' concept of energy security, published in 2005, calls for an increase in underground gas storage capacities by 5 bmc by 2020. See also Beltransgaz' official website at: http://www.btg.by/proizvodstvo/hranenie/. There is no official information on Belarus' crude oil reserves, but they can be estimated at 20 days; in addition, the country has, as per administrative regulations, a ten

Lacking nuclear-generation facilities in its territory, Belarus is largely dependent on imported gas for electricity generation.

On the other hand, during this period Belarus was—and continues to be—one of the most important transit countries for Russian gas exports to Western Europe. In 2009, some 20 percent of Russia's total gas exports outside the CIS and the Baltic states, and over one-third of Russian oil exports to the EU, went through Belarus.[17] Transit through Belarus offers the shortest route from Russian oil and gas fields to the main Western European markets. This transit potential, however, is limited by technical problems: in particular the state of disrepair of Belarus' pipeline system, most of which was built in the mid-to-late 1960s. (More details on Belarus' oil transit role are provided in the later part of this chapter.)

A comparison with another important transit state, Ukraine, highlights the strengths and weaknesses of Belarus' counter-power as a transit state. Although both countries' role in the transit of Russian oil is largely similar, Belarus' 20 percent role in gas transit gives it much less bargaining power than Ukraine's 80 percent role. The structure of ownership of the main gas pipelines further diminishes Belarus' bargaining power. While Ukraine owns most of the high-volume gas transit pipelines crossing its territory, only one of the two main gas-transit pipelines crossing Belarus (the Beltransgaz pipeline) belonged to Belarus during the 1991–2011 period; Gazprom owned the Yamal pipeline (which in 2007 carried 63 percent of all gas transported through Belarus).[18] Of all the countries which the Yamal pipeline crosses, Belarus is the only one where the pipeline itself belongs to Gazprom, which also has a long-term lease for the land it uses. Thus, only slightly more than a third of Russian gas transported through pipelines was carried out by national pipeline operator Beltransgaz; this limited Belarus' techni-

day reserve of heating oil (*mazut*). Elena Rakova, personal communication, January 2011. A 2010 official document makes reference to a 61-day reserve *capacity* for heating oil in 2009, see http://www.pravo.by/webnpa/text.asp?RN=C21001180#Зar_Утв_1 (accessed September 15, 2011). The Concept of Energy Security to 2020, approved in 2007, calls for the establishment of 90-day reserves of heavy oil, but sets no deadline for the project. See www.president.gov.by/press34523.html#doc.

17 Broadly understood, Belarus' transit role also includes the oil indirectly exported through Belarus (i.e., shipped as crude oil to Belarus, refined there, and sold to Western Europe as refined oil products).

18 Data for 2007 from IPM), *MIB 2008*, 33. In the original agreement (1994) Belarus gave Gazprom a long-term lease on the pipeline (Zagorskaya et al., *Belarus. 1991–2006*, 51). A 2005 agreement, negotiated in the midst of broader discussions on the price of gas supplies to Belarus, formalized Gazprom's ownership of the Belarusian segment of the pipeline. *MIB 2007*, 29. The Beltransgaz pipeline network is used to transit Russian gas to the Baltic States and Kaliningrad, while the Yamal pipeline transits gas to Poland and further West.

cal and legal ability to obstruct gas transit. These limitations grew stronger in 2010 when—as will be discussed in Chapter 5—Beltransgaz itself became a 50–50 percent Russian (Gazprom)–Belarusian joint venture. Thus, despite taking into account its transit role, Belarus' objective counter-power vis-à-vis Russia was limited. As seen in Graph 3.5, despite increased oil transit volumes, Belarus' percentage role in the transit of Russian oil to non-CIS states has steadily diminished.

Energy in the context of the Russian-Belarusian relationship: Virtual integration, real deterioration

The broader ties with Russia provided a second context for Belarus' management of the energy relationship during this period.

The formal integration process

Energy ties took place in the context of the development of a formal relationship between Belarus and Russia. A Monetary Union Treaty was signed in 1994. After protracted negotiations, in April 1996, both countries signed a Commonwealth Agreement; and, in April 1997, the Treaty on the Union of Belarus and Russia. In December 1999, a new Union Agreement, including detailed specifics on its implementation, was signed. While much in these agreements remained vague or was never implemented (such as a plan for monetary union by 2005), they still held an important symbolic value, and set the basis for closer cooperation in military and strategic areas, which proceeded much more successfully.[19]

Some aspects of the integration process produced clearly positive results for Belarus. Increased access to Russian markets starting in 1995 as a result of the Customs Union agreements, the import-substitution effects of increasing import duties for imports from third countries to Russian levels, and the devaluation of the Belarusian rouble and the accompanying sharp fall in wages and price levels compared to Russian ones, all stimulated growth and GDP recovery. In addition, once Russia's economy started to recover, this had a positive effect on Belarus' economic growth as well.

19 See also Danilovich, *Russian Belarusian Integration*, 67. Danilovich argues that the 1996 Treaty on a Community of Sovereign Republics, characterized by internal contradictions and devoid of measures for concrete implementation, was clearly "not intended to carry out integration."

Belarus became, in fact, the first post-Soviet state to reach 1992 GDP levels (in 2003), after the sharp fall of the first post-Soviet years.[20] In a depressed Russian economy, low-cost (and often low-quality) Belarusian consumer goods found an important market, with Russia receiving nearly 80 percent of some of Belarus' main exports (such as refrigerators) in the mid-2000s.[21] (Belarus' GDP growth, however, was not only the result of improved access to Russian markets, but of the fact that a process of economic transformation—with all its painful side-effects—had not started.)

Virtual integration, real deterioration

The formal integration process, however, masked growing contradictions in the Belarusian-Russian relationship. Although these tensions remained largely under the radar for most Western observers until around 2001, there had been clear signs since 1997.[22] In addition to political differences, such as those related to Lukashenka's toying with the idea of a Union State presidential bid, economic differences could be seen in the attitudes towards the conditions of monetary union and economic integration, and in Belarus' abuse of an open border with Russia.[23] Little real economic integration took place in practice in the first years after the signing of the Union agreement in 1997, in great part because of lack of real cooperation on the part of the Belarusian government. Agreements on a single currency also remained unimplemented, mainly due to the Belarusian side's insistence on retaining significant control over emission decisions, and to the reticence of the Russian Central Bank to tie the Russian economy to that of a country which remained largely unreformed and thus faced very different economic problems from those faced by Russia. The pattern was clear: constant talk of unification, especially from the Belarusian side, but little in terms of real economic integration. In 1997, Boris Nemtsov, the former Russian deputy prime minister, was describing the Belarusian leadership's talk about union with Russia as a political game: "On the one hand, there is constant talk about economic integration; and, on the other, all possible juridical, administrative and economic obstacles are created to prevent this integration from really happening."[24]

---

20 Calculated from World Bank database, available at http://devdata.worldbank.org/query/default.htm.

21 Source: Ministry of Statistics of the Republic of Belarus, 2005–2007, cited in Romanchuk, "The Belarusian Republic," 8.

22 See Balmaceda, "Myth and reality."

23 See Balmaceda, "Belarus as a transit route."

24 Interview with Nemtsov, "Rossiâ stroit."

These realities have led a number of authors to describe the Belarusian-Russian relationship during this period as a game of "virtual integration," where both sides had much to gain from constant declarations, posturing and outdoing each other in their support of a Union state, but much less to gain from real integration.[25] Thus, actual integration was replaced by a game of virtual integration played out for political purposes by both sides. For the Russian side, virtual integration was relatively cheap, and yielded high short-term political dividends, especially in contrast with breaking ties with Lukashenka, which could entail high political costs vis-à-vis the Russian electorate. For the Belarusian side, the integration discourse was used to lobby for continued high levels of support from Russia, but without allowing a real integration that could threaten President Lukashenka's power. A central contradiction here is that, rather than using the economic benefits accrued from the relationship with Russia as a stimulus to inch closer to reform policies similar to those pursued in Russia during the Yeltsyn and early Putin administrations, Belarus used the relationship as an escape route to avoid any crucial reforms in the economy.

Authors such as Yafimava have argued that some of the Russian-Belarusian gas conflicts were a result of the failure of both states to establish a real union.[26] Yet, it could be argued that it was actually the *lack* of institutionalization of significant aspects of the relationship (understanding the "lack of institutionalization" not only in terms of a lack of establishment of a real union but also the fact that many formal agreements were not adhered to) and vagueness about its future that allowed Lukashenka to keep extracting energy rents and subsidies from Russia. For example, under a situation of full integration with Russia, Belarus would have been unable to maintain export duties on oil products which were different from Russia's, a situation that (as will be discussed in a later part of this chapter) created important profits for Belarus, but led Russia to lose billions of dollars of income in the process.[27]

Below, we discuss this issue in terms of the actual managing of gas and oil relations during this period.

---

25 When gas relations finally seemed to sour for good in late 2006 when Russia started talking about charging Belarus $200/tcm, opposition leader Aliaksandr Milinkevich commented much to the point: "Ten years of the building of an ephemeral state, on which many politicians and common people put their hopes ... and suddenly it turns out that everything failed. *But this is simply punishment for a lie that was [forcibly] initiated and cultivated.*" Milinkevich, quoted in Karnej, "Rossijskij gaz-2007: Belorussiâ vzvolnovana." Emphasis mine.

26 Yafimava, *Post-Soviet Russian-Belarussian*, 19.

27 As noted by Karbalevich, the reality of incomplete integration (i.e., combining integration and sovereignty) was not only politically and economically advantageous for Lukashenka, but also psychologically preferable for the Belarusian population. See Karbalevich, *Aleksandr Lukashenko*.

Gas: External Management in the "High Years," 1994–2004

Aleksander Lukashenka came to power at a time of serious gas supply and payment problems; in September 1994 Russia again suspended fuel shipments to Belarus over unpaid fuel bills. This pressure led to the attempt, immediately after the September 1994 cut-off, to sign an agreement which gave Gazprom partial ownership of Beltransgaz, in exchange for the resumption of gas deliveries. However, this agreement was not ratified by Belarus' Supreme Soviet. Thus, the first priority for Lukashenka regarding relations with Russia was not to gain economic or energy independence, but to create a deeper relationship with Russia in order to lift the country out of its economic crisis.

Once the initial payments crisis had been overcome through a "zero option" agreement (discussed below), the outline of a gas strategy began to take shape, with two general goals emerging as policy priorities: first, ensuring low prices, while maintaining *and increasing* gas supply volumes from Russia; second, limiting the real impact of any actual gas-price increases by extracting related concessions, mainly through low-interest stabilization loans intended to soften the impact of price increases (as had been the case with a $40 million export credit to Belarus as compensation for the higher prices in 2002,[28] and a $175 million loan provided shortly after the gas price increases of January 2004).

Some of the ways these goals were pursued were by presenting Belarus as an unavoidable transit gatekeeper, by "selling" the promise of joint Russian-Belarusian control over the country's gas-transit system, and by making sure that any gas price increases by Gazprom would create high political costs for the Russian leadership vis-à-vis its own domestic electorate. These strategies became especially clear through the cases of Yamal, Beltransgaz, and the negotiations on gas supplies and prices, which we discuss below.

Gas transit: the Yamal pipeline and the "gatekeeper" myth

A first crucial element in Belarus' management of its gas dependency on Russia during this period was the attempt to present the country as both the gatekeeper and the most reliable transit state for the transit of Russian oil and gas to Western markets. This element was especially visible in the case of nego-

28 See Europa Publications, ed., *Eastern Europe, Russia and Central Asia 2004*, 147.

tiations around the Yamal pipeline.[29] Although many conflicting issues concerning the pipeline would not become apparent until after 2004 (discussed separately in Chapter 5), the history of the project during 1994–2004 illustrates the ways in which Lukashenka sought to present Belarus (and himself personally) as a reliable but unavoidable gate-keeper for the transit of Russian gas to Western Europe.

The Yamal pipeline, called "the project of the century" when building began in 1994, represents Belarus' most important gas transit project to date. During this period, it was also the most important component of Belarus' claim of a special relationship with Russia. Yamal was conceived as a vast project involving the development of the Yamal gas fields in Siberia and the transportation of this gas to Western Europe via a 6,670-km pipeline, passing through Belarus, Poland and Germany; the total price tab for the project was estimated at $36 billion. (The terms of Belarus' participation in the project, as well as Russia's growing commitments towards gas transit through Belarus until 2015, were noted in the Long-term Agreement on Supplies and Cooperation between Gazprom and Beltransgaz signed in 1994, the first in Lukashenka's presidency.)[30]

Given Gazprom's situation at the time, the Yamal pipeline was of central importance for the company's domestic and global strategy. Despite Gazprom's economic prowess, its short-term economic situation in the mid-1990s was highly problematic; and, lacking the investment resources needed to develop new gas fields with higher start-up costs, it sought to increase medium-term revenues by seeking to gain a stake in Western European gas markets and to enter into their profitable domestic gas distribution business before these countries could tap into alternative suppliers. This strategy required a safe and dependable gas-delivery system. As energy relations between Russia and Ukraine became increasingly problematic in the 1990s,[31] Russia became keen to use a possible Belarusian-Polish corridor to reduce transit via Ukraine. This need coincided with, and boosted, President Lukashenka's view of himself and Belarus as irreplaceable partners for Russia. Yamal also seemed to embody Lukashenka's view of integration in the post-Soviet space, by rewarding the advocates of closer economic union with Russia and punishing those post-Soviet states who opposed it (as Ukraine was perceived to do). Lukash-

29 On the Yamal pipeline, see also Sahm and Westphal, "Power and the Yamal pipeline."

30 Zagorskaya, et al., *Belarus. 1991–2006*, 31.

31 The main issue at stake was the large-scale disappearance of Gazprom gas from the export pipeline going through Ukraine.

enka's position echoed the views of many in Moscow who were happy to see pressure on Ukraine—in the form of reduced transit revenues—to adopt a more pro-Russian foreign-policy stance. This fitted well with Lukashenka's positioning of himself, not only as Russia's only reliable energy transit partner, but also as its most loyal, "last" ally.

Yamal was also important for Lukashenka's domestic power, as it represented an important influx of investments which could be used to modernize Belarus' aging gas-transit system, bolstering the president's domestic image as someone irreplaceable to Moscow. Yamal also placed a solid economic actor, Gazprom, behind the political project of Belarusian-Russian integration, giving it a powerful lobbyist. So, for a while at least, Belarusian and Russian interests in the transit area coincided, putting into motion a project that, once started, would take on a life of its own. In fact, many Belarusian opposition figures saw Gazprom's transit interest as the main motivation for the establishment of the Belarus-Russia Union in 1997.[32]

Beltransgaz: fighting for control, selling the dream

The second element of Belarus' gas strategy during 1994–2004 concerned Lukashenka's response to Russia's long-standing interest in acquiring control over its energy-transit infrastructure. This response involved selling the promise of joint Russian-Belarusian control over the country's gas-transit system, while actually seeking to retain control over it. This was especially visible concerning the case of gas transit company Beltransgaz, which owned Northern Lights, one of the two major pipelines transiting Russian gas through Belarus (the other being Yamal, directly owned by Gazprom).[33] The dynamics of negotiations on its possible purchase between 1994 and 2004, discussed below, provide a prime example of the ways in which Belarus sought to man-

32 Some opposition leaders, such as Stanislau Shushkevich, Belarus' first head of state, saw the proposed union as being only to the economic advantage of Gazprom. See *Kommersant*, 29 April 1997. Others, like Anatoly Lebedko, feared the West and Russia could find a common understanding based on their common interest on gas imports to Europe through the Yamal pipeline, but at the expense of democracy in Belarus. See Lebedko, "I v vozduh čepčiki brosali," 2. Paniushkin and Zygar' also argue that one important reason the West (and Russia) remained silent about growing authoritarianism in Belarus was because of their common economic interest in the Yamal pipeline, as they did not want anything to threaten the continuous supply of gas to Western Europe through the pipeline. Panjushkin and Zygar' , *Gazprom*, 127.

33 In addition, Beltransgaz operates a 7377-km network of pipelines of various diameters, two underground gas storage facilities, a network of gas compressor stations, and a variety of social facilities for its employees. From Beltransgaz's official website available at http://www.btg.by.

age its gas relationship with Russia during these years: seeking to gain maximum possible subsidies and rents for Belarus, but without giving up control and ownership of important economic assets.

Gazprom's attempts to gain control over Beltransgaz were closely related to both the Russian government's desire to strengthen its grip over Belarus, and to Gazprom's value-added chain-and-export strategy. Repeated attempts in the 1990s had failed due to disagreement between the parties, especially around the issue of how the company would be valued. Gazprom's estimates were regularly lower than those offered by the Belarusian side. (In 1993, discussions had started on a possible joint venture and Gazprom's acquisition of shares in Beltransgaz in exchange for part of Belarus' accumulated gas debt. The agreement was not finalized, however, as Premier Kebich left office in 1994, and the agreement was not ratified by the Belarusian parliament.) A second attempt came in the form of a debt-for-shares offer from the Belarusian government in 1995, but failed due to sharply differing valuations of the company.[34] After this attempt, the idea of using a shares-for-debt approach as a means of dealing with Belarus' debt to Gazprom was temporarily left aside, replaced by a "zero option" agreement waiving over $1 billion of Belarus' gas debt to Gazprom in exchange for a number of military and other concessions (discussed in the next section).

A third attempt took place in 1998, when the idea of creating a joint system to which Belarus would contribute two planned gas pipelines (Torzhok-Ivatsevichi and Torzhok-Dolina) and Russia the planned Yamal-Europa pipeline, was discussed. Once again the issue of how to calculate the value of each partner's contributions hampered any final agreement. A new attempt in the following year also floundered, as the Belarusian side realized that, on paper, its contribution would amount to only $400,000 as opposed to Gazprom's $3 billion, leaving it with little representation in the consortium's top management. Moreover, such a joint venture would have given Gazprom control, not only over gas supplies, but also over gas distribution in Belarus, a prospect opposed by the Belarusian side.[35]

A new burst of activity preceded the September 2001 presidential elections in Belarus; Gazprom's significant informal help in Lukashenka's campaign was predicated on the expectation that, after the elections, negotia-

34 Gazprom's valuation was $90 million, Belarus' $900 million. Zagorskaya et al., *Belarus. 1991–2006*, 52.

35 See Tikhon Klishevich, "Istoriâ bor'ba za `Beltransgaz'," www.dw-world.de November 29, 2006 (accessed August 5, 2006) and Sekhovich, "Założniki truby," 19.

tions on the corporatization of Beltransgaz and the creation of a joint venture would go forward successfully.[36] The April 2002 agreement, "On the Establishment of equal conditions in the area of price policy," (signed on the basis of the Union State agreements), making available to Belarus similar gas prices as those available to nearby areas of Russia, was predicated on the same expectation.[37] However, little real progress took place after the elections (although Russia fulfilled its part of the agreement by selling gas to Belarus at domestic Russian prices, Belarus did not fulfill its side of the agreements).[38] Thanks to a restructuration of its gas debt in 2001 Belarus received a temporary respite on the pressure to privatize the company as a means to deal with the debt. However, under pressure from a 50 percent reduction in gas supplies by Gazprom in mid-November 2002 (discussed in the next section), the process of privatizing Beltransgaz started to move again; a law lifting existing restrictions on Beltransgaz's privatization was passed by the Belarusian parliament shortly thereafter. In addition, the late 2002 decisions by the EU and the US to refuse visas to Lukashenka and other Belarusian leaders as response to human rights violations most likely also played a role, as the fear of falling into total isolation may have moved Lukashenka to seek better relations with Russia. But this new attempt to privatize Beltransgaz also failed, as in 2003 Lukashenka made new demands (in particular, a $5 billion valuation of the company—contrasting sharply with the Russian valuation at $1 billion—as well as asking for new investments and gas supply guarantees).[39]

Although the future of Beltransgaz would not become clear until after 2006, the dynamics of the negotiations in 1994–2004 provide a good sense of the main tactics favored by the Belarusian government during this period. These tactics were characterized by two elements. First, delaying the "moment of truth" (much in the same way as it had been delayed in the process of Belarusian-Russian "virtual integration" in general) in Beltransgaz's privatization through constant promises, but few concrete results. Second, seeking to tie negotiations on the future of Beltransgaz with discussions on the future of Gazprom's gas supplies and prices to Belarus. The motivating factor behind these tactics was Lukashenka's strong desire not to share ownership of Beltransgaz with Gazprom. However, this was not so much the result of a clear

36 Urban and Nikolskii, "Bez pridannogo."

37 See also the agreement on the development of relations in the gas sphere ("Soglašenie o razvitii otnošenij v gazovoj sfere") signed by Belarus and Russia on 12 April 2002.

38 Urban and Nikolskii, "Bez pridannogo."

39 Klishevich, "Istoriâ bor'ba."

conceptualization of Belarus' separate economic interests as different from Russia's, but of domestic considerations: the fear that the presence of any strong economic actors might challenge Lukashenka's own personal power.[40]

Politicization of price and debt negotiations

A third element of Belarus' gas strategy during this period was concerned with the politicization of negotiations on gas prices, and of any incident in which gas prices would be increased, or volumes lowered. Although between 1992 and 2002, Belarus formally purchased gas from Russia at commercial prices (i.e., prices affording the seller some level of profit above and beyond cost recovery), trade conditions changed significantly within this period, providing ample opportunities for the politicization of negotiations.[41]

In the 1992–1994 period, uncertainty about the forms of this trade, together with a sharp decline in Belarus' liquidity, led to Belarus' accumulation of a significant debt and periodical gas supply reductions, the most significant occurring in September 1994. After 1995's unsuccessful attempt at a debt-for-shares swap involving Beltransgaz, in 1996, after Belarus' gas debt had reached more than $1 billion, a different approach was pursued. A so-called zero option agreement in 1996 established that Belarus would be pardoned its gas debt accrued up to that date ($1.27 billion),[42] in exchange for a number of military and political concessions: forfeiting any claims to Russia for the costs of ecological damage created by its military bases in Belarus; for the compensation of Chernobyl victims; for the removal and processing of nuclear weapons; and leasing to Russia, free of charge, two military telecommunications units for a 25-year period (a naval communications unit in Vileika and a radar station in Hantsevichi/Gantsevichi).[43]

---

40 Other analysts have emphasized Lukashenka's own perceptions about the economy as a source of his insistence on Belarus' not ceding control over such assets. In particular, they have noted his emphasis on the importance of physical control over the "real" sector of the economy (such as factories, pipelines, and other physical infrastructure), as opposed to less tangible assets such as services and intellectual property, and less tangible means of control and profits such as through the financial sector. See Elena Rakova, personal communication, January 27, 2011. See also Karbalevich, *Aleksandr Lukashenko,* 441, 445.

41 In the Russian/post-Soviet context the term "commercial prices of gas" is used to denote prices affording the seller some level of profit above and beyond cost-recovery; these, however, are not necessarily the same as market prices.

42 Danilovich, *Russian-Belarusian Integration*, 62. Other sources put the amount at "close to $1 billion." Sekhovich, "1991–2006. Itogi. Gazovaâ otrasl'."

43 See Zagorskaya et al., *Belarus. 1991–2006*, 53. In connection with the Strategic Arms Reductions Treaty (START), in 1992 the leaders of Belarus. Ukraine, and Kazakhstan agreed to eliminate all their nuclear

In contrast with Ukraine, where a similar "zero option" agreement in 1995 had faced significant opposition, little open opposition was seen in Belarus.[44] The agreement also had a number of indirect effects: as noted by Belarusian analysts, it was following this agreement that barter and non-cash operations in the gas sector—as discussed in Chapter 4—opening the door to corruption and rent-seeking, became especially common.[45]

Thus, despite the formal continuation of gas purchases from Russia at commercial prices, after 1996 the actual burden on Belarus decreased significantly, as barter and other non-cash arrangements (in the early 2000s covering some 80 percent of gas purchases) and the existence of multiple exchange rates significantly reduced the prices.[46] Starting that year, Belarus and Russia moved to a "single balance of energy resources," further eroding the basis for a Belarus-based conceptualization of energy security.[47] In this single balance for Belarus and Russia, the production plans of Russian companies, as well as exports to Belarus were noted, but without prices being set in advance. The balance also spelled out how much domestically produced oil Belarus would be allowed to export each year. This was especially important as—as long as Belarus could rely on cheaper Russian crude to keep its refineries working at full capacity—the export of domestically produced oil, with a production cost of $30-60 per ton (2004 and 2006) while world prices were many times higher, was especially profitable for Belarus, yielding a net profit of c. $86 (2004) to $119 per ton (2006).[48]

After the Russian economic crisis and devaluation of 1998, the gas prices paid by Belarus went down (from c. $50/tcm to $30/tcm in 1999), remaining around that level until 2002. This made the gas import prices paid by Belarus during this period two or three times lower than those paid by its neighbors.[49] Nevertheless, Belarus' payment problems continued, and it continued to press for a price reduction. In April 2002, President Lukashenka

weapons within a seven-year period and to join the Non-Proliferation Treaty (NPT) as non-nuclear weapons states. By November 1996, Belarus had removed to Russia all the SS-25 missiles and nuclear warheads based in its territory.

44 As part of the 1997 Black Sea Fleet and subsequent agreements, Ukraine received a significant energy debt relief in exchange for a 20-year contract leasing Black Sea Fleet bases in Crimea to Russia at a reduced rate and the relinquishing of an additional share of the Fleet.

45 Zagorskaya et al., *Belarus. 1991–2006,* 53.

46 IPM, "Rost cen na gaz," 8, Footnote 4.

47 The balance of energy resources, a Soviet legacy, is s volume-based plan specifying plans for the production of specific types of fuel and their use in various sectors of the economy.

48 Tatsyana Manenok, personal communication, January 29, 2011.

49 Zlotnikov, "Faktor nomer 1."

achieved one of his most important goals: the agreement "On the establishment of equal conditions in the area of price policy" reduced prices further by establishing that Russia would sell gas to Belarus at the same (domestic) price as industrial consumers in Russia's fifth region, Smolensk. Thus, the basic price of gas charged by Gazprom to Belarus was reduced to c. $22/tcm in May 2002, one of very few examples of gas price reductions in the post-Soviet era. This arrangement—in principle without an expiration date—remained in place until 2004.[50]

Despite the agreement's stipulation on charging Belarus Russian domestic prices for gas, there was plenty of space for negotiation and disagreement, as it applied only to the quantities established in the yearly agreements between Gazprom and Belarus, c. 10 bcm out of Belarus' yearly consumption of c. 18 bcm, providing a constant source of disagreement.[51] The story repeated itself yearly: the amounts set in the Gazprom-Belarus yearly agreement usually ran out by November, and discussions on how much gas would be supplied, and at what prices, resumed shortly afterwards. In addition, on at least one occasion during this period there were disagreements about the amounts of gas in the yearly agreements themselves, as the state-to-state agreements between Belarus and Russia stated a larger amount than the Gazprom-Belarus agreements.[52]

These contradictions and tensions had become clear by early November 2002, when Gazprom, arguing unpaid debts and delays in the privatization of Beltransgaz, reduced gas supplies to Belarus by 50 percent, and demanded an increased price of $150/tcm instead of the domestic Russian price, thus providing the first open signal that relations between Belarus and Russia had seriously deteriorated. Belarus' politicization of gas negotiations was made clear through its reaction to this incident. The immediate response was decisively angry. The Foreign Ministry called the reduction in supplies "a premeditated attempt to exert economic pressure";[53] President Lukashenka argued that the decline in supplies was a reprisal for Belarus' refusal to give Gazprom control over the country's gas system.[54] Lukashenka also threatened to charge world-market rates for the transit of Russian gas through Belarus. Most

50 The first agreement, on April 12, 2002, on equal pricing conditions, did not have an end date. A second agreement stated that, by July 1, 2002, Belarus would register a gas transit joint venture with Gazprom on the basis of Beltransgaz, with the implication that the agreement on domestic gas prices would only be valid should the venture be created. See Aparina, "Trojnaâ udavka."

51 See IPM, "Rost cen na gaz," 8.

52 See Prime-TASS.

53 Novozhilova and Sekhovich, "'Gazavat' po-gazpromovski," 1, 6.

54 *Belarus Today*, 9 November 2002.

importantly, Lukashenka sought to politicize the issue by tying it to broader issues in the relationship, presenting a bill for services rendered by Belarus in the context of the Belarusian- Russian union. Yet the crisis dissipated in less than two weeks, with Belarus agreeing to pay an outstanding debt of $250 million, the Russian Central Bank agreeing to provide a $40 million export credit to Belarus as compensation for the higher prices,[55] and the Belarusian government promising to introduce legislation to eliminate the ban on privatizing Beltransgaz.[56] This created a pattern that would become increasingly visible after 2004.

However, with little further movement on the privatization of Beltransgaz, and with no reaction from Belarus to increasingly direct hints from Moscow that domestic Russian gas prices might be canceled should the situation around Beltransgaz not start developing in a more desirable direction,[57] on September 12, 2003, Russian Prime Minister Mikhail Kasianov signed a decree cancelling his recommendation to Gazprom that Belarus be charged domestic gas prices; on January 1, 2004, Belarus started to pay $46.68 per tcm of gas. This remained significantly lower than prices charged Western European importers, but no longer represented as large a discount vis-à-vis most other post-Soviet states as that in place before (see Table 3.1).

The discussion of gas supplies in the 2002–2004 period brings to the fore the question of supplies by non-Gazprom sources, first and foremost Itera. Itera—itself enjoying a privileged relationship with Gazprom—entered the Belarusian market in 1997; from 1999 to 2004 it (and, to a much lesser extent, other independent suppliers such as TransNafta and Sibur, itself a Gazprom sub-unit)[58] supplied around 30 percent of Belarus' imports, reaching 38 percent in 2004. Interestingly, as long as Belarus was having difficulties paying in cash, (in order to avoid payments arrears), Gazpron "allowed" independent companies to supply about a third of the Belarusian market. However, once payment discipline increased around 2003 and Belarus started to pay predominantly in cash, Gazprom moved to gain more direct control of the market. Itera's supplies to Belarus ceased in 2004.[59]

55 See *Eastern Europe, Russia and Central Asia 2004*, 147.

56 Tomashevskaya, "Lëgkaâ pobeda," 1.

57 Around the summer of 2003, Putin indirectly let it be known that domestic gas prices for Belarus would be maintained only in case a joint venture between Beltransgaz and Gazprom was formed. See Zhbanov, "Komu – gaz, komu – pedigree."

58 Bruce, "Friction or fiction?" 17.

59 Itera would reappear in 2007 as key investor in a large project for the building of the Minsk-City Business Center, a project that was cancelled in 2012.

TABLE 3.1 PRICING OF GAZPROM'S GAS TO BELARUS, SELECTED FSU STATES, AND GERMANY, 1991 AND 2001–2011, IN US$/TCM

	Belarus	Ukraine	Moldova	Germany (price at border)
1991	0.25	0.25	0.25	108.3
2001	30	42	80	139.4
2002	29.5	42	80	96.0
2003	35.6	42	80	125.5
2004	46.68	50	80	135.2
2005	55	50	80	212.9
2006	55	95	160**	295.6
2007	118	135	172	293.1
2008	126.8	179.5	232	472.9
2009	151	232.4*	263	318.8
2010	185	252 (Q4)	252*	292.4
2011	265	400 (Q4)	400 (Q4)	381.5

* Estimated. ** Effective July 1.

Sources:
All 1991 prices estimated from IEA, *Energy Policies of Ukraine.*
Belarus prices: 2001–2004: Table 3.2; 2005–2009: Stern et al., *The April 2010 Russo-Ukrainian,* 7; Rakova, "Ènergetičeskij sektor" 2011; various press sources.
Ukraine prices: 2001–2004: Pavel and Chukhai, "Ukrainian Gas;" 2005–2009: Stern et al., "The April 2010 Russo-Ukrainian," 7; various press sources.
Moldova prices: 2001–2004: various press sources; National Agency for Energy Regulation (ANRE), 2010; "Sredneevropejskaâ cena za gaz;" 2011; Muntean, "The first consequences," 1.
Border price in Germany, Econstats, "IMF Commodities."

Itera's role as a supplier added a number of new elements to Beltransgaz's relationship with Gazprom. From the perspective of the conditions of supply, the murky relationship between Itera and members of the Gazprom management raised the possibility of misuse of personal connections for personal profit, as the company enjoyed privileged and low-cost access to Gazprom's resources, while taking away its most profitable business (as it was allowed to charge higher prices and did not have to put up with payments arrears).[60] From the Belarusian perspective, supplies from Itera and

60 See Guillet, "Gazprom's Got West Europeans Over a Barrel," and Hermitage Capital Management, "How should Gazprom be managed," 4, cited in Global Witness, "It's a Gas," 35.

Table 3.2: Gas supplies to Belarus from Gazprom and other suppliers, 1999–2004

	1998	1999	2000	2001	2002	2003	2004
Supplies by Gazprom, in bcm	14.8	12.2	10.8	16.2	10.2	10.2	10.2
Supplies by Itera and other independent suppliers, in bcm*	1.1	4.3	5.8	5.1	5.9	6.2	6.4
Imports from Itera and other independent producers, as % of total supplies to Belarus	6.96	24.57	34.93	23.94	36.64	38.80	38.55
Prices charged by Gazprom to Beltransgaz, in US$/tcm	50	30	30	30	17-22	30**	46.68
Average price of imported gas, in US$/tcm	N/A	N/A	N/A	30	29.5	35.6	46.68

* De facto overwhelmingly supplies from Itera. ** End-of period values.

Sources:
Yafimava, *Post-Soviet Russian-Belarussian*, 58–59, 106; Dashkevich, *Jenergeticheskaja zavisimost'*, 20 (on the basis of data from the Energy Ministry and the OAO Beltransgaz).
Data for average import prices from Sekhovich, "1991 -2006. Itogi. Gazovaya otrasl'."
Data for 1998 prices charged by Gazprom from Zlotnikov, "Faktor nomer 1-*Rossiâ.*"

(to a much lesser extent) other independent suppliers, added both some flexibility and a complicating factor to the relationship with Gazprom. (As noted before, the 2002 agreement with Gazprom on gas prices did not cover the totality of Belarus' yearly import requirements.) One illustration is provided by the November 2002 crisis. In June 2002, Itera had cut gas supplies to Belarus by half after accumulating a $24 million debt; full supplies resumed in July after a partial payment, but were later cut again. The Belarusian side responded by arguing that, as supplies from Itera had declined, supplies from Gazprom—significantly cheaper, at around $24/tcm vs. $36 for Itera—should increase to fill the gap, a change Gazprom was not interested in.[61] It has been argued that Belarus' decision to reduce purchases from Itera (and thus, to allow the contract to be cancelled due to growing debt) was related to the expectation that (in contradiction with the writ-

61 Energy Minister Vladimir Semashko, cited by Chelnok, "Belarussiâ oplatit' staryj gaz cenami za novyj" *Gazeta.ru*, November 5, 2002.

ten agreement) the April 2002 agreements would allow it to purchase *all* of its gas from Gazprom at domestic Russian prices.[62] This was part of a pattern of Belarusian behavior where, although not denouncing existing agreements, Belarus would simply ignore them.[63]

Oil: external management during the "High Years," 1994–2004

If a very public politicization seemed to be the hallmark of Belarus' management of its gas relationship with Russia, in oil matters there seemed to be much less public positioning. This may have been due to the fact that less public negotiations with the heads of Russian oil companies ("oil oligarchs") proved to be more useful in that area, or simply to the fact that in the oil area there were no major crises until late 2006 that could have elicited a public response. These differences may also have had to do with differences in the structure of ownership on the Russian side. Whereas Gazprom continued to be largely state-owned and state-controlled throughout this period, the oil sector remained mostly under private control. This naturally affected the counterparts of any negotiation; it also mattered in public relations terms, as Lukashenka could present Gazprom as having a certain responsibility vis-à-vis Belarus as Russia's partner in the joint Union State (something harder to argue for in the case of oil companies).

If, in the years immediately following Lukashenka's access to the presidency in 1994, the immediate priority in the oil area was to assure Belarus' oil refineries could be put to work again after their near collapse in the early 1990s, by the late 1990s, a more proactive strategy was taking shape. Two central pillars of this strategy were the attempt to maximize Belarus' transit role, and to extract the maximum possible rents from the oil-refining and re-exporting business. In both processes, the production and value-added chains linking Russian producers with actors in Belarus were also crucial. Although Belarus was able to reap important benefits, these two areas were also deeply contested in the relationship with Russia.

62 See Klishevich, "Gazovaâ vojna zaveršilas'?"

63 Other examples include the (non) sharing of oil export duties throughout the late 1990s and early 2000s and the situation in 2009 where Belarus, in the second part of the year, ignored the price increase imposed by Gazprom, continuing to pay the previous prices.

Before turning to the main areas in Belarus' management of its oil relationship with Russia during this period—oil transit, oil refining, and the modernization and control over main refineries—a brief excursus is needed to clarify the various roles played by Russian oil in Belarus during this period.

Russian oil in Belarus: types, players, and value-added chains

With the exception of small amounts produced locally, during the 1994-2004 period most of the oil consumed in Belarus came from Russia, much of it through barter ("clearing") agreements signed as early as 1993. This Russian oil was not a single, uniformly tradeable good, but could be conceptually divided into four distinct groups of marketable goods, each with its particular value-added chain linking it to specific actors in Russia, Belarus, and further markets, each covered by specific taxes, duties, and regulations, and each with its own particular niche in Russian-Belarusian relations.

The first group was Russian crude oil transited to the West through Belarus, for which the country simply received transit fees. In this area, the main subject of negotiations with the Russian side during this period (with oil pipeline operator Transneft) was the level of transit fees to be paid to Belarus. The second group was oil intended to cover Belarus' domestic needs (in 2009, around 6.3 Mt out of total supplies of 21.5 Mt). Traditionally—perhaps because of the political integration rhetoric between Russia and Belarus—this oil was isolated from discussions on the applicability of Russian taxes and duties; from the signing of the Customs Union agreement in 1995 to as late as 2011, Russia did not charge export duties on it. (As will be discussed in Chapter 5, however, the question itself of how much oil Belarus would need for domestic consumption—and, thus, how much oil should remain immune to decisions on Russian export duties—was a deeply contested one and the subject of difficult negotiations between the partners.)

A third group was oil *purchased, owned, and refined* by Belarusian refineries for export as oil products to Russia and, mainly, Western Europe. The fact that the resulting oil products were exported to Western markets made an important difference, as this meant Belarusian refineries could export them at world prices, while paying lower-than-world oil prices for the oil it imported. A fourth group concerned oil used in tolling operations (*davalcheskaya neft'*), oil not owned by, but processed by Belarus' refineries and mostly returned to Russia as oil products or sold in Western European markets.[64] ("Tolling" refers to operations where oil or another good is transferred for processing, without changing ownership.)

This oil remained the property of Russian oil companies or other tolling operators. Throughout this period, such oil has amounted to half or more of all oil refined in Belarus, c. 10 Mt in the mid-2000s. Specifically tolling arrangements were especially attractive to Russian oil companies because in tolling operations they could retain ownership of the oil (simply paying a fee for its refining), which meant they also retained the profits from the export of the refined products to Western Europe. (So, assuming the same refining price, supplying oil to Belarus on tolling terms would allow the Russian supplier to keep 100 percent of the profit from the resulting oil product exports, while selling this oil to the Belarusian refinery would mean the Belarusian refinery would keep most of the profits, with the actual distribution of profits between both sides determined by the price at which the oil was sold to the Belarusian side.[65]) Thus, with other factors being equal, Russian companies would ideally have preferred to refine 100 percent of their oil on the basis of tolling operations, and to keep the profits from exports at higher prices.[66] Yet it is important to keep in mind that Russian oil companies were not the sole tolling operators. In addition, a variety of other, usually smaller, companies also conducted similar operations, purchasing oil from Russian companies, having it refined on tolling terms, and exporting the refined products to Western European markets.

Not surprisingly, oil refined in Belarus and then exported as oil products to Western Europe (around 10 Mt/year if we count both tolling and non-tolling operations) provided the largest profits for those actors involved in these operations: Belarusian refineries, Russian oil companies involved in tolling operations, or other resident (Belarusian) oil-tolling operators (often referred

64 Thus, this oil could be subdivided into oil sold as refined products in Russia and (as a fifth category) sold as refined products in Western Europe.

65 Refining prices charged to Russian companies by Belarusian refineries have been estimated at around \$30/t in 2007–2010, \$36 in 2011, and \$41 in 2012.

66 At times, as in 2010, the portion of the oil exported by Russia for use in tolling operations and intended for return to Russia was offered special taxation privileges by the Russian side, opening the door to possible abuse by oil traders, who could designate, for taxation purposes, this oil as intended for return to Russia as oil products, but have these oil products actually shipped to third markets where they could be sold at a higher price. Oil market analyst Mikhail Krutikhin, quoted in Ivan Trefinov, "Minsk otstupil do leta," available at: http://www.svobodanews.ru/content/article/1942311.html (accessed May 20, 2011). See also Dmitry Budrin, quoted in "Èksperty v gostâh u Vitaliâ Portnikova," www.svobodanews.ru, January 28,2010, transcript available at http://www.svobodanews.ru/content/transcript/1942934.html (accessed May 10, 2011).

to as *davaltsy*), which acted as *de facto* intermediaries, buying crude oil from Russian oil companies and refining it on the basis of tolling schemes.

These exports to Western Europe were also the most profitable for the Belarusian budget, as, in addition to receiving the raw materials (crude oil) for these oil products on a duty-free basis, Belarus also received all (until 2006), or a portion (2007–2009) of the export duties on the resulting exports. (As will be discussed in Chapter 5, despite written agreements stating otherwise, during 1995–2006, Belarus kept the totality of these export duties.)

Operations with each of these four groups of oil involved different types of Russian, Belarusian and trans-border actors, a different role for Belarus in the value-added chain of Russian companies, and a different basis for Russian companies' interest in collaborating with Belarusian actors. Figure 3.3 provides an overview of these actors.

Specifically within the segment of oil intended for export, tolling operations (encompassing both oil refined for sale to Russia and to Western markets) constituted an important sub-sector, where two main types of actors were especially active. The first type of actor was *neftetreideri* directly related to Russian oil-producing companies (most importantly LUKoil, but also the subsidiary companies of Russneft, the Alians group, and TNK-BP).[67] It must be noted that the role and interests of Russian companies and their local subsidiaries differed at times: while some companies (for most of this period in particular Rossneft and Surgutneft) were interested mainly in selling oil to Belarusian refineries, others (notably those Russian companies having their own petrol station chains in Belarus, such as Slavneft-Start and LUKoil-Belarussia) were more interested in refining oil for sale in their own petrol stations.[68]

The second type of actor in this segment were formally independent Belarusian and Russian tolling operators, acting as intermediaries for the importation of Russian oil (such as "Tripl," discussed in Chapter 4). In some cases, these were involved in murky operations concerning the origin of the oil supplied from Russia.[69] As they dealt mainly with documentation and not

67 As per Interfax data, in 2007 the relative role of various Russian oil companies in the supply of oil to Belarus was as follows: Surgutneftegaz, nearly 30%; Rosneft 25%; Sibneft 13%; LUKoil 11%; Slavneft 10%; Russneft 6.5%; and 6.5% "other suppliers." See: http://www.interfax.by/node/1019767 (accessed May 13, 2011). This distribution is largely representative of the situation in the late 2000s.

68 Elena Rakova, personal communication, January 2011. Some LUKoil materials refer to its Belarus daughter company using the official name of the country (i.e., LUKoil-Belarus), but an even larger number to its unofficial Russian usage (LUKoil-Belarussia).

69 This also refers to the so-called "unaccounted-for oil" (*neuchtennaya neft'*, sometimes also referred to as *kriminalnaya neft'*), i.e., oil stolen at or near the production source, an especially significant phenomenon in the 1990s. See Zaiko, "Leonid Zaiko."

Figure 3.3 Main actors in the Belarusian oil market, 1994-2011

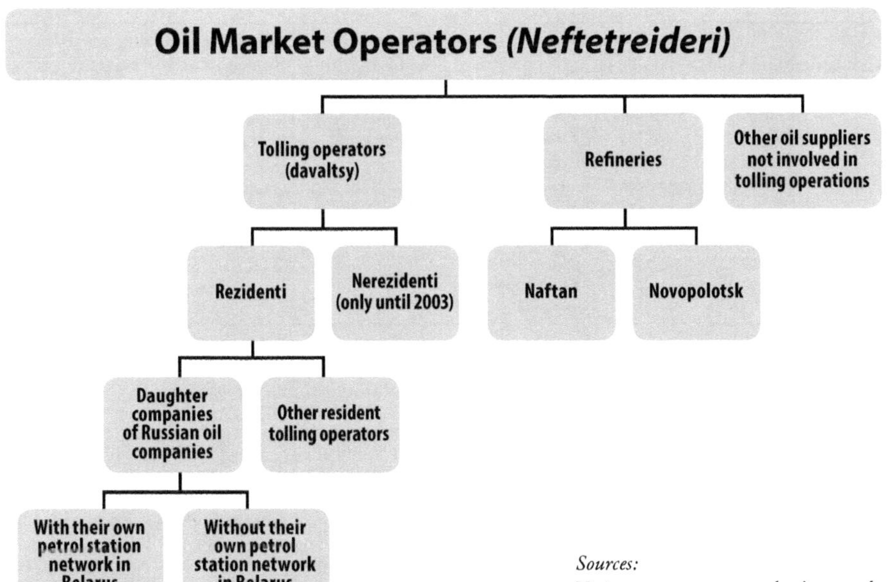

Sources:
Various press sources, author's research.

with actual physical oil volumes, these were often small firms with only a few employees; even if profits margins were low, the high volume of transactions allowed them to reap very high profits per employee.[70]

The possibility of profiting from oil operations involving Belarus and, in particular, from the price differences between low-cost crude oil imported from Russia and the high price at which refined oil products could be sold in Western European markets did not exist in an institutional vacuum. Rather, domestic conditions and regulations, both formal and informal, as well as specific Russian-Belarusian agreements, affected various actors' ability to benefit from this general foreign trade situation. Not all actors were equally significant at all periods, or even allowed to participate in the informal division of oil rents in all periods. Table 3.4 provides an overview of these actors' changing roles during the period 1994–2011. These actors included, in addition to the actors noted above, Belarusian state or semi-state structures: not only oil producer Belarusneft and the Belarusian Oil Company, but, most importantly, the Naftan and Mozyr refineries, which, in addition to carrying out for-pay refining as part of tolling operations, also refined and exported oil owned by themselves.

70 Leonid Zlotnikov, personal communication, January 21, 2011.

TABLE 3.4 BELARUSIAN OIL-MARKET PLAYERS: KEY DEVELOPMENTS, 1994–2011

	1990s	1999–2003	2003–2006	2007–2010	2011
Refineries (Naftan, Novopolotsk)	Early-mid 1990s: due to cash-flow problems, unable to buy enough oil to refine at full capacity, return to tolling operations to keep working.	Refineries return to work at (near) full capacity as changing conditions in Russia (reinstatement of oil export duties in 1999) help attract for-refining oil volumes due to Belarus' lower export duties.	Record profitability as Belarus' oil products exports reach an all-time high.	Introduction of Russian export duties for a significant part of oil supplies to Belarus increases costs and reduces the profitability of Belarus' refineries.	Increased refining activity, but refineries' profitability further reduced due to higher oil prices.
Belorusskaya Neftennaya Kompania				Established in 2007 to centralize the export of oil products.	
Tolling operators (*davaltsy*) including both Belarusian and Russian, resident and "non-resident" companies, large and small	System established in the early 1990s to help gain access to oil volumes despite refineries' liquidity problems.		Many tolling operators pushed out of the refining-and-export market by members of the Presidential Administration, opening the market to companies such as Belaya Rus'.	Now subjected to double duties, tolling operations, become unprofitable .	Higher oil prices make tolling operations less attractive to Russian companies than direct sales.
Russian oil companies (a single company could play multiple roles: sale of crude oil to refineries; refining through tolling schemes; supplies to own petrol stations in Belarus.)	Mainly present through non-resident operations.		After a 2003 decree, non-resident companies banned from oil trading and tolling operations; major Russian oil companies establish their own subsidiary companies in Belarus.	Loss of interest in tolling operations due to double taxation.	Higher oil prices make direct sales more attractive than tolling operations.

Sources: Various press sources, author's research.

Pricing

Although not as heavily subsidized as gas, oil prices charged to Belarus during this period were significantly (about 40 percent) lower than world market ones. (See Table 3.8). Although the price of Russian oil sold to Belarus increased sharply in 2000 (from an average of $46 to $119 per ton),[71] it

71 Data for 1999 from Alesin, "Ob ickrennocti družby kreditorov c dolžnikami," 17.

remained significantly below international prices; in fact, the per-ton difference between the prices charged to Belarus and world market grew significantly from 2001 to 2004.[72] These low prices had to do with the tax and customs agreements between Belarus and Russia, with the nature of the political relationship between both states, and with the fact that Russian oil companies were able to reap large profits through their refining businesses in Belarus.

Oil transit

Although better known in the West for its role in gas transit to Western Europe, oil transit was actually even more central in Belarus' external management of its energy dependency. Until 2000, some 50 percent of Russian oil exports to non-CIS markets went through Belarus, most of it through Druzhba, the most important pipeline transporting Russian oil to Western Europe. Throughout the 1990s and early 2000s, Russia used the possibility of transiting oil through Belarus instead of Ukraine as a safeguard of sorts against Ukraine's perceived or real demands for increased transit fees from Russia.[73] (This was technically possible, as Druzhba starts in Russia and later divides, already on Belarusian territory, into northern (Belarus) and southern (Ukrainian) branches, with the Belarus branch having a larger capacity (720,000 barrels per day (bbl/d) as opposed to 500,000 bbl/d for the southern branch). In addition, Belarus transited oil via rail, significant as this transit amounted to 12–18 percent of total transit.[74]

Although there were no major problems with the transit of Russian oil through Belarus from the time of Lukashenka's coming to power in 1994 to the conflict of late December 2006 (discussed in Chapter 5), much can be learned about the dynamics of the relationship by looking at a 2002–2004 controversy over ownership of an oil products pipeline belonging to the Zapad Transnefteprodukt company. Following a long period where Belarus failed to recognize Russian ownership over the pipeline,[75] in 2002 a battle ensued on the matter. In this case, in contrast with that of the company's Ukrainian equivalent (Yugo-Zapad Transneftprodukt), lax contractual regulations between the Belarusian

72 IMF, "Republic of Belarus: Selected Issues," 9–10.

73 Belarus' role in the overall transit of Russian crude oil (including to non-EU states) grew from 28% to 45% between 1999 and 2004, before declining to 36 % in 2007. Kostiugova, "Perspektivy učastiâ," 4.

74 Calculation based on data on transit via railway, addendum to *Postanovlenie Soveta Ministrov Respubliki Belarus' ot 28 iûnâ 2005 g.*

75 Russian ownership was contractually established.

GRAPH 3.5 TRANSIT OF RUSSIAN OIL VIA BELARUS, IN MILLION TONS AND % OF RUSSIAN EXPORTS TO NON-CIS STATES, 2000–2010

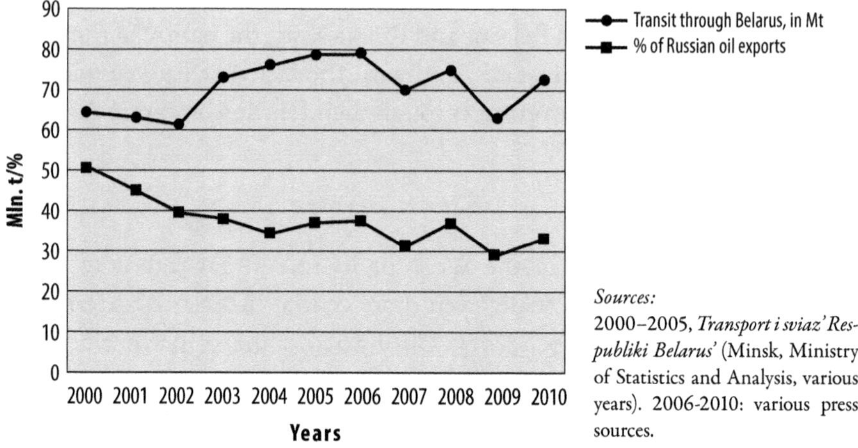

Sources:
2000–2005, *Transport i sviaz' Respubliki Belarus'* (Minsk, Ministry of Statistics and Analysis, various years). 2006-2010: various press sources.

and Russian sides may have contributed to the confusion. In 2004, it became clear that, should Belarus not recognize Russian ownership of the pipeline, it might not receive the full 18Mt of oil from Russia it was expecting for 2004, threatening its growth targets for the year and significant refining and reexport revenues. As a result of this threat, Belarus accepted Russian ownership, but it also received certain concessions: it would be able to influence the actual work of the company by, for example, playing a role in the setting of transit fees, instead of these being set only by Russia's federal energy commission, and which on occasion had been set so low that the company could not cover its costs.[76]

Oil refining, modernization, and ownership of refining companies

Belarus' main source of energy rents turned out to be not transit *per se*, but the refining and re-exporting of Russian oil under especially favorable trade terms. Rather, a stable oil-transit role became important, as it helped make attractive the supply oil to Belarus and Belarusian refineries, acting as a guarantee of continued supplies. Cooperation between Belarus and Russia in the oil refining area was an obvious proposition given the dependencies and synergies inherited from the centralized Soviet energy system. Belarusian refineries provided Russian oil companies with important logistical advantages, as

76 Transit fees for oil products were also increased effective 2004: from $0.59 to $0.89 per ton per 100 km. Manenok, "Spor isčerpan."

it is often more efficient to supply the nearby Russian oblasts with oil refined in Belarus than in Siberia or the Volga region, where many Russian refineries are located. Belarus had some of the largest and most modern oil refining facilities in the USSR; in 2007 its total oil refining activity of approximately 20 Mt per year was larger than that of much larger Ukraine (18 Mt).[77] With a refining capacity many times larger than domestic oil production, the crude oil supply crisis of the first post-independence years had led to the near collapse of the sector, which between 1991 and 1995 went from using 88.1 percent of its production capacity, to 31.6 percent.[78] However, it is important to avoid the impression that until 2002, the sector was not profitable. First, it must be kept in mind that the worst of the crises was over by 1997. Secondly, even these first years of crisis produced a more complex picture: while the sector may not have been profitable as a whole, certain operations within the sector, especially the payment for various services with unaccounted-for (presumably stolen) oil in the unstable and unregulated environment of the early 1990s, was extremely profitable for some players.

Yet by the late 1990s, the crisis had not only been surmounted, but the oil-refining sector had been so revitalized as to become one of the country's most important sources of foreign revenue. Between 1994 and 2004, we see a total transformation of the sector into the main source of income for the Belarusian state. This did not happen spontaneously, but as a result (in addition to a number of external circumstances) of a conscious policy on the part of the Belarusian government, intended to make it attractive (through tax breaks and other incentives) for Russian oil companies to supply oil to Belarusian refineries via tolling operations. In fact, if in the early 1990s the allowing of tolling operations was seen as a last-resort measure intended to attract oil to Belarusian refineries given the refineries' sheer financial inability to purchase on their own the crude oil to be later refined, by the late 1990s it had evolved into a conscious policy intended to attract Russian oil to Belarusian refineries. Lower export duties on refined oil products levied by Belarus in comparison with Russia served as an important incentive for Russian producers (see Table 3.11).

At times, some of these arrangements, involving VAT and preferential export duty rates, were making Belarus a *de facto* offshore operation for these

77 Ukraine's total refining *capacity*, at 55 Mt per year, is significantly larger than Belarus' 40 Mt, but through most of the 2000s was less fully utilized than Belarus'. Rakova, "Reformy administrativnymi metodami."

78 Aleksandr Matyas, "Analiz osobennostei, faktorov i istochnikov ekonomicheskogo rosta v Respublike Belarus." Published in *Nashe Mnenie*, nmnorg.by, 2005. (Accessed June 13, 2008).

Graph 3.6 Destination of Belarusian refined oil products exports, in percentages, 1996–2010

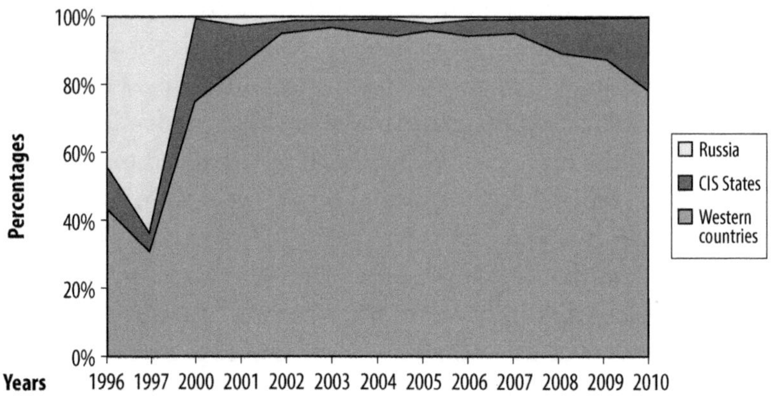

Note: no data available for 1998–1999.
Sources: Compiled by Leonid Zlotnikov on the basis of official Belarusian trade statistics, 1996–2010.

companies.[79] The effects of such policies were clearly seen in 1999–2000. When Russia reinstated oil export duties in 1999 after a four-year hiatus, there was an immediate increase in the supply of oil and oil products to Belarus, and an even more marked rise in the exports of oil products from Belarus (see Table 3.8).[80] In addition, as shown in Graph 3.6, there was a clear shift in the direction of these exports, with significantly increased exports to Western European markets.

European Union states played an important role in Belarus' cycle of energy rents. The strong demand for Belarusian oil products in EU markets was crucial, and was the main reason why Belarus could turn theoretical oil trade advantages from Russia into actual profits. Indeed, the c. $1.2 to $11b in yearly revenue from oil products sales between 2001 and 2007 (see Tables 3.7 and 5.4) was made possible by large oil product purchases from EU states taking place

79 New Value-Added Tax (VAT) regulations that entered into effect in January 2005 (establishing that VAT taxes would be levied by the receiving side) created new opportunities for Belarus to manipulate the regulations to create an additional offshore situation in order to attract Russian oil supplies. To make the situation easier on *neftetreideri* and other oil importers (who under the new VAT regulations would have had to pay the VAT to the Belarusian budget, to be returned subsequently to the Russian budget) Belarus started to allow them to credit part of their export duties to the money owed as VAT payments, de facto reducing the effective rate of export duties on oil products, already significantly lower than Russia's. This created new losses for the Russian budget and new tensions in the Belarusian-Russian relationship, and was an important factor leading to the January 2007 oil crisis. See Leonid Zlotnikov, personal communication, December 13, 2008.

80 Under pressure from the IMF, Russia abolished export duties on oil in 1995, but these were reinstated in 1999 as a result of the 1998 crisis.

even when political relations were less than ideal.[81] Thus the question arises – given the fact that income from such sales was so critical for the Lukashenka regime, and given Lukashenka's problematic human rights record, should the importing countries have considered the ultimate economic sanction against Lukashenka: a ban on these imports? Throughout the entire 1994–2011 period of ups and (mostly) downs in relations with the EU, although economic sanctions were used against individual members of the Lukashenka regime (freezing of accounts in EU banks, for example), an outright ban on the importing of Belarusian oil products was never seriously discussed. While such a ban was never on the US agenda for the simple reason that it did not import oil products from Belarus, in 2007, 2008 and 2011, the US imposed sanctions on Belneftekhim and several associated companies; these sanctions stemmed not only from human rights issues but were also a response to Belneftekhim's collaboration with Iranian companies allegedly supporting that country's nuclear program.[82] While there is debate as to the real impact of these sanctions on the volume of US-Belarus trade (as Belneftekhim does not export to the US, and the general level of Belarusian exports to the US has remained small) the sanctions, by freezing all assets of these companies under US reach and prohibiting US persons from engaging in commercial or financial transactions with Belneftekhim and other associated companies, may have had a strong indirect impact.[83]

Table 3.7 shows that an important point had been reached in 2004: for the first time, Belarus' income from the export of oil and oil products was able to more than compensate total expenditures for oil and oil-product imports. This was a major change, not only from the role played by the sector in the thin early 1990s, but also during the Soviet period. Although, at the peak of their pre-independence work in 1989, Belarusian refineries produced some 40Mt of oil products (higher than at any time after 1991),[84] their role in exports and in

81 Technically, the Netherlands and the UK were by far the largest importers, as the most important import ports and further distribution hubs for oil products are located in these countries.

82 On the August 2011 sanctions against Belneftekhim and associated companies Naftan, Grodno Azot, Grodno Khimvolokno and Belshina, see IPM, *Ezhemesiachnii obzor ekonomiki Belarusi* (Belarus Monthly Economic Review (thereafter *BMER*) 9/108, September 2011.

83 According to a US representative, in the three years between the imposition of the first sanctions in November 2007 and 2010, Belarus' exports to the US went down exponentially, from over $1b per year in 2007 and 2008, to $0.175 in 2010. Michael D. Scanlan, US temporary Charge D'Affairs, cited in Belapan, "Sankcii protiv," February 28, 2012. For data on foreign trade between the US and Belarus, see the US Census Bureau database for Trade in Goods with Belarus. Belarus responded to the August 2011 sanctions by freezing its participation in a U.S.-led program of exchange of highly-enriched uranium for low-enriched uranium used for research purposes.

84 By 1993, this had been reduced to 13.6 Mt. *Belarus Energy Sector Review 1995*, 46.

TABLE 3.7 BELARUS: FOREIGN TRADE OF OIL AND OIL PRODUCTS, 2000–2004

	2000		2001		2003		2004	
	Million tons	Billion US$	Million tons	Billion US$	Million tons	Billion US$	Million tons	Billion US$
Export of oil products	7.78	1.358	7.66	1.21	10.56	1.96	12.96	3.3
Export of oil	0.35	0.062	-	-	0.8	0.144	1.55	0.31
Total export of oil and its products	8.13	1.42	7.66	1.21	11.36	2.104	14.51	3.61
Import of oil from Russia	12.01	1.636	11.91	1.38	14.89	1.988	17.81	3.232
Import of oil products from Russia	1.075	0.21	0.167	0.02	1	0.148	1.18	0.16
Total import of oil and its products	13.085	1.846	12.077	1.4	15.89	2.136	18.99	3.392
Import price of oil to Belarus from Russia US$/ton		136.2		115.8		133.1		181.5
Price of Russian oil exports to non-CIS states US$/ton		145		156.4		181.2		233
Belarus' income from oil and oil products' exports after paying for imports of oil and oil products		-0.426		-0.19		-0.032		0.218

Sources: Calculated on the basis of Ministry of Statistics and Analysis of the Republic of Belarus, *Foreign Trade of the Republic of Belarus. Statistical abstracts.* (Minsk, yearly), *Rossiâ v cifrah. Oficial'noe izdanie. Federal'naâ služba gosudarstvennoj statistiki*, Moscow, 2008; and (for data on the first half of 2008) the statistical compendium *Social'no-èkonomičeskoe položenie Rossii*, Nos. 1–7, 2008. Special thanks to Leonid Zlotnikov for his help in preparing this table.

foreign-currency earnings flowing to Belarus was much more limited, if only because much higher levels of domestic consumption at the time meant there were fewer oil products available for export, and because the related profits were accrued by the central Soviet state, not by Belarus as a separate entity.

The rags-to-riches transformation of Belarusian refineries was made possible by the natural synergies between Belarus' and Russia's energy infrastructures, by the new possibilities created by the incomplete integration process, and by Belarus' conscious policies in the area. The formal political integration process also played an important role, as it provided certain guarantees, both to Belarus (that the Russian oil companies would keep their sup-

TABLE 3.8: BELARUS' TRADE BALANCES IN OIL AND OIL PRODUCTS, 1996–2004, IN MILLION TONS

Year	Domestic production	Import of oil and oil products	Supplies (production + imports)	Export of oil and oil products	Domestic use	Percentage of domestic oil use covered by domestic production (domestic production/domestic use)	Oil and oil-product exports as % of overall exports
1996	1.86	11.11	12.97	3.71	9.26	20.0	10.8
1997	1.82	11.24	13.06	2.96	10.10	18.0	8.6
1998	1.83	10.10	11.93	3.30	6.08	30.0	7.8
1999	1.84	9.90	11.74	3.70	6.20	29.6	9.1
2000	1.85	12.10	13.95	8.10	5.85	31.6	20.2
2001	1.85	12.00	13.85	8.10	5.75	32.1	18.2
2002	1.85	14.50	16.35	10.50	5.85	31.6	20.9
2003	1.82	15.80	17.62	11.36	6.25	29.1	22.7
2004	1.80	18.00	20.70	14.10	6.60	27.2	27.4

Sources: Ministry of Statistics and Analysis of the Republic of Belarus, *Foreign trade of the Republic of Belarus. Statistical abstracts* (Minsk, yearly). Note: data under oil and oil-product exports for 1998 and 1999 are from total exports of energy resources Table 2.2 in Rakova, "Energeticheskii sektor," 2010: 7), and differ slightly from the 2001–2010 data from the Ministry of Statistics, which covers only trade in oil and oil products.
Data for oil volumes for 1998 and 1999 estimated from the Russian statistical yearly *Vneshnaya Torgovlia* (Moscow, various years).

ply commitments) and to the Russian oil companies (that it was safe to invest in Belarus' refinery sector); the abolition of customs barriers made it possible for Russian companies to enter into advantageous schemes involving oil refining in Belarus. No less important was the role played by the Belarusian government, which helped Russian oil companies maximize profits through special arrangements such as tolling operations. Last but not least, the Belarusian government engaged in an aggressive refinery modernization program, aimed at increasing the production of EU-standard, higher value-added light oil products and gasoline, able to fetch higher prices in Western European markets. (Indeed, such modernization was one of the few means available to

Belarus to maintain and increase profitability (refining margins) even in the face of increased crude-oil prices.[85]) This policy is all the more remarkable when looked at in the context of trends in the rest of the Belarusian economy, where factories remained outdated and extremely energy-inefficient. This strategy was clearly part of a strategic goal of rent-maximization at the domestic as well as the external level. As a result of this modernization process, Belarusian refineries could process oil more efficiently than the average Russian refinery, making their "refining margin" (the difference between the price of a ton of oil and that of the oil products refined from it) often much higher than those of Russian refineries.[86]

A division of labor was soon established: Russian companies would produce oil in western Siberia, supply some of it to Belarus, where Belarusian companies would refine it, and the profits of sales to Western Europe would be shared by both sides. As would become increasingly clear from 2007, however, how these profits and rents were divided between various involved actors would become a major issue of contention, not only between Belarus and Russia, but between various actors in each country.

Central to Lukashenka's management of oil issues was his desire to attract Russian capital for refinery modernization, while at the same time seeking to prevent Russian companies from taking control of these refineries. Indeed, even at times of extremely tense relations with Russian oil companies (as in the example of relations with LUKoil in the mid and late 1990s)[87] investments were secured for the modernization of oil refineries. This takes us to the issue of the struggles for the control of the Naftan and Mozyr refineries, which we discuss briefly below. (Chapter 5 discusses these conflicts in the post-2004 period.)

The Mozyr refinery

Since Belarus' independence, Russian oil companies (and especially LUKoil, Yukos, and Slavneft) had shown an interest in acquiring full or partial ownership in Belarus' two refining complexes, Mozyr and Novopolotsk.

---

85 The issue would become especially important with the increases in oil prices in 2011, when, it was calculated that for Belarus' refining to be profitable under the new conditions, it should reach a 93% level of deepness of refining, while it was only around 70% in 2010. Manenok, "NPZ balansiruût."

86 *Kommersant* notes that while in Russia (late 2010) such refining margin was negative, in Belarus it amounted to around $22/t. Azarov, "Rossiâ i Belorussiâ."

87 For details of the ups and downs of this relationship, see Zagorskaya, *Belarus. 1991–2006,* 149–157.

Of these two refineries, a degree of private ownership was easier to establish in Mozyr, which was also the most coveted by Russian investors. The refinery's strategic location as the western-most refinery from which derivates produced from Russian oil could be exported to Western Europe,[88] and its being one of the most modern refineries in the CIS,[89] explains this interest. Established in 1975, it was privatized in 1994, with 42.7 percent of its shares belonging to the Belarusian state, 42.6 percent to Slavneft (until 2002 a Belarusian-Russian joint venture);[90] 12.2 percent to MNPZ Plus (owned by the company's employees and former employees); and 2.4 percent to other investors.[91] Despite the common interests discussed above, relations with the Belarusian government throughout the second half of the 1990s were not smooth, with the Belarusian side accusing its Russian partners of taking important decisions without properly consulting Belarus. [92]

The Naftan refinery

The Belarusian government's keenness to modernize its refineries was especially evident in the case of the Naftan (Novopolotsk) refinery. In contrast with Mozyr, the overwhelming majority of Naftan's shares (99.8 percent) remained in state hands even after the company's transformation into a shareholding company in 2002.

In the mid-1990s, LUKoil and Yukos repeatedly proposed the creation of a joint venture with Naftan. Although an agreement was reached in 1995 stipulating their participation in the modernization of the refinery in exchange

---

88 Mozyr is located some 200 km from the Polish border and 50 km from Ukraine.

89 Vladimir Kapustin, presentation at the conference "New possibilities of oil refining and transport in the CIS and the Baltics," Odessa, 10–12 June 2004, as cited in *Ukrainian Oil and Gas Report,* June 18, 2004. Accessed via the Internet Securities, Inc. portal, available at www.securities.com (thereafter ISI).

90 Until Slavneft's full privatization in 2002, Russia (the State Property Fund, together with the Ministry of State Property) held 75% of the company's shares, Belarus (the Ministry of State Property) 10.8%, and foreign shareholders 11.2%. In November 2002, Belarus sold to Sibneft its package of shares in the company, followed by Sibneft and the Tiumenskaya Neftennaya Kompania (TNK) jointly winning an auction for 74.95% of Slavneft's Russian shares briefly thereafter. As a result, Sibneft and TNK ended up owning 98.95% of shares in Slavneft, including Slavneft shares in companies such as the Mozyr refinery. On the battle for control for Slavneft on the Russian side, see Fortescue, *Russia's Oil Barons,* 108; and Teplov, "Obesslavlennaia SLAVNEFT," *Infobank Oil and Gas Monitor,* 13 June 2002 (via ISI).

91 The refinery has nearly 4,000 workers, and in 2005 its market value was assessed at $1.1b. The assessment was made by Belarus' National Academy of Sciences in cooperation with Belarusian and Russian experts and using Western methodologies. See "Mozyrskij NPZ ocenili v 1,1 mlrd. Dollarov."

92 In 1997, Lukashenka made accusations that, although a significant share of Mozyr belonged to the jointly owned Slavneft, the Russian government had sold a large amount of company stock without consulting Belarus. Interview with Aleksander Lukashenka, *Delovoy Mir,* December 18, 1997, 1, 3.

for participation in its privatization, the deal did not come to fruition, as neither company was granted special conditions as originally agreed.[93]

In 1999, the government began an ambitious modernization program aimed at increasing Naftan's refining depth (the ratio of obtained oil products to the original quantity of crude oil), which increased from 59 percent in 1997 to 71.6 percent in 2005.[94] (Starting in late 2004 Naftan was able to produce EU-standard diesel fuel.) Naftan's profitable exports helped finance significant investments in its modernization, and also helped the refinery compensate for reduced-price sales to the chronically unprofitable domestic (especially agricultural) market.

This modernization process kept alive the interest of Russian oil companies. In a pattern similar to that followed by Gazprom, LUKoil and Slavneft supported Lukashenka's 2001 re-election bid in exchange for his promises that Naftan would be privatized. This promise, however, was not kept, leading to a cooling of relations.[95] Despite the fact that the deal did not go through, refining in Belarus continued to be highly profitable to Russian companies, especially as it allowed them to overcome some of the export limitations related to pipeline capacity set by Russia's Transneft,[96] essential for these companies to gain access to the profitable Western European refined oil products market. Similarly, oil re-exports via Belarus (in the form of refined oil products) became a way for Russian companies to override limits in oil production and exports agreed to with OPEC at times when the organization requested a reduction in oil exports—such as in 2001—as a response to falling world oil prices.[97]

Patterns of energy privatization negotiations with Russia

Taking the energy sector as whole, during the 1994–2004 period there seemed to be a pattern to the Belarusian government's dealing with Russian privatiza-

93 Vadim Sekhovich, "Belorusskaâ promyšlennost': V novyj god - s novymi hvorami," *Belorusskaya Delovaya Gazeta*, December 29, 1997, 19.

94 Manenok, "Stavka na povyšenie."

95 See Feduta, *Lukashenko: Političeskaâ Biografiâ* and Liakhovich, "Palitychny kantekst napJaredadni parlJamenckih vybaraw i referendumu," in *NajnowshaJa gistoryJa bjelaruskaga parlJamentaryzmu*. (Minsk: Analitychny Grudok, 2005). Online version available at http://kamunikat.fontel.net/www/knizki/palityka/parlamentaryzm/index.htm (accessed May 21, 2011).

96 A September 1999 order by Russia's minister of fuel and energy, Viktor Kalyuzhny, made Russian crude-oil deliveries to refineries in Belarus equivalent to deliveries to Russian ones. Interfax, Daily Financial Report, September 21, 1999, FBIS-SOV-1999-0921.

97 See "Gor'kij nefteklapan." Although not a member of OPEC, Russia agreed to voluntary export limitations.

tion proposals: going ahead with the agreement in its planning stages, when maximum concessions could be achieved from the Russian side (for example, LUKoil's and Gazprom's support for Lukashenka's 2001 presidential bid), only to later create a number of obstacles to the actual carrying out of the deal. Gazprom's reactions to unfulfilled promises on the sale of Beltransgaz most often involved the threat of a cut-off in supplies and price increases, but these increases were usually offset by special compensation credits provided by the Russian state. Indeed, it would seem as if the logic of self-interest on the part of Russian companies worked only up to a certain point. When Belarusian-Russian relations were just about to go truly sour, Russian leaders seemed to find sufficient strategic arguments to step in and provide continued support to Belarus.

Domestic management of energy issues, 1994–2004

Gas: domestic management during the "high years"[98]

Gas and more gas

A crucial element of Belarus' management of its energy situation during this period was the increased reliance on gas. This growing dependence on gas was not simply a legacy of the Soviet period which Belarus had no choice but to live with, but a conscious policy aimed at keeping production costs under check thanks to increasing the role of low-price Russian gas, as opposed to more expensive fuels.[99] Thus, from 1990 to 2007, the role of gas in the country's Total Primary Energy Supply (TPES) grew from 43 to 65 percent.[100] The role of gas in electricity generation grew even more dramatically, from 48 percent in 1992 to 95 percent in 2005,[101] as many electricity generation stations were refitted to work on gas when gas prices for Belarus became especially competitive from the late 1990s. This made the role of gas in electricity generation significantly higher than in gas-rich Russia itself (where its role in gen-

98 As most electricity in Belarus is generated through gas, this section includes electricity as well.

99 See IPM, "Rost cen na gaz," 7.

100 Ibid. A World Bank study puts the 1990 role of gas in TPES lower, at 17.7%. World Bank, *Belarus Energy Sector Review 1995*, 9.

101 Data for 1992 calculated from Graph 1, von Hirschausen and Rumiantseva, "Èkonomičeskie aspekti," 92 (on the basis of IEA data). Data for 2005 from Pavel and Rakova, "Improving Energy Efficiency."

eration was around 43 percent in 2003 and 45 percent in 2005).[102] Although already by 2001 (when gas accounted for 58 percent of TPES) official policy declarations were calling for a reduction in the role of gas in the country's TPES to 48 percent by 2015,[103] by 2008 the role of gas had not been reduced, but had increased to some 65 percent. As a result of these policies, Belarus became one of the world's most gas-dependent countries, surpassing such gas-rich countries as Russia, where the role of gas in its TPES was 53.4 percent in 2005. Gas was also crucial as, with around 80 percent of Belarus' exports consisting of highly energy-intensive products, cheap energy (mainly gas-generated electricity) became central to the country's export competitiveness.[104] Gas also became essential for the production of some of Belarus' most important exports, chemical fertilizers (nitrogen and potash fertilizers);[105] the nitrogen fertilizer company Grodno Azot alone used a fifth of the total gas volume imported by Belarus.[106]

Analyzing the important role of gas in the Belarusian economy also highlights the importance of developing a differentiated picture of Belarus' energy dependency, and of the role of various types of primary energy supplies in its economy. Both oil and gas—and the rent streams associated with each of them—were crucial for the Belarusian economy, but in different and not necessarily interchangeable ways. Gas (and, in particular, inexpensive gas) was important for the general supply of the population (heating, cooking, and electricity generation) and as a basis for the functioning of all industries using electricity. Thus, gas also contributed to lowering the export prices of Belarusian products. The role of oil, on the other hand, was no less important, but was more concentrated on specific sectors of the economy. Oil and its derived products

102 Data for Russia from (2003) IEA, *Russian Electricity Reform,* 21–22 and (2005) Mitrova, "Natural Gas in Transition: systemic reform issues."

103 See Šyrokaŭ, "Mit dem Wind," 84–95.

104 The overall resource intensity (including energy intensity) of Belarus' products is four or five times higher than that in highly developed countries. Zlotnikov, "Žestkaâ posadka."

105 In 2005, potash fertilizers, which use a large amount of energy (usually gas) in the production process, accounted for 6.2% of Belarus' exports. By 2006 nitrogen fertilizers (*azotnie udobrenie*) whose production not only depends heavily on gas as a source of energy, but also as a raw material (as gas constitutes 80% of the material needed for its production), accounted for 0.5 % of Belarus' exports. See Sawyer, "Natural gas prices impact nitrogen fertilizer costs," available at: http://www.ipm.iastate.edu/ipm/icm/2003/4-14-2003/natgasn.html (accessed October 23, 2008). By 2005–2006, Belarus' chemical industry, including fertilizers, accounted for almost 20% of Belarusian industrial production and nearly 25% of exports. Sekhovich "1991–2006. Itogi. Neftânaâ i neftepererabatyvaûŝaâ otrasl'."

106 In 2004, Grodno Azot (which in addition to fertilizers, produces a number of important chemical products), used around 22% of Belarus' total gas imports. "Bez iliuzii," *Belorusskii Rynok* No. 35/619, September 6, 2004.

(especially gasoline, diesel, and heavy oil) was a crucial (and hard to substitute with other fuels) input for the transportation and agricultural sectors. By the late 1990s, however, the primary use of oil for domestic needs had taken a back seat to the use of oil for refining and re-export, to the point that for most of the 2000s, only about one third of the crude oil imported by Belarus was used for such purposes, with the balance used in refining-and-export operations.

Pricing policy and selective cross-subsidization

An important element of Belarus' domestic gas policy during this period—and a significant particularity of the Belarusian case as compared to other post-Soviet cases—is the fact that, in general, payments by end consumers covered (and at times provided a significant premium over) the gas prices Belarus was charged by Gazprom.[107] Such an emphasis started to develop after 2000, with household gas prices growing much faster than inflation in the 2000–2003 period.[108] (At the same time, prices for residential users were consistently lower than those charged industrial users, which deviated from the usual practice in developed economies where (taking the EU as an example) residential gas prices were some 20–50 percent higher than those charged to industrial users.)[109]

This practice set Belarus apart from most post-Soviet states. While cost-covering residential electricity and gas tariffs are a common international practice, during this period it was somewhat unusual in a post-Soviet context where countries such as Ukraine routinely charged consumers and industries prices lower than the import prices paid to Russia and other gas suppliers, thus creating chronic losses. So the first particularity of the Belarusian model after 2000 was the fact that, in overall terms, domestic prices charged for gas and electricity covered the costs for imported gas. The second particularity concerns the way various domestic users were affected: while the agricultural sector and residential consumers enjoyed low prices, much of the cost was borne by the bulk of industrial enterprises.[110]

107 By December 2003, for example, gas prices charged residential end-consumers amounted to 150% of the import prices paid by Belarus. IPM, "Rost cen na gaz," 14.

108 See Centre for Social and Economic Research, *The economic aspects*, 144. The faster-than-inflation growth of household prices can be partially explained by the need to catch up from extremely low prices up to 2000.

109 IPM, "Rost cen na gaz," 15. For electricity prices charged the population and industrial users in 2001–2004, see Dashkevich, *Jenergeticheskaja zavisimost'*, 64 (Table 7). Residential prices are usually higher than industrial ones due to the relatively higher distribution costs. See also Table 1 in IPM, *MIB 2008*, 12.

110 IPM, "Rost cen na gaz," 3. As will be discussed below, a number of hand-picked industrial enterprises also received preferential prices.

Industrial users were also subjected to price increases after 2000. Notably, when in 2002 Belarus started to receive Gazprom gas at lower, domestic Russian prices, prices paid by industrial enterprises did not decrease. This created an even larger difference margin than the year before: a total of some $503.4 million, as calculated by Yafimava.[111] Although some Belarusian and Russian commentators have argued that some of the mark-ups paid by domestic gas consumers went to increment the Presidential Administration's budget, little evidence has been provided.[112] In any country, end prices need to be higher than import prices in order to cover distribution and capital upkeep expenses. In the case of Belarus, to import prices, a mark-up is added by Beltransgaz and a second one by national distributor Beltopgaz. In both cases, the mark-ups are intended to cover each enterprise's costs (such as capital, labor, raw materials, and some profits). In order to restrict tariff growth due to increases in gas import prices, profit and mark-ups are often artificially held down by the government, which hampers the further development of gas distribution enterprises.[113] After 2006, when Gazprom would acquire a stake in Beltransgaz, the size of Beltransgaz's mark-up would become a key area of disagreement between the two sides.[114]

The role of populism in Lukashenka's way of conducting and "marketing" end-consumer gas pricing policies should not be neglected, however. Residential consumers were subsidized as a group, rather than offered targeted need-based subsidies as recommended by international organizations.[115]

Gas sold in liquid petroleum (LPG) form in cylinders—especially used in the non-gasified countryside—was particularly subsidized.[116] This is significant given the fact that a significant portion of Lukashenka's supporters are rural residents

111 Yafimava, *Post-Soviet Russian-Belarussian Relationships*, 56. Yafimava's calculation of the difference margin for 2001 considers only the gas supplied by Gazprom and assumes the price paid for gas from Itera and other independent suppliers was no less than the price paid by industrial consumers.

112 In 2002, during a gas confrontation with Belarus, a Gazprom representative argued the Belarusian government was using part of the price difference between gas import and domestic sale prices charged by Beltransgaz to fill "the so-called extra-budgetary funds, used by Lukashenka and his entourage to finance large-scale projects." Savelev, in RFE/RL program,"'Gazpram' zaJawlJaje.".

113 Rakova, personal communication, February 28, 2011.

114 Ibid.

115 Some groups of residential consumers (war veterans and the disabled, among others) received special low prices, but these were based on group membership and not income. In general, non-targeted subsidies actually amounted to a larger subsidy to wealthier households than to poorer ones. See Rakova, "Ènergetičeskij sektor Belarusi," 9, 23; and (on subsidies per wealth group), Agenstvo politicheskoi ekspertizi, "Segodnâ deševyj svet".

116 IPM, "Rost cen na gaz,"12. Rakova described the cycle of energy cross-subsidies as follows: "bottled gas for the rural population [and even *dacha*-owners] is subsidized by higher prices charged city-dwellers. Gas used for heating homes in the winter is subsidized by higher prices for gas used for cooking purposes. Energy used for heating purposes is subsidized by electricity; electricity for residential use is subsidized through higher prices charged enterprises." Rakova, "Tarifi i lgoti."

highly dependent on LPG gas cylinders for cooking and other uses.[117] This went hand-in-hand with a renewed program of gasification of the countryside, with dedicated programs passed in 1999, 2001 and 2003.[118] By 2007, 90 out of 110 cities, and 60 out of 110 "urban-type villages" were heated by (centralized) gas-operated systems.[119] Populist considerations also explain why price increases in presidential election year 2001 were much less pronounced than in 2000 and 2002.[120] Similarly, in 2004, Lukashenka declared that household energy prices could not be increased by more than two percent each month, even when import prices were rising more quickly[121] and the promise could not effectively be maintained.

Another way of looking at the question of subsidies for end consumers is to analyze the degree to which the tariffs paid by household users covered the operating costs of various energy-related services. Table 3.10 gives us a sense of this situation by looking at the degree to which household payments for various gas-related energy services (in addition to gas for cooking, electricity and heating prices are relevant indicators, as they are mainly gas-generated) covered costs in 2001–2010. The trend is clear: in general, cost-covering was achieved from 2003 to 2007, but declined after the 2007 increase in gas prices.[122] (Off figures for heating are related to the significantly higher level of subsidization of these services.)

How does this picture of relatively high cost-recovery levels fit in with views of Belarus using low gas prices from Russia to subsidize its industries? First and foremost, it should be kept in mind that prices were relatively low to start with, so an element of implicit hidden subsidization was always present. Secondly, part of the difference between the prices paid to Gazprom and those charged to end users was retained by the state and contributed toward its budget, to be further used to subsidize goods so that they subsequently enjoyed a competitive price advantage when exported.[123] Moreover, some industrial

117 As of the mid-2000s there was a marked difference in levels of gasification between city (79%) and countryside (14%) households. Energy Ministry of the Republic of Belarus, cited in Yafimava, "Belarus," 146.

118 See Yafimava, "Belarus," 145.

119 IPM, "Rost cen na gaz," 7.

120 Centre for Social and Economic Research, *The economic aspects*, 144.

121 See Zhbanov, "S novym gazom."

122 However, it must be kept in mind that calculating household gas prices in Belarus is complicated by the absence of comparable time-series data, and by the coexistence of a variety of prices, for example for cooking, heating in winter, and hot water, applied differentially to apartments with and without central heating. Moreover, some types of gas (for heating and hot water) are usually metered, while others are not, with prices being charged on a per person basis.

123 Makarov, (Itera's president), interview in *Gas Matters*. See also "Gazprom Not Happy with Belarus," RFE/RL, 12 November 2002.

Table 3.9 Gas import prices and prices paid by end users, in US$/tcm, 1999–2004

	1999	2000	2001	2002	2003	2004
Price paid by Beltransgaz to Gazprom	30	30	30	17–22*	30	46.68
Average price of imported gas**	N/A	N/A	30	29.5	35.6	46.68
Average price of gas paid by end users	N/A	N/A	56.7	49.9	51.6	67.0
Price paid by industrial users to Beltransgaz	N/A	40–55	40–55	N/A	60–65	70

* For the period from January 1 to April 1, the price, as calculated by the IPM, was higher, at US$30/tcm.
** The average price of imported gas includes both the basic amounts purchased from Gazprom at fixed prices, plus additional supplies purchased from Gazprom or other suppliers at higher prices.

Sources:
Yafimava, "Post-Soviet Russian-Belarussian Relationships," 58 (Table 2.2); and Dashkevich, *Jenergeticheskaja zavisimost',* Table 3. (On the basis of data from the Energy Ministry and the OAO Beltransgaz.)
Data for average import prices and average final consumer prices from Sekhovich "1991–2006. Itogi. Gazovaya otrasl'."

enterprises were charged preferential gas prices: in general, 50–80 percent of the official price.[124] Although the list was not made public and there was no clear criteria for inclusion, companies which were usually offered such preferences included the electricity monopoly Belenergo, some petrochemical companies, and some light industries.

Oil: Domestic management during the "high years"

Domestic management in the oil area was concentrated on three areas: seeking state control of refineries and their modernization process (discussed above); maintaining profit margins from the domestic sale of oil and oil products; and extracting certain concessions from refineries and Russian oil companies that would allow the government to subsidize certain domestic sectors, especially agriculture.

As regards prices charged to domestic users, the same general trends observable in the gas sector were also at play in the oil sector, especially cost-

124 IPM, *MIB 2008*, 34.

Table 3.10 Cost coverage by tariffs for expenditures for services provided by communal services provider ZhKKh, in % (January 1st of each year)

	2001	2002	2003	2004	2005	2006	2007	2008	2009	2010 (preliminary)
Average price of imported gas from Gazprom, US$/tcm	30	17-22	30	47.88	55	55	118	126.8	151	185
Level of cost coverage for expenses related to electricity	37.6	54.9	120.0	107.3	98.9	101.1	117.5	82.0	59.0	N/A
Level of cost coverage for expenses related to heating, in %	17.0	34.0	75.3	50.8	41.8	36.5	37.4	46.7	40.0	20.6
Level of cost coverage for expenses related to natural gas (for cooking), in %	29.6	58.4	150.8	143.8	141.1	144.2	157.5	67.0	57.0	N/A

Sources:
Ministry of Economics of the Republic of Belarus, IMF, 2007; Republic of Belarus: Statistical Appendix. Preliminary data for 2010 from:
www.nest.by/content/uroven-vozmeshcheniya-uslug-zhkkh-v-2010-godu-ne-prevysit-25.
Gas import prices from Tables 3.1 and 3.9.

covering end-user prices. In fact, high taxes and the long-standing price policy which was held by national petrochemical concern Belneftekhim often made the price of oil products (such as gasoline) inside Belarus higher than in neighboring states which were paying higher import prices.[125] Most sales of oil products were cost-covering, with the exception of those in the agricultural sector, which were cross-subsidized by higher prices charged to other end consumers. In general, domestic sales were profitable for the state due to the high level of taxes (often nearing 50 percent of the prices) levied on them, but not so much for the oil companies (including Russian companies) them-

125 According to Romanchuk, as of 2002, the price of gasoline (A-92 and A-95 types) was 36–40% higher than in Russia and Ukraine. Romanchuk, "Degradacià monopolista." In 2008, taxes comprised almost 50% of the retail price of gasoline, compared with 34.1% in Russia. Mikhail Osipenko, deputy chairman of Belneftekhim, quoted in Rublev, "Naš benzin," 1.

selves, which, on the other hand, were able to compensate for these losses through their export profits.

Russian oil companies working in Belarus were subjected to a number of requirements, for example that they supply the agricultural sector with a certain volume of oil products at highly discounted prices, in particular, diesel supplies at planting or harvest times.[126] In addition, they were usually only allowed to refine on a tolling arrangement basis up to 50 percent of the oil imported to Belarus, and were obliged to sell 50 percent of their oil to Belarusian refineries, guaranteeing them high profits.[127] Despite requirements such as these, Russian oil companies continued to benefit from their work with Belarusian refineries, which allowed them to avoid the heavy export duties and export limitations imposed by the Russian state on direct oil exports.

In summary, and looking at both the oil and gas sectors, it is clear that the rent-maximization strategy observable in the external management of Belarus' energy situation was also pursued domestically. Its most important element was a cost-covering price policy vis-à-vis domestic consumers, where domestic prices were set sufficiently high as to cover import prices. Within this general policy, however, differential prices were charged to different users, with subsidies to residential and rural users financed by the higher prices paid by other users ("cross-subsidization"); and by the energy-trade macro rents accrued by the country as a whole. This was part of a broader rent-extraction and redistribution cycle which allowed Lukashenka to secure (relatively) high levels of popular support through large subsidies to rural areas, sustaining full employment, and steadily improving salaries and living standards.

Belarus, Russian energy, and macro-level rents

Having looked at Belarus' gas and oil policies during the "high years" of 1994–2004, let us summarize the types of energy rents accrued by Belarusian actors during this period. (Chapter 5 discusses energy rents in the post-2004 period.) These rents may be categorized as accruing either at the macro-economic (discussed here) or micro-economic levels (discussed in Chapter 4).

126 Elena Rakova, personal communication, January 2011.

127 See "Gor'kij nefteklapan."

Macro-level rents accrued in the Belarus-Russia relationship through the indirect subsidization of the economy through lower-than-international gas and oil prices; the possibilities opened up by barter arrangements; the extra income created by transit fees; the direct and indirect re-export of energy sources; taxes paid by energy companies; and through semi-legal and illegal energy transactions. (Above and beyond these energy-specific advantages, preferential access to Russian markets brought additional benefits, augmented through profitable barter arrangements.) Although these rents accrued at the macro-level, affecting the country as a whole, they also benefited President Lukashenka politically, as they made possible the survival of his regime by helping to delay painful economic reforms.

Lower-than-international gas and oil prices

The first and most obvious way in which Belarus benefited financially from the energy relationship with Russia during 1994–2004 was through importing gas and oil at prices much lower than those prevalent in Russian trade with Western Europe or other former Soviet states. According to IMF estimates, the subsidy effect of selling Belarus gas and oil at preferential prices amounted, in 2004, to 10 percent of the country's GDP, with 6–7 percent being the result of subsidized gas prices, and three percent being the result of oil prices.[128] Such preferential energy pricing brought complex issues to the fore concerning the relationship between business and the state in Russia. For much of this period, Gazprom was asked to sell gas to Belarus at domestic Russian prices but, in exchange, received a number of indirect advantages from the Russian state. The situation was complicated by the fact that Gazprom, with its web of personal and corporate interests within one company, could hardly be considered a typical private enterprise. Although the Russian government may have had more of an interest than Gazprom in supplying Belarus with gas at domestic Russian prices in exchange for a certain level of political loyalty, Gazprom's calculation was more complicated. Gazprom, as a corporation, had an interest in maximizing profits and in charging market prices to both domestic and foreign buyers.

128 According to the IMF, the subsidy effect of low gas prices amounted to 11.5% of GDP in 2000, and to 6.1% in 2005. IMF, "Republic of Belarus," cited in IPM, "Rost cen na gaz," 16. However, the exact amount of such subsidies is extremely difficult to calculate given the large role of barter and other barter-like operations at the time.

When Gazprom sold gas to Belarus at preferential prices, it was also doing so for the sake of good relations with, and indirect benefits from, the Russian state.[129] Russian oil companies—at this time still controlled mainly by private actors—were not asked to subsidize supplies to Belarus as heavily as Gazprom was in the case of gas. Instead, in the case of oil, issues related to these companies' own value-added chains played the prominent role: the profits that could be made from refining and re-exporting through Belarus, and their ability to avoid Russian export quota limitations through these.[130] These two examples bring to the fore how impossible it is to speak of a single "Russia" acting vis-à-vis Belarus, and how the existence of a multitude of actors in Russia, with different priorities and interests, played a role in the relationship.

Barter

The profit generated by special pricing schemes had to do not only with low prices, but with the widespread use of barter, and the high prices assigned to Belarusian products in exchange for Russian oil and gas. In the mid-to-late 1990s, barter accounted for about 50 percent of the total commodity turnover between the two countries, and for 74 percent of Belarus' energy imports from Russia.[131] In 1998, it was estimated that by buying from Belarus as part of these barter arrangements (instead of from cheaper suppliers) Russia was therefore losing—and subsidizing the Belarusian economy by—a further US $200–300 million a year.[132] Barter deals included a crucial element: so-called coefficients governing the way the barter equivalencies would be calculated. The Belarusian government was able to push through "coefficients" especially favorable to it: according to one source, as high as 1.27 in the late 1990s, which meant that the price of Belarusian products used for the barter calculations was increased by 27 percent, which "automatically reduced the real price of the gas purchases."[133] Added to the effect of multiple exchange rates up to 2002, this created important discounts and possibilities for price manipulation.[134]

129 See Balmaceda, "Russia's Central and Eastern European."

130 Manenok also talks of *premii* (special rewards) paid to Russian oil companies for supplying oil to Belarus. Manenok, "Valûtnyj ručej."

131 See Selivanova, Èkonomičeskaâ integraciâ," 324 and World Bank, "Belarus: Window of Opportunity," 119 (Table 4.12). According to Yafimava, in 1997 only 8% of Belarus' payments to Gazprom were conducted in currency. Yafimava, *Post-Soviet Russian-Belarussian Relationships*, 105, Footnote 197.

132 Zlotnikov, "Vyzhivanie ili integracija?," 84.

133 Sekhovich, "1991–2006. Itogi. Gazovaâ otrasl'," and Dashkevich, *Jenergeticheskaja zavisimost'*.

134 During much of the period up to 2002, the official exchange rate was between two and three times higher than the market one. Other rates also differed substantially.

Barter was important not only as a means of financing energy imports, but also as a means to stretch the impact of energy-related compensation credits provided by Russia. Referring to the mid-2000s, Feduta describes this cycle of barter-related subsidization as follows. Gazprom supplies gas (for example, a billion dollars' worth of gas) to Belarus on credit terms, after which, citing problems with payment collections from Belarusian consumers, Belarus fails to pay back in full (while actually forcing domestic industrial users to pay for the gas in full). Later, Belarus pays Russia back, but only half of the amount. In this way, "quite a bit of money appears in the budget"[135] (in fact, 1.5 billion—the still unreturned credit from Gazprom, plus the money paid by Belarusian companies for gas), which President Lukashenka "channels into the agricultural sector—that is, to his electorate." The debt vis-à-vis Gazprom is paid back with Belarusian products, bartered at especially advantageous prices for Belarus. Thus, the regularly provided compensation credits, together with the premium prices paid by Russia to import large amounts of goods produced in Belarus on the basis of still-subsidized Russian gas, reduced the actual impact of gas price increases, providing an important source of stability for the regime. This was also so because—in contrast with loans from the IMF and other financial institutions—these were seldom conditional on economic reforms.

Thus, Lukashenka's ability to maintain favorable-terms barter trade in the Belarusian-Russian gas trade could be considered one of his main short-term successes in the relationship with Russia. The downside, however, was that this allowed the Belarusian economy to continue focusing on outdated, uncompetitive goods, for which there was a limited demand and which could only be "disposed of" through barter with Russia. The fact that this production was the result of cheap government credits, and of high production targets often imposed by decree on enterprise managers, only increased the broader negative effects of such policies. (Indeed, throughout the period covered by this book, parallel to elements of private economic activity, especially in retail trade, Belarus continued to use Soviet-era mechanisms such as central planning, five-year plans, the imposition of production targets on individual companies, and administrative price controls.)

However, Belarus' ability to rely on the Russian market to absorb noncompetitive goods came under increased strain after 2003, when now wealthier Russian consumers started to be able to afford higher-price imports. If in 2003 $600m in unsold goods had accumulated in Belarusian warehouses, by

135 Feduta, *Lukashenka*, 575.

2005, the amount had increased to $1 billion and to some $1.4 billion by January 2007.[136] This change was accompanied both by changes in the structure of Belarusian exports (a growing role of oil products) and in the country's orientation away from Russian and towards EU markets.

Income from transit fees

During 1994–2004, gas transit fees charged by Belarus remained extremely low by international standards, in a setup where these low transit fees were largely offered in exchange for low prices on Russian gas. Due to the high volumes involved, however, they provided an annual income of around $250 million. It is estimated that, in 2004, Belarus was able to cover 14.8 per cent of its gas purchases from Gazprom through transit services.[137] Similarly, transit fees charged to Russian oil companies remained extremely low (at about 50 percent of that charged by neighboring states)[138] and remained unchanged between 1995 and 2007. At $168m in 2006, the income accrued by Belarus strictly from oil-transit activities was relatively modest.[139] However, low oil transit fees played an important indirect role: they made it especially attractive for Russian oil companies to transit their oil exports through Belarus to the West and, thus, encouraged the supply of oil to Belarusian refineries. Thus, low transit fees were a crucial factor in assuring access to high profits through oil refining and the export of refined products.[140] Similarly, in the case of gas, low transit fees can be seen as an incentive for supplies to Belarus.

Energy re-exports: oil refining and re-exports

Of all the sources of income related to Russian energy, none proved more profitable to Belarus than the direct and indirect re-export of energy sources, first and foremost the export of refined oil products to Western markets.[141]

136 Romanchuk, "V strane slučilsâ bum," and Rakova, "Reformi." By January 2007, the value of such unsold production was equivalent to 53.4% of monthly production. Rakova, "Reformi."

137 Dashkevich, *Jenergeticheskaja zavisimost'*, quoted in Romanchuk, "Do gazovogo Armageddona."

138 In 2007, transit fees for oil were increased by an average of 30%, to $3.5/t for oil transported West to Poland through the Yamal pipeline, and to $1.5/t for transport south to Brody. Even after the 2007 increases, however, transit fees, calculated in cost per ton/100 km, were approximately half of those charged by Poland and Ukraine. See Manenok, "Po ŝadâŝej stavke."

139 Scherbo, "Tranzit." From 2009 to 2012 Scherbo was Belarus' Minister of Transport and Communications.

140 See Kostiugova, "Perspektivy učastiâ Belarusi," 6.

141 This mainly concerns heavy oil products such as diesel fuel, heavy heating oil and lubricant oils, which compose 70 per cent of Belarus' exports of oil products. Manenok, "Sozdaetsâ valûtnyj goseksporter."

While not re-export in the a narrow technical sense of the word, in broad terms, the refining and re-sale of crude oil as oil products can be considered a type of oil re-export (crude oil comprises 80–90 percent of the raw material for refined oil products). Here, the essential mechanism of rent creation was the importation of crude oil from Russia at low prices—and free from any export duties levied by Russia—and its refining and subsequent re-export at world prices, which meant Belarus could profit not only from the value-added process and the difference between custom-made Belarus prices and international ones, but would also receive related export duties.[142] Belarus' significant oil products' exports profits during this period were made possible by the combination of lower-than-market and only slowly rising import prices for oil, and on the other hand, the rapidly increasing demand and prices for oil products in Western European markets at a time when refining facilities in EU states were not able to keep up with demand.[143] As a result, the weight of oil products' exports in Belarus' overall exports grew massively during this period: from 9 percent in 1999 to 27.4 percent in 2004.

A central element of the oil refining and re-exports rents story is the fact that the practice that was actually followed concerning the division of oil duties between Russia and Belarus (i.e., Belarus receiving all duties on its oil-product exports, while Russia charged no export duties on oil sold to Belarus) was in clear violation of agreements signed between both countries. The 1995 Agreement on a Customs Union prescribed that both states would apply the same customs duties towards third countries;[144] the agreement also prescribed that proceeds from export duties should be divided on a 85:15 basis (i.e., that 85 percent of receipts should go to Russia, and 15 percent to Belarus.)[145] Yet until January 2007, Lukashenka was able to keep the totality of those revenues in Belarus. A related and equally contested issue concerned the level of export duties applied by Belarus and Russia. According to the 1995 Agreement on the Establishment of a Customs Union between Russia and Belarus (Article 12), as well as an agreement on the unification of custom rules and

142 As noted before, however, until 2007 these duties we not significant, constituting less than 1.5% of budget revenues.

143 The relative deficit of refining capacities in EU states changed after 2005 with the building of several new refineries.

144 Article 2.8 of the December 1999 Treaty on the Creation of a Union State restates the same point (i.e., that both sides will apply the same import and export duties).

145 Point 3, sub-point B, *Soglashenie o Tamozhennom Soiuze Rossii i Belarus* (1995). For other related items, such as goods produced in Belarus from wood and metal imported from Russia, a different division of export duties was set up: 60% to Russia and 40% to Belarus.

Table 3.11 Export duties on light oil products, in US$/ton, levied by Russia and Belarus, 2005–2007

Year	Russia	Belarus	Belarus duty as % of Russia's duty	Difference per ton
2005 (November)	134	68	51	66
2006 (November)	158	57	36	101
2007 (December)	138	76	55	62

Sources:
Calculated on the basis of data in Sekhovich, "1991–2006. Itogi. Neftânaâ i neftepererabatyvaûŝaâ otrasl'," and Tatiana Manenok, "Benzinovyj signal." Numbers have been rounded to the next entire numbers.

on the creation of a single customs system within the Union of Russia and Belarus (signed on January 29, 2001), both countries were obliged to apply the same level of export duties. However, Belarus continued to delay full implementation of the agreement.[146]

Table 3.11 presents a snapshot of these differences in export duties on oil products during 2005–2007. It must be noted, however, that data from this table is for indicative purposes only, as it presents an accurate but somewhat simplified picture. A full picture would include a number of additional items for which data is not publicly available, such as different export duties for different qualities of refined oil products, as well as average annual duties. Russian duties changed according to average oil export prices per ton.

How can Russia's acquiescence with Belarus' failure to divide oil export duties as agreed be explained? First, Belarus used a variety of explanations to avoid handing over to Russia its share of the duties. At first the argument—invoked in private discussions—was that the duties applied by Belarus were negligible and, thus, did not merit sharing with Russia.[147] Later, as new rules prescribing the application of VAT on a "country of destination" as opposed to on a "country of production" basis entered into effect (2005), Belarus argued that the collected export duties should not be subject to the agreed 85—15 division, as they were being counted as part of the VAT paid by the

146 Manenok, "Benzinovyj signal," When in 2004 Russia voiced serious concerns about the issue, Belarus increased its duties and there was a short (three month) period when the duties levied by both Belarus and Russia were indeed the same. But the balance was lost again when Belarus failed to increase its duties when Russia did in April of 2004. By November 2006, the difference in export duties on oil products had grown significantly, with Russia charging duties nearly three times higher than those charged by Belarus. Sekhovich, "1991–2006. Itogi. Neftânaâ i neftepererabatyvaûŝaâ otrasl'."

147 Author's interviews, Minsk, January 2011.

Russian oil suppliers.[148] Perhaps one reason for Russia's lack of zeal in applying the agreement had to do with the fact that in the mid-1990s world oil prices were rather low, meaning low oil export duties as well so Russia's interest in fully applying the agreements was not as strong; once oil prices started to increase rapidly around 2004, Russia acquired a much stronger real impetus to claim its half of the export duties.

Yet, undoubtedly part of the explanation for Russian acquiescence with Belarus' pre-2007 lack of compliance had also to do with Lukashenka's ability to politicize the relationship with Russia, and to apply political pressure on Russia as discussed below. In addition, it must be kept in mind that Belarus' refusal to share with Russia export taxes on oil products, while disadvantageous for the Russian budget, benefited Russian oil companies. This in turn contributed to Belarus keeping export duties at an extremely low level, as such policy provided an incentive for Russian oil companies to continue exporting through Belarus.[149] This tells us that, in order to understand this question, we need to look at the diverse value-added chains in Russia's oil sector during this period, how they were affected by Russian and Belarusian trade regulations, and how they, in turn, affected the preferences of concrete actors in Russia's oil sector. These regulations affected Russian oil companies and oil oligarchs very concretely, making it possible for them to gain additional profits at the expense of lowered revenue for the Russian budget in the form of foregone export duty revenue.

Within this context, how to understand Russia's 2007 policy change concerning the sharing of oil export duties between Belarus and Russia? In addition to the increased cash value of the issue (given the sharp increase in prices for oil and oil products from 2004), changes in the structure of the Russian oil sector also help us understand these changes: with increasingly centralized control over the oil business in the wake of the virtual destruction of Yukos, it would only be expected that those central structures also wanted to acquire a greater control over oil export duties as well.

148 Although not focusing on the case of Belarus, Shiells, "VAT Design and Energy Trade" provides a good overview of the connection between VAT issues and Russia's energy trade with its post-Soviet neighbors.

149 This situation is reminiscent of that around gas trade in Ukraine 2006–2009 when gas supply monopolist RosUkrEnergo was able to offer some "advantages" to Ukraine by, arguably, cheating both the Ukrainian state and Gazprom (with the acquiescence of some in its high management) of its own profits, while providing important players in both Ukraine and Russia important profits. See Balmaceda, *Energy Dependency*, Chapter 4. Milov argues Gazprom's generous support of RosUkrEnergo during this period included giving the company $1.25 b in profits from gas trade with Turkmenistan it could have received itself. See Milov and Nemtsov, *Nezavisimyj ekspertnyj doklad*. In contrast with the Ukrainian case, however, the benefits received from the Russian budget formally seemed to have been received legally, as a result of available loopholes.

Tax income from oil and gas companies

A related source of revenue was the tax and duty income received from energy sector companies.

For most of the period until 2007, Belarusian export duties on oil products remained low, contributing less than 1.5 percent of the yearly budget revenue during 2004–2006. However, it was exactly these low export duties which helped Belarus attract Russian oil for refining. Other tax sources were also important, with the Mozyr and Naftan refineries accounting for over 10 percent of tax payments to the consolidated budget in the mid-2000s (11.62 percent in 2006, 10.51 percent in 2007); and the largest oil traders (LUKoil-Belarussia, Yunivest, Tripl, and Interservis) supplying a further 3.54 percent in 2007.[150] This was in addition to the tax revenue provided by Beltransgaz, 4.27 percent of the total in 2007. To these, we should add the less formalized non-tax contributions, or "informal taxes" made by energy companies discussed in Chapter 4.[151] After a significant increase in 2007, export duties on oil products started to provide around 10 percent of the total income of the Belarusian budget.[152]

Energy-rents-driven populism, energy culture and Lukashenka's relationship with the Belarusian electorate

Belarus' "Energy-political model": energy rents and rising living standards

This chapter has concentrated on the macro-level rents accrued by Belarus in its energy trade with Russia during 1994–2004. These rents provided important sources of stability for the Lukashenka regime. In Belarus' own brand of "energy-political model," these rents helped stabilize the system through four central roles: Firstly, through the subsidization of the economy as a whole—an impact calculated at almost 10 percent of GDP in the mid 2000s—without forcing the country to engage in painful economic reforms; this support also

150 Romanchuk, "The Belarusian Republic," 16–17, calculated on the basis of data from the Ministry of Tax Collection.

151 Following Gaddy and Ickes, informal taxes can be defined as nominally voluntary but *de facto* mandatory contributions needed to be made by a business in order to survive. Gaddy and Ickes, "Resource Rents." See also Gaddy and Ickes, *Russia's Virtual Economy*.

152 Calculated by the author from data by Leonid Zlotnikov. See also Manenok, "Valûtnye donory."

translated into higher GDP rates, also important for propaganda purposes.[153] Secondly, increasing hard-currency earnings from the export of oil products to Western markets allowed the Belarusian government to maintain a high (some would say artificially high) value for the Belarusian rouble vis-à-vis the dollar. This was crucial for the government's social policy, as it made imported consumer goods increasingly accessible to the general population. Thirdly, energy-related income made possible the targeted support of specific areas crucial for Lukashenka's electoral support, or to reward, at his discretion, loyal regions or groups within his electorate,[154] for example, rural areas,[155] and the police and security forces, an area where salaries were reportedly increased significantly between 1994 and 2007. More generally, thanks to the special oil trade relationship with Russia, the significant rise in world oil prices in the mid 2000s meant a huge economic boom for Belarus, contributing to steady wage increases, which grew from an average $100 per month in 1997 to $420 in June 2008.[156] As Zaiko and Romanchuk (Ramanchuk) state, "Russian petrodollars allowed all of us to live beyond our means [...] from the director to the doorman."[157]

Energy-rents-driven populism as a source of political support

The economic advantages received by Belarus from the particular organization of energy trade with Russia were crucial for the increase in living standards during this period. In turn, Lukashenka's use of rising living stan-

---

153 "Istočnik rosta," citing IMF, "Rapid growth in Belarus." Dashkevich calculated that paying $46.68/tcm instead of $80 allowed Belarus to have a growth rate of 11% in 2004, instead of the 8.1% that he would prognosticate under $80 per tcm prices. Dashkevich, *Jenergeticheskaja zavisimost'*.

154 Feduta, *Lukashenko,* 418–419, and comments by Leonid Sinitsyn, former Vice-PM in the first Lukashenka period, quoted in ibid., 414.

155 Feduta, ibid., 515 puts the connection as follows: "Lukashenka takes this money [i.e., the direct or indirect gas subsidies from Russia] and channels it to the agricultural sector – that is, to his electorate." Zaiko and Romanchuk argue that support for the struggling (in decline from its Soviet-time zenith since the Chernobyl accident of 1986) countryside, provider of the most steadfast Lukashenka electorate, costs the Belarusian state $1–1.5 b per year, "approximately the same as the indirect Russian subsidization." Zaiko and Romanchuk, *Belarus' na razlome,* 145. Although the actual figure quoted by Zaiko and Romanchuk may be inaccurate as the true size of Russian subsidization of Belarus, the general principle makes sense.

156 If, in 1997, average monthly salaries amounted to $100 in dollar equivalent, by late early 2007 they had increased to nearly $300. For 1997 data see *Human Rights Watch Report 1998*. For 2007 data see *Belarus News*. Real wages grew by 17.7% in 2006. IPM, *BMER* 1/64, January 2008, 1. Data for 2008 from IPM, *BMER* 9/72, November 2008, 1. On the growth of real wages in Belarus see also World Bank, "Belarus: window of opportunity." A note of caution must be exercised when presenting average wage data in dollars, as the results achieved depend strongly on the exchange rate at any given time—something that, as discussed in Chapter 4, can be manipulated by the state, and also has little meaning if not presented in real purchasing power terms.

157 Zaiko and Romanchuk, *Belarus' na razlome*, 142.

dards (as opposed to a program of national or ethnic revival, for example) as means to bolster his legitimacy built upon deep roots in the Soviet period. In many ways, Lukashenka's "energy-political model"[158] could be seen as a continuation of the social contract in place during the high-growth 1970s and closely associated with the rule of First Secretary of the Communist Party of Belarus Piotr Masheraw, 1965–1980.[159] This "social contract" was based on the state's provision of extensive services to the population—including reliable energy services—and the expectation of steadily increasing living standards.

In addition, the relative weakness of a national platform as basis for political mobilization and Belarus' historical legacies also created a basis for Lukashenka's legitimation through rising living standards.[160] The legacy of World War II devastation, in particular, made a significant part of the population prone to a resigned and even passive attitude, best reflected by the Russian-language phrase *"Hot' by ne bylo vojny,"* loosely translated as "we can bear anything—just spare us war." This helps explain both the relative lack of political mobilization, and the population's positive reception of a "social contract" which provided stability and rising living standards. (That such policies were ultimately unsustainable seemed to seldom come into the picture, however.)

Explaining the success of Lukashenka's external energy management, 1994–2004

Manipulating asymmetrical interdependence

How do we explain Belarus' ability to maintain such preferential treatment from Russia?

One central key to Lukashenka's external management of the relationship was his ability to turn around the balance of forces in the relationship in the context of Belarus' objectively limited energy counter-power vis-à-vis its much larger and more powerful ally.

158 See Balmaceda, "At a crossroads," 79–91.

159 See Haiduk, "Social Contract," 8, and Silitski, "From Social Contract to Social Dialogue," 157–159.

160 Leschenko credits Lukashenka with creating something close to a national ideology, but one not based on ethnic exclusivity, but on an ethnically inclusive collectivistic and egalitarian view of the nation. Leshchenko, "The National Ideology."

Given the reality of Belarus' limited bargaining power vis-à-vis Russia in the economic and energy areas, one would have expected a much narrower field of action for the Belarusian side, and less of an ability to carry out its policy preferences. In reality, however, as shown in this chapter and Chapter 5, between 1994 and 2006 Lukashenka's Belarus was able to extract much larger energy benefits and concessions from Russia than would be warranted by this balance of power.

The key to this was connected with Belarus' military and strategic importance for Russia, and with Lukashenka's ability to politicize the economic and energy relationship. Concerning the former, it is important to keep in mind the country's important geographical position as the former Soviet Union's westernmost state, a comparative advantage the value of which increased after Estonia, Latvia, and Lithuania joined NATO in 2004. Given Russia's complicated relationships with the Baltic States and Ukraine during this period, Belarus both provided Russia with the most convenient access to the West and to its own Kaliningrad Oblast, and remained the sole zone of Russian influence on the borders with NATO.

Starting in the late 1990s, Belarus' military infrastructure became integrated into Russia's military planning, and a coordinated military exercise schedule was established. In addition, Russia installed its state-of-the art Volga early-warning system (covering its western airspace and completed in October 2003) at the Hantsevichi/Baranovichi base, replacing a facility in Latvia which Russia had lost use of. Also, the deployment of S-300 anti-aircraft missile systems to Belarus in 2005–2006 made the special relationship with Belarus invaluable for Russia from a military perspective.[161] In 2009, both countries signed a treaty integrating their air-defense systems.[162]

Looking specifically at the energy sector, if to a large extent one can agree with analysts such as Yafimava in that "Belarus' financial ability to withstand price increases is precisely what determines the limits of its bargaining power" in disputes with Gazprom,[163] this is not the end of the story. Indeed, President Lukashenka's greatest political coup—both in terms of securing his own hold on power and of securing important energy macro rents for Belarus as a whole—was his ability to manipulate the political and psychological aspects

161 On military cooperation, see Reppert, "The Security Dimension,", and Deyermond, "The State of the Union."

162 The February 2009 agreement, however, was only signed after significant delays and misunderstandings (2009–2010 developments in the military cooperation area are discussed in Chapter 5). See Pilloni, "The Belarusian Russian." On military cooperation see also Reppert, "The Security Dimension," and Deyermond, "The State of the Union."

163 Yafimava, *Post-Soviet Russian-Belarussian Relationships*, 46.

of the relationship with Russia and make his country significantly more important to the Russian leadership than would be warranted for purely economic reasons. Our picture of the asymmetrical interdependencies between Belarus and Russia would be incomplete without taking into account Lukashenka's political and psychological power vis-à-vis Moscow which, as we will discuss further, allowed him to compensate for a lack of economic counter-power during much of the 1994–2011 period.

Lukashenka, energy, and Russia's collective self-esteem

Lukashenka's turning of weakness into strength was achieved overwhelmingly through the consistent politicization of the relationship with Russia, though it remains to be explained why the Russian side, having objectively significant instruments of counter-power at its disposal, went along and played along with this politicization. The answer to this question lies above and beyond Russia's military interest in Belarus, at another level, having to do with the role Belarus could play in Russia's national interest from the perspective of what Alexander Wendt has called its "collective self-esteem" dimension (i.e., a "group's need to feel good about itself, for respect or status.")[164] It is exactly this element which, in addition to the military-strategic element, helps us to understand why Russia, having objectively significant instruments of counter-power at its disposal, largely went along with Lukashenka's demands in the energy area, until at least 2007.[165]

Lukashenka's strategy in this area relied on capitalizing on the trauma of loss of empire by manipulating the Russian elites' psychological insecurities stemming from the dissolution of the USSR, offering a self-esteem boost in the form of an alliance with Belarus, which was directly or indirectly presented not only as an alliance with Russia's "last ally" but as promise of a revived Union. In this way, Lukashenka was selling not only the "Belarusian model," or Belarus

164 Wendt, *Social Theory*, 236.

165 Belarus was certainly not the only post-Soviet state to receive some form of energy preferential treatment: for most of the period up to 2005, other post-Soviet states such as Ukraine, Moldova, and Armenia received Russian gas at prices well below average European ones. For all these cases (also including Belarus), those lower prices can be explained by a mixture of factors, including Russia's desire to continue playing an important role in these economies, in addition to the specific interests of Russian energy players, tied to these countries through specific political ties and value-added chains. What sets the Belarusian case apart is not only the fact that it became the only post-Soviet state with a legal claim to receive gas at domestic Russian prices (2002–2004), but because of the especially profitable *oil* trade conditions it enjoyed.

as an ally, but the *idea of Russia as a continuation of a strong and successful Soviet Union*, which remained deep in the longings of Russian citizens. Such messages were carefully targeted to the Russian leadership and the Russian public at large.[166] A first, crucial audience to address was the broader Russian electorate, especially in the provinces, cultivated through regular visits until 1999 and targeted press conferences after that.[167] At least until 2004, when the heavy influx of oil and gas dollars into the Russian economy started to chip away at Belarus' comparatively higher living standards, Lukashenka was successful in selling to the average Russian citizen the image of the country as an order-and-stability paradise, sharply contrasted with a Russia portrayed as characterized by chaos, unstable wages, and corrupt capitalism. In addition to selling the image of Belarus as Russia's "last remaining ally," Lukashenka, perhaps most importantly, sought to present himself as "last defender of the USSR," an idea with a powerful resonance given the "Belavezh complex" (perceived guilt for the demise of the USSR) experienced by those leaders who signed the December 1991 Belovezh Agreement on the dissolution of the USSR. In doing so, Lukashenka invariably presented the argument that, in contrast with Russian leaders, he had not signed the agreement.[168] Most importantly, Lukashenka used the political and psychological value of his endorsement (as well as the endorsement provided by the building itself of a Union State with Russia) as means for a curious trade: contributing—by association—to specific leaders' domestic popularity in Russia, in exchange for economic support for Belarus. This was seen, for example, in the case of Boris Yeltsyn, where, thanks to integration agreements with Belarus, Yeltsyn "once again appeared to the Russian masses as collector of [Russian] lands' ('*sobiratel' zemel'*')."[169]

Lukashenka used a dual-pronged approach with the Russian leaders, pursuing a direct relationship but also using his popularity with the Russian masses to exert pressure. The issue of his political ambitions within a single

166 Interestingly, there seemed to be an apparent contradiction between Lukashenka's marketing himself to the Russian public as an ally of the idea of a strong and successful Soviet Union and—at least at times of crisis in the relationship—as the defender of Belarusian interests and sovereignty against Moscow's imperialist encroachment. That he was able to seemingly successfully move between these two roles or discourses may be the result of his close-to-the-people populist rhetoric and oratory ability.

167 Between 1996 and 1998, Lukashenka visited more than half of Russia's regions and provinces. See Drakokhrust and Furman, "Belarus and Russia," 243.

168 There seems to be some controversy as to the accuracy of this statement, however. See Lindner, "The Lukashenka Phenomenon," 84.

169 Portnikov, "Krasnaâ Metka," 7. On Yeltsyn's use of the unification process with Belarus (especially discussions on monetary union) as a way to "seek advantage in his domestic struggle for power," see Danilovich, *Russian-Belarusian Integration*, 41–47.

state presents an interesting example. As early as December 1997, Lukashenka repeatedly declared his interest in establishing a joint presidency—with significant powers—for the Belarusian–Russian Union State, and to eventually hold this post.[170] The underlying logic here is that Russian leaders, uneasy about a possible Lukashenka run for a joint presidency, but also afraid of eliciting the wrath of their own voters should they "let Belarus down," were eager to neutralize Lukashenka's role in domestic Russian politics, and found it was safer to do so (at least outwardly) by embracing him and his goals—hoping to benefit from being associated with his popularity—than by opposing him openly. One of the reasons Lukashenka was able to do this was because of the particular combination of circumstances at the time, in particular the fact that Yeltsyn found himself under strong pressure from the Communist leadership in the Duma in the eve of the 1996 presidential elections.[171]

Through the manipulation of the internal element inside Russia, Lukashenka was able to put himself in an excellent position to pressure (or, some would argue, extort) the Russian leadership. As Vadim Dubnov, editor of the Russian journal *Novoe Vremia*, neatly put it, "Lukashenka turned the status of being 'Russia's only real brother' into a natural monopoly, no less significant than Gazprom's monopoly on Belarus."[172] As will be discussed in Chapter 5, as the energy relationship with Russia began to sour, this strategy would continue, but in a somewhat different incarnation.

Conclusion

This chapter analyzed some of the main ways in which the Belarusian government dealt with its energy situation during 1994–2004, a period characterized by the transition from a crisis-ridden energy system to one where oil refining became one of the state's most important sources of revenue. Rather than conceptualizing its almost exclusive reliance on Russian energy as a dangerous dependency, Belarusian leaders saw it as a profitable opportunity. Indeed, the main elements of the energy relationship were pursued in such a

170 Ibid., 100–101.

171 Ibid., 63–70.

172 Dubnov, in RFE/RL program, *Pratskii Akzent.* On the impact of the energy conflict with Russia (and Lukashenka's use of it) on the Belarusian national consciousness, see the comments by philosophers Velentin Akudovich and Uladzimir Matskevitch and historian Hennadz Samusevich, in RFE/RL program, *Pratskii Akzent.* Romanchuk refers to similar processes as being related to the "monetization" of non-material assets. Romanchuk, "The Belarusian Republic," 3.

way as to generate the maximum possible macro-level rents, in turn used by the regime to keep the economy growing and to solidify Lukashenka's hold on power. If anything prevented further integration between both systems, and Belarus' further subordination to Russian energy capital, it was not so much a sense of apprehension vis-à-vis increased dependency on Russia, but President Lukashenka's fear that such capital could create alternative sources of power in Belarus, threatening his own personal power base.

While the macro-level rents discussed in this chapter were exceptionally important for the short-term survival of Lukashenka's regime, they are not the end of the story. In addition to such macro-level rents associated with the particular modalities of Russian-Belarusian energy relations, there were also economically and politically important micro-level rents that could be accrued from the relationship. We turn to these in our next chapter.

4

Nomenklatura Players, Energy Corruption, and Belarus' "Energy-Political Model"

Chapter 3 provided an overview of Belarus' energy relationship with Russia in 1994–2004, and of the main types of macro-level energy-related rents accrued by Belarus during this period. These rents included the indirect subsidization of the economy through lower-than-international gas and oil prices, barter arrangements, extra income from transit fees, the direct and indirect re-export of energy resources, and taxes paid by energy companies. As discussed in Chapter 3, although these rents accrued at the macro level, affecting the country as a whole, they also benefited President Lukashenka politically, as they made the survival of the regime possible by helping delay painful economic reforms.

A complete picture of the situation is not possible, however, without considering the role of micro-level energy rents in Lukashenka's Belarus (i.e., the concrete benefits received by specific economic actors). In doing so, new insights are also gained about the question of the sources and limits of President Aleksander Lukashenka's power and his relationship with various social, economic and bureaucratic groups. Thus, this chapter looks beyond the purely bilateral relationship to gain additional insights into the real system of energy policy-making in Belarus, and its relationship with the larger political system.

This chapter looks first at the dynamics of energy-related rent seeking, and at known instances of energy corruption in Belarus during 1994–2004. Then it asks what this means in terms of our understanding of the country's overall political dynamics. The third part places energy micro-rents within the context of the country's overall energy rents accrued during this period, and of the country's "energy-political model."

Energy rent-seeking and corruption

Energy rent-seeking in Belarus: from macro-rents to micro-rents

Most discussions of energy in Belarus focus on the macro-economic level (i.e., the benefits accrued by Belarus as a whole, as a result of preferential energy relations with Russia and given a largely state-controlled energy sector).[1] The macro-level significance of these rents has been, undoubtedly, immense, with the impact of rent-like Russian energy subsidies and preferences calculated at nearly 10 percent of GDP in the mid 2000s. The impact of macro-level rents is also the one which is easiest to show and document. However, any realistic discussion of the impact of energy rents in Belarus would not be complete without a discussion of the micro-rents that could be accessed by specific individuals or specific groups, including through corrupt activities, and of President Lukashenka's degree of control over these.[2]

The chapter's focus on micro-level rents complements the macro-level perspective presented in Chapter 3, with the two levels being synergistically inter-related. Thus, for example, the large-scale use of barter in gas trade in the second half of the 1990s facilitated the growth of micro-level rents-producing corrupt activities, as "coefficients" governing the way barter equivalencies would be calculated were administratively set, often with great latitude, opening new possibilities for arbitrage schemes and rent-seeking. Similarly, the import of crude oil from Russia at low prices and free of any export duties levied by Russia (1999–2006), and its refining and subsequent re-export at world prices, opened the door for substantial rent-seeking by those companies able to receive quotas for oil import, its processing, and the subsequent export of resulting oil products.

Despite the dearth of open information, there is much indirect evidence of corruption in the Belarusian energy sector during 1994–2011. We know that the large number of administrative regulations affecting private business gave bureaucrats important gate-keeping powers, creating attractive corruption pos-

1 Of Belarus' two oil refineries, one (Naftan) is around 96% state-owned, while the Mozyr refinery is jointly owned by the Belarusian state and private investors, with around 43% of shares in state hands. Belarus' gas transit system remained under the sole ownership of the Belarusian state until 2007.

2 As discussed in Chapter 1, "rent seeking" does not necessarily amount to corruption. While rent-seeking refers to "the attempt by an individual or entity to obtain unjustifiable high profits, often through the illegal or semi-legal manipulation of the economic environment (including by lobbying, bribing, or the use of privileged information)," corruption refers more specifically to the use of public office for private gain.

sibilities. We know that corruption increased significantly in the mid 2000s, exactly at the high point of oil-related profits accrued by Belarus.[3] Available information on the wave of privatizations that took place in the late 2000s also tells us that, although less developed than in Ukraine or most other post-Soviet states, *nomenklatura* privatization was also taking place in Belarus.[4] We also know that much of the capital brought in from abroad to privatize these companies was actually Belarusian, temporarily "parked" in tax havens in countries such as Switzerland and Cyprus.[5] We also know about conflicts over control of various rent-seeking opportunities between various groups in the Presidential Administration, and about how such conflicts expanded to various branches of the security apparatus as well.[6] The next section presents the main dynamics of micro-level energy rent-seeking in Belarus during this period.

Micro-level rents: main dynamics and concrete schemes

An analysis of several corruption cases, examined in the context of the processes described above, can give us important clues about the dynamics of corruption and micro-level energy rents. An important caveat is needed here, however: these cases did not come to light "by themselves" from below, but were specifically brought up by the state in connection with concrete individuals. We know little about the cases that *did not* make it into the open, or

3 According to Transparency International, Belarus' ranking in the Corruption Perceptions Index increased (higher rankings refer to higher levels of corruption perceptions compared with other countries) from number 53 (2003) to 74 (2004) to 151 (2006). (See Transparency International Corruption Perceptions Index 2004.) It must be noted, however, that these rankings do not purport to measure corruption directly, only the perception of corruption.

4 Ninety-three percent of shares of the bicycle and motorcycle manufacturer Motovelo, were sold to a Russian-origin company in 2007 for the unusually low price of $7.2 m. Velcom was sold in August 2007 for an undisclosed sum to a Cyprus company, which, three months later, sold it to Mobilcom Austria. On Velcom and Motovelo, see "DlJa chago Raman Abramovich prylJataw u Mjensk?"

5 On the return of Belarusian capital, see also Yaroslav Romanchuk, quoted in Feduta, *Lukashenko*, 592. Others have pointed to the high level of investments from Swiss tax-havens (in 2001, 38% of foreign investments to Belarus came from Switzerland, and, in 2006, 66.4%) as indirect evidence that Belarusian capital deposited abroad may be involved. Some authors have used the fact that many investments have come from Switzerland, well known as a home to dubious companies such as RosUkrEnergo, as circumstantial evidence for the participation of "laundered" *nomenklatura* Belarusian capital in the Belarusian privatization process. See for example Zhbanov, "Zolotuû akciû."

6 The best example of such confrontations was a July 2007 incident where the head of the State Control Committee was beaten up by KGB officials dressed as policemen, which brought into the open the often unspoken reality of conflict between various competing security structures. On the 2007 confrontation between the KGB and the Ministry of Internal Affairs (MVD), see Romanchuk, "Belarus: perestrojka ili perezagruzka?" and Marples, "Lukashenka removes KGB Chief."

were not prosecuted at all.[7] Nevertheless, we can learn much from the information available.

On this basis, let us consider the two main mechanisms available for micro-level energy rent-seeking and corruption during this period: first, the system of *zachety* (also known as bills of exchange or IOUs) related to gas, especially widespread in the post-Soviet area in the mid-1990s. *Zachety*, a response to the chronic lack of liquidity during this period, formalized a barter-like chain of exchange, where for example, a gas distributor would supply gas to a company and would be paid partially in bills of exchange (IOUs). In turn, with the help of intermediary companies such as Itera, these IOUs could be used to partially cancel its tax liabilities vis-à-vis the state. In the case of Belarus in the 1990s, such methods were widely used by a broad range of companies facing liquidity problems, including flagship companies such as the Minsk Automotive Factory (MAZ).[8] As bills were seldom traded at face value, but various levels of discount were applied to them depending on the level of risk, the discount applied is key to understanding rent-creation through this mechanism.[9] By manipulating differences in the level of discount at various stages in the chain of payments, a significant profit could be made. Although we lack much concrete evidence on how such operations worked in Belarus, it is widely believed that such operations were an important part of the Presidential Administration's business during Ivan Tsitsiankow's (Ivan Titenkov) tenure as head of its Property Management Division (*Upravlenie Delami Administratsii Prezidenta*) during 1994–1999.[10] The widespread use of barter in Belarusian-Russian gas trade from 1995 to 2002 made *zachety*-based rent-seeking especially attractive during this period. As late as 2001, 80.1 percent of gas supplied domestically in Belarus was paid by non-cash means: 50 percent by payments in kind (barter) and 30.1 percent in debt transfer and clearance schemes, including *zachety*. Non-cash payments decreased drastically after that, reaching only 12.5 percent in 2004.[11] The issuing of bills of exchange was banned in 2004.[12]

7 For information on some of those cases that were prosecuted but not brought into the open, see Rublevic, "V 'liderah' po korrupcionnosti - upravdelami prezidenta." For a discussion of other, never prosecuted corruption schemes involving oil products see Romanchuk, "Degradaciâ monopolista."

8 Elena Rakova, personal communication, January 2011.

9 See also Gaddy and Ickes, "Russia's Virtual Economy."

10 Zagorskaya et al., *Belarus. 1991-2006*, 53. Other authors translate *Upravlenie Delami Prezidenta* as "Presidential Property Office." The Upravlenie Delami is part of the much larger Presidential Administration.

11 Data from Ministry of Energy of Belarus, in *MIB 2006*, 20 (Table 2).

12 An exception was made for the Ministry of Finance in 2004 to pay its debt to Itera.

A second important source of rents had to do with the cycle of import, refining and re-export of oil imported from Russia under especially favorable conditions, which gave local actors (especially tolling operators, so-called *davaltsy*) access to significant added-value and arbitrage profits due to the large price differentials involved.[13] Significant profits in the sector could be accessed, and rents shared, through both legal and illegal means.

One of the most profitable means for oil-related rent-seeking, as will be discussed below, involved illegal activities: the sale of refined oil products to foreign buyers at prices significantly lower than market ones, creating a loss for the refinery or company officially involved in the trade, in exchange for bribes. Similarly, oil could be purchased by Belarusian refineries from Russian companies at higher than usual-for-Belarus prices, also in exchange for kickbacks transferred to the offshore accounts of the managers in charge. It must be noted, however, that not all oil-related micro-rents were related to corruption or illegal activity: anyone receiving quotas for the import of oil to Belarus could earn a significant profit legally, given the fact that, at least until the change of oil trade conditions in 2007, very significant profits could be made from the difference between crude oil import prices from Russia and the price at which refined oil products could be sold in Western European markets. The issue remains, however, as to the role of corruption in accessing these quotas, an issue we discuss in the next section as part of our discussion of rent-seeking by business working outside the Presidential Administration.

Three main levels of micro-level energy rent-seeking in Belarus

From the information currently available, we can talk about three main micro-levels at which the acquisition and further distribution of gas and oil rents took place in Belarus: of individual players within the Presidential Administration; the Presidential Administration *as an institution*; and of businesses outside the Presidential Administration.

13 As discussed in Chapter 3, daughter companies of Russian oil companies also conducted tolling operations.

The first micro-level: individual corruption

A first micro-level had to do mainly with medium-level operations by some of Lukashenka's associates at the Presidential Administration and other important state bodies and state-owned energy companies, acting mainly in an individual capacity.

Belaya Rus' and Galina Zhurawkova, 2001–2004

The first case of individual-level energy corruption by a member of the Presidential Adminstration to receive broad coverage came to light following the 2004 arrest and subsequent trial of Galina Zhurawkova (from 2001 to 2004 head of the Administration's Property Management Division).[14] Having taken over from Uladzimir Gancharenka (Vladimir Goncharenko, head of the Property Management Division 1999–2001) at a time of crisis in the Administration's business operations, it was largely thanks to her efforts that the Administration was able to recover and develop as an important business and rent-seeking system. Zhurawkova was able to bring new business areas into the Administration's fold, in particular tobacco, sugar imports, and trade in confiscated goods.

Due to a special confluence of events—in particular, a sugar imports supply crisis in the summer of 2001—Belaya Rus', a company closely associated with Zhurawkova and the Presidential Administration, was able within a short period to secure a virtual monopoly on sugar imports, and also to gain control of large segments of other markets. These included the cigarette, fish, tractor, alcohol, timber, health resorts, as well as coal and oil products businesses.[15] As the company started to become active in oil, and was becoming one of the strongest tolling oil traders (*davaltsy*) in the country, its connections landed it a 50 percent quota for oil refining from petrochemicals consortium Belneftekhim as well as other special perks.[16]

During the corruption trial of some of Zhurawkova's Belaya Rus' associates, one of the prosecution's claims was that Belaya Rus' head of oil products sales, Sergei Stepanov, had not returned $2.2 million received—and deposited

14 After her trial and sentencing to four years in prison for large-scale stealing in 2005, she was immediately pardoned by Lukashenka, and has kept a low profile since then.

15 Zygar' and Svirko "Člena 'sem'i' sdali organam." Belaya Rus' had been poorly managed and nearly bankrupt by the time Zhurawkova took office.

16 Feduta, *Lukashenko,* 458; and (on the Belneftekhim quota), Barnatovich, "Biznes Vlasti."

abroad—for the sale of oil products.[17] Other corruption-related accusations involved the fact that the Russian companies for which Belaya Rus' arranged oil refining were allowed to purchase the resulting oil products at prices significantly lower than market rates, in exchange for transferring funds to private accounts.[18] While this was the first time that a Belaya Rus' official was brought to justice, murky business operations were not new for the company, which had used a variety of related schemes in its dealings in sugar trade, cigarettes, and fish.[19] Operations involving either straightforward smuggling—of vodka in particular—or the abuse of an open border with Russia (which had been ongoing since before Zhurawkova's tenure), were highly damaging to relations with Russia. This was especially so in the late 1990s, as the Russian budget suffered important losses as a result of tax evasion, while Belaya Rus' and private Russian actors were making significant profits.[20]

It is hard to imagine that such operations could only take place at the individual level, without the backing of the Presidential Administration as an institution. In fact, the Zhurawkova case is of particular interest, as it unveils how business rules and regulations were changed at the insistence of the Administration's Property Management Division, in this case to ease other tolling operators out of the oil imports and refining business, so that this market could be taken over by Belaya Rus'.[21] This was part of a much broader phenomena where Presidential Administration companies would be granted far-ranging privileges, from preferential access to National Bank credits, to tax and duty-free status, to, in many cases, a virtual monopoly on supplies to state organizations.[22] From the case of the fish-supply business—the sector for which the most information is available—we also know of situations where preferences granted to Administration-related companies were provided at the expense of the actual state company responsible for that sector.[23] While there is good reason to believe that some of the same dynamics present in the Administration's business operations in the sugar, cigarette, and fish markets

17 Zygar' and Svirko, "Člena 'sem'i' sdali organam."

18 At first, \$1 or \$2 for each ton of oil sold, and later also 30% of their profits, with the transferred sums amounting to around \$3.6 m per year. See Barnatovich, "Biznes Vlasti," referring to the prosecution's report (*vybody sledstvia*) in the case.

19 On trade in sugar and cigarettes, see Barnatovich, "Biznes Vlasti."

20 See Balmaceda, "Belarus as a Transit Route."

21 On the role of the Upravlenie Delami Prezidenta in the easing out of other tolling operators (*davaltsy*), see Barnatovich, "Biznes Vlasti."

22 See Feduta, "Skazka o zolotoj skumburii." See also Levsina, "Belorusskuû verhušku."

23 On fish and fish-products trade under the aegis of the Presidential Administration, see Feduta, "Skazka o zolotoj skumburii," and Levsina, "Belorusskuû verhušku."

were also present in oil operations, there was one central difference between them: the much higher profits that could be accessed through oil operations. This had to do with the significantly higher arbitrage gains available through the export of high value-added products such as oil, as compared to items like sugar, fish and cigarettes, which were sold in the domestic Belarusian market and where the locally added value-added component was minimal.

The Zhurawkova case is also highly illustrative of inter-group confrontations for access to energy rent-seeking opportunities. As Belaya Rus' and Zhurawkova became increasingly active in the oil market, their interests started to collide with those of others already working in that area, in particular members of Belarus' most important "clan" at the time, that associated with Viktar Sheiman (Viktor Sheiman), at this point Prosecutor General, the security services and the KGB. Although press reports have most often associated Sheiman with the weapons-export business, it is widely understood that he and his associates also had interests in the energy sector, and that Zhurawkova's advance in that area was highly unwelcome.[24] Feeling pushed out of their market, Sheiman's group responded by starting "to blackmail their bureaucratic competitor."[25] Thus it is likely that Zhurawkova was prosecuted not so much because of corruption itself, but mainly because of transgressing unwritten rules as to how rents related to the Presidential Administration should be divided, and because of her encroaching into the rent-seeking territory of other actors, in particular Sheiman.

The growth of Zhurawkova's energy business led to conflict not only with Sheiman, but also with Ivan Bambiza, head of the petrochemicals complex Belneftekhim, who reportedly fought hard to keep Zhurawkova from penetrating Belneftekhim, refusing to provide her and associated companies (Belaya Rus' and Belvneshtorginvest) with the needed quotas for access to refining and re-exports.[26] Zhurawkova's complaints "to the very top" (where, as a friend of Lukashenka from his youth, she had special connections) meant Bambiza had no choice but to finally acquiesce to providing the needed quotas. However, he only did so reluctantly, creating so many conditions (concerning supply deadlines, quality, and prices) so as to make it extremely hard for Zhurawkova's company to make use of them. This time, the response from the top to Bambiza's lack of cooperation was more resolute: an investigation on Bambiza and the

24 On Sheiman and the energy business see Sukhovenko, "Oligarhi Lukašenko." On Sheiman and weapons exports, see "UCP Urges V. Sheiman" and (for background) Berger, "Belarusian Weapons Exports."

25 Feduta, *Lukashenko*, 458. See also Zhurawkova's declaration at her trial, cited in Ankudo, "'Vinovataâ â...'."

26 Dan and Sacuk, "Neftânye vojny."

making public of results of previous investigations into Belneftekhim. In addition to other accusations, it was argued that, by buying oil at artificially high prices (instead of at the lower prices offered by other companies, including at least one associated with Zhurawkova, Belvneshtorginvest), Bambiza had created a loss of $8–10.5 million for Belnefekhim in 2000.[27]

The Naftan Refinery Case, 2004

In 2004, a new corruption case was revealed at the state-owned Naftan refinery, whose two top managers[28] were accused of profiting from corrupt deals through the selling of refined oil products at artificially low prices to companies in neighboring Latvia and Lithuania; presumably, they had received kickbacks—deposited into offshore accounts—in exchange. Competition for rent-seeking possibilities also seemed to have been an element in this case. One of the accused, Naftan's Commercial Director Dzmitry Bandarchuk (Dmitry Bondarchuk), argued that some representatives of the "power structures" (*silovie struktury*), who had been entrusted with exercising oversight over the refinery, were unhappy about him having chosen one set of oil-trading companies to work with, instead of their own favorites.[29] It was also argued that the real reason for the attack on Naftan was political: the fact that Kanstancin Chasnavicki, (Konstantin Chesnovitskii), General Director of the company, had not been able to secure in his region the level of voter support expected by President Lukashenka in the Fall 2004 referendum to remove presidential term limits.[30]

Most of the cases of corruption that were officially discussed during this period were related to oil operations. So what may explain the fact that we did not see any open scandals in the gas sector? One reason for the lack of high-profile cases in the gas area may have had to do with the even lower level of transparency and lower visibility of any private interests involved in the gas sector as compared to the oil sector. At the same time, the complex value-added chain of oil refining and (re)export, in conditions of the special Belarusian-Russian relationship, provided especially large opportunities for micro-level rent-seeking.

---

27 Ibid. Under pressure from some in the Presidential Administration, Bambiza resigned from his position as head of Belneftkhim, and became one of several vice PMs, in charge of agricultural issues. See Sekhovich, "1991-2006. Itogi. Neftânaâ i neftepererabatyvaûŝaâ otrasl'."

28 General Director Konstantin Chesnovitskii and Commercial Director, Dmitry Bondarchuk.

29 Ankudo, "Triškin 'Naftan'." By *silovye struktury* is most likely meant the KGB, which kept a close eye on refinery transactions and without whose approval "not a single ton of oil came into Belarus." Declarations of Aleksandr Borovsky, paraphrased in "Borovskij uhodit ot otveta."

30 See Dovnar, "Glava 'Belneftehima' postradal za rossijskuû neft."

The second micro-level: the Presidential Administration and energy business

A second micro-level at which we can analyze energy rent-seeking in Belarus concerns the Presidential Administration as an institution, as well as President Lukashenka himself.

From the officially published materials on the Zhurawkova corruption trial, we know that the energy (and, especially, oil-related) business was a central area of rent-seeking by individual actors within the Presidential Administration. From this, we can also deduce that it was also quite important for the Administration as a whole. We know from a variety of sources that much of the proceeds from Administration-related businesses (including energy-related business) went to the Administration's budget, a budget which—as a result of the 1996 referendum—is neither required by law to be disclosed, nor subject to any outside oversight. One of Belarus' most-respected journalists, Sviatlana Kalinkina, editor of *Narodnaya Volya*, has called the oil business "that which forms the extra-budgetary Fund of the Presidential Administration."[31]

Estimates vary, but there is agreement that the Administration had access to very significant funds.[32] How were these accrued? While we have little information about other sources of income, it is clear that the Administration's business activities played an important role. After a particularly unsuccessful tenure by Uladzimir Gancharenka as head of its Property Management Division,[33] the early 2000s saw the Administration's expansion into a major business and rent-seeking empire, an accomplishment closely related to Zhurawkova's tenure in the position between 2001 and 2004. While some

31 See comments by Kalinkina, in "Pavinjen zastacca al"bo Shejman al"bo Viktar Lukashenka."

32 Estimates—all unconfirmed—on the size of this budget vary, but according to various estimates in the early 2000s it ranged between c. $3b– $10b a year, compared to the country's GDP of $23.1b and official budget of c. $11.6b in 2004 (GDP data from Table 5.3). At its height, the Presidential Administration machinery is estimated to have employed up to 5,000 people, effectively becoming a shadow government (author's interviews, Minsk, November–December 1997, November 2001, and March 2004). In 2004, former Prime Minister Mikhail Chigir estimated the yearly turnover (*oborot*) of Presidential Administration-related business at $1 b. See Zygar' and Svirko "Člena 'sem'i' sdali organam." Other observers have estimated the Administration's income (from budget assignments and its own business operations) as "equalling the size of the entire budget of the Republic of Belarus," although this assessment seems to be vastly exaggerated. See Danilovich "Understanding Politics in Belarus," 23. According to former head of the Presidential Administration Ivan Tsitsiankow, during his time at the Adminstration (1994–1999), it encompassed more than a hundred companies with a total of 19,000 employees. See Titenkov, "Lukašenko nužno projti."

33 Illustrative of this is the fact that the firm Belaya Rus' associated with the Administration had according to one source, run up a deficit of some $1.7 m. Information from Aleksander Murashko's statement at his 2004 trial for misuse of office for personal gain, as reported in Barnatovich, "Biznes Vlasti."

have emphasized the profit made by the Administration—or people within it—through business directly involving its own companies such as Belaya Rus', others have emphasized its role as an "informal bank" of sorts, lending start-up funds to various businesses, and later receiving these back with interest.[34] Most likely, both schemes were at play.

What was Lukashenka's personal role or benefit from this system? Analysts disagree on this issue. Some see him as having made a significant personal profit from corrupt deals.[35] Other commentators, such as Feduta, emphasize Lukashenka's weak understanding of the dividing line between Presidential Administration funds and his own, and his use of these funds not necessarily or only for his own enrichment, but for pursuing chosen policies and dealing with crisis situations by providing cash support to key players at critical times.

The third micro-level: business outside the Presidential Administration

A third micro-level at which we can analyze energy rent-seeking in Belarus concerns the role of *large-scale businessmen working outside the Presidential Administration*, who were able to access energy rents both in the gas and oil areas. In gas, such profits were acquired largely through barter and promissory note operations, especially during the heyday of non-cash operations in the late 1990s. In the oil area, profits stemmed largely from tolling operations and the difference between crude oil import prices from Russia and the price at which refined oil products could be sold in Western European markets. While, as discussed in Chapter 3, significant macro-rents could be accessed by the state in this area from taxes, export duties, and the trade balance benefits implied by the large-scale export of refined oil products at world prices in conditions of preferential oil trade, significant micro-rents could be accessed as well by those individuals or companies receiving oil importation, refining and re-export quotas. This situation raises a red flag, as it is clearly at odds with prevalent perceptions of Belarus under Lukashenka as a state-controlled economy. Given the significant rents that could be accessed through this business, the question arises as to why Lukashenka did not move to immediately establish state control of the sector, doing away with middlemen (commonly referred to a *neftetreideri* or *davaltsy*), in the mid-1990s counting in the doz-

34 Leonid Sinitsyn, former vice PM in the first Lukashenka period, quoted in Feduta, *Lukashenko,* 414.
35 See for example Suzdaltsev, interview in DW-World.

ens.[36] Although refineries—which maintained profitability rates of 21–28 percent between 2001 and 2006—also benefited, it was first and foremost individuals who gained the most, and not necessarily the refineries *as companies*, as they had to turn over their profits to the state.[37]

Although many individual *neftetreideri* were eased out of the field around 2003 and—as will be discussed in Chapter 5—the government moved to gain more centralized control of the area in 2006–2007, they were never completely removed from the market. This is all the more surprising given the fact that plans for the establishment of a state oil-trading company had been under discussion since at least 1999,[38] given state attempts to keep refineries under its tight control, and given that centralized control over Belarus' second largest source of export revenue (potash fertilizers) had been established in 2005 with the creation of the Belorusskaja Kalijnaja Kompanija (Belarusian Potash Company).[39] This delay, or disinterest, in establishing a state monopoly over oil operations may be explained in a variety of ways. One possible explanation focuses on the fact that, given the massive cost of oil imported from Russia for refining (c. $3.2 -5.66b per year in 2004–2006) and the constant cash flow it required, the state depended on private *davaltsy* for financing those imports.[40] A second possible explanation would focus on the role of quotas and the *davaltsy* system as most beneficial in order to maximize the rent flow to the Presidential Administration and/or to the president himself.

Access to the most profitable oil refining operations, especially tolling, was restricted to those granted specific oil import and tolling quotas; access to these quotas was tightly controlled by the president and his close entourage.[41]

36 Although most often used to refer to individual oil traders, the term *naftotreider* technically means any persons or organizations involved in oil trade, from individuals to the refineries themselves (see Figure 3.3). Author's interviews with Belarusian energy experts, Minsk, January 2011.

37 Leonid Zlotnikov, personal communication, January 21, 2011. This was true of both state-owned Naftan and semi-privatized Mozyr, as the state retained an important role in both. However, up to which point Naftan and Mozyr developed and retained separate corporate interests independent of those of the state or of their top managers is an area where further research is needed. Data on refinery profitability from (for 2001) IMF Country Report Belarus No. 06/316, 19 (Table 16), and (for 2002–2006) IMF Country Report Belarus No. 07/311 Statistical Appendix, 19 (Table 16).

38 Manenok, "Vse resursy v odnih rukah."

39 As of the late 2000s, the company controlled over 30% of the world market of potash fertilizers.

40 In addition, *neftetreideri* were often able to "find" and import additional amounts oil from Russia, often at prices lower than those set in the state-to-state agreements, helping to bring refineries back to working at high capacity—a problem through the mid-late 1990s—and to bring additional income to the state in the form of export duties. Author's interviews, Minsk, November 8, 2006.

41 Referring to decisions on the importation of oil to Belarus by private traders, Aleksandr Borovsky, until his arrest in 2007 head of the Naftan refinery, noted in 2008 that "not a single ton of oil came into Belarus

(An alternative means of distributing these quotas could be through auctions, for example.) Available evidence points to the fact that receipt of such quotas took place, at least partially, in exchange for contributions to the president and the Presidential Administration.

These contributions could take place either in the form of informal taxes such as expected donations to special government projects, or of less clearly-defined contributions, usually referred to by local analysts as *dan'* (tribute).[42] The extent of these contributions is unknown, but we know the president depended on them for the carrying out of high-cost prestige projects, as well as for additional cash flow to the Presidential Administration. One of Belarus' richest businessmen, Juri Chyzh (Yuri Chizh), may have received oil quotas in exchange for such contributions. In a June 2007 interview with *Forbes*, Chyzh described how this happened. "I went to the top leadership and said: give me a quota for oil trade and I will direct the profits to the development of 'Dinamo' [the football club]."[43] In a February 2012 ranking, the Belarusian independent online newspaper *Ezhedevnik* rated Chyzh as Belarus' second-most successful and influential businessman.[44]

Private companies able to receive such quotas were able to access significant profits through the importing of Russian crude oil at low prices and free from any Russian export duties, and its refining and subsequent re-export at world prices. Evidence of their profitable operations can be shown by of the amounts they contributed to the state budget. We know, for example, that in the mid-2000s (the first half of 2006), taxes paid by the largest oil traders contributed 5.42 percent of consolidated budget revenues and 2.72 percent of GDP. In particular, a single company, Yunivest-M, led by presidential sup-

without the approval of a special commission composed of representatives of the Finance Ministry, Economics Ministry, KGB and other state agencies. But the commission's decisions were to be confirmed personally by Aleksander Lukashenka. [...] Beleftekhim just collected the applications [for oil import] and presented them to the commission." Declarations of Aleksandr Borovsky, paraphrased in "Borovskij uhodit ot otveta."

42 On formally voluntary but "expected" contributions, see for example Presidential ukase 291 of July 7, 2003 on "O dopolnitel'nyh merah gosudarstvennoj podderžki futbol'nyh klubov" ("On supplementary measures for state support of soccer clubs"), establishing a system by which all higher-level Belarusian soccer clubs "receive financial support from a number of enterprises chosen by the president." Interfax.by, "Igry oligarhov."

43 Chizh, in Forbes. Forbes adds: "The Belarusian higher leadership has a weakness for team sports – and they gave Chizh the quotas." Chizh was the owner of the Dinamo football club.

44 The first place went to Vladimir Peftiev, chairman of Beltekhexport, a company associated with weapons exports and since 2011 included on the list of individuals on a EU visa ban as sponsor of the Lukashenka's regime. (See Sekhovich, "200 samyh uspešnyh i vlijatel'nyh biznesmenov Belarusi-2011.") Chizh closely avoided being placed on the list himself thanks to a veto from Slovenia, a country where he has close business contacts.

porter Anatoliy Ternavskiy, provided 2.04 percent of all consolidated budget revenues, or 1.02 percent of GDP during this period.[45]

Russian actors and Belarusian rent-seeking

The rent-seeking discussed above added complexity to the Belarusian–Russian energy relationship by involving an additional layer of actors and interactions, and moving it from the purely bilateral level. The question thus naturally arises: up to which point were Russian actors involved in these deals? Although we lack specific evidence on this issue, we can make an assessment based on observations from related areas.

First of all, let us remember that the type of *de facto* oil trade regime in place between Belarus and Russia between 1995 and 2006 not only benefited the Belarusian budget, but also individual Russian oil producers, who, using Belarus as a conduct for oil exports, were able to avoid Russian oil export duties, paying significantly lower Belarusian rates instead. Secondly, from the oil-related corruption cases that became public, we know that they often involved the export of oil products at reduced prices, or the purchase of crude oil at inflated prices, in exchange for kickbacks from foreign, often Russian, partners.

Thirdly, we should not exclude the possibility of Russian involvement in indirect forms of corruption, such as those related to Russian energy companies' contributions (directly or indirectly) to Lukashenka's electoral campaigns, most clearly seen in the run-up to the September 2001 presidential elections. Chapter 3 discussed this support in terms of Lukashenka's broken promises to privatize important energy objects (in this case the Naftan refinery) after the 2001 elections. Yet, a no less important perspective on this story has to do with the possibility of corruption. Although Vagit Alekperov (LUKoil) and Mikhail Gutseriev (Slavneft) were not able to cash in on Lukashenka's promises, at least one exchange of favors took place. It has been argued that, in the election year, Slavneft donated $5 million worth of fuel and mechanized harvesters to collective farms, and $450,000 for a shelter and rehabilitation center (*Dom Miloserdya*) in Minsk, thus providing free political advertising for Lukashenka.[46]

Above and beyond the involvement of specific Russian actors in corrupt deals, it is important to keep in mind that it was, in many ways, the specific details of concrete Russian- Belarusian agreements at any given point (for

45 Centre for Social and Economic Research, *The economic aspects,* 282.
46 Sekhovich, "1991–2006. Itogi. Neftânaâ i nefteperer abatyvaûŝaâ otrasl'."

example, concerning the level and applicability of export duties) that would make one or another type of corrupt operation attractive or even possible. In other words, issues such as whether Belarus would be required to impose oil products export duties similar to those used by Russia, and whether crude oil imports to Belarus should take place on a duty-free basis, played an important role in creating profitable options for specific actors.

ENERGY RENT-SEEKING, LUKASHENKA AND THE BELARUSIAN *NOMENKLATURA*

The cases of micro-level energy rent-seeking and corruption discussed in this chapter are important as they allow a more nuanced view of Aleksander Lukashenka's relationship with other important domestic players, as well as of various mechanisms used by him to gain and maintain control over the state apparatus. The system of energy rent-seeking described above reflected, fuelled, and helped shape the broader relationship between Lukashenka and the *nomenklatura*.

ENERGY RENTS, VERTICAL CONTROL AND COOPTATION IN LUKASHENKA'S RELATIONSHIP WITH THE *NOMENKLATURA*

Lukashenka and the *nomenklatura*: historical background

Lukashenka's relationship with the *nomenklatura* took place in the context of a complex process encompassing two parallel but interrelated developments: on the one hand, his increased control over the country's formal political institutions, and on the other, increased control over more informal *nomenklatura* processes.

Lukashenka's growing control over formal political institutions was formalized by the results of the November 1996 referendum and the resulting changes to the constitution which dissolved the country's last democratically elected parliament and replaced it with a more pliable National Assembly.[47] This allowed

47 The "old" parliament continued to function underground for some time, and distinguished itself from the "new" parliament loyal to Lukashenka (the National Assembly) by using the name "13th Supreme Soviet" or "Supreme Soviet of the 13th Session."

for the establishment of an undisclosed budget for the Presidential Administration; a 2004 referendum removed presidential term limits.[48] The autonomy of local governments was also abolished, with the heads of regional administrations becoming appointed by the president.[49] These trends were solidified by the growing presidential takeover of judicial and legislative powers starting in 2005, with Article 3 of the 2008 Civil Code giving presidential decrees (*ukazi*) the prerogative in case of conflicts between such decrees and the code.[50] At the same time, the National Assembly and other representative bodies—already under *de facto* presidential control—continued to lose influence, being sidelined by new centers of power such as the Presidential Administration, where all important decision-making started to be concentrated.[51]

The story of micro-level energy rent-seeking told in this chapter is also the story of Lukashenka's gradual easing out of the old Soviet *nomenklatura* to establish his own system of vertical control, largely by building up the Presidential Administration as most important center of economic power, decision-making, and informal lobbying;[52] by late 2001, he had succeeded in easing out representatives of the traditional *nomenklatura* from most positions of power.[53] At the same time, Lukashenka moved to gain increased personal control over important state companies. Starting in 1997, experienced top managers, including those at the largest energy companies, Belneftekhim and gas operator Beltransgaz, started to be replaced by cadres with no experience in the area, but who had strong connections with the president.[54] Rent-seeking considerations most likely played a role here, as the new managers typically did not have their own, clearly shaped energy rent-seeking interests and sector-specific networks in place, and thus, could be more easily swayed to follow presidential preferences in this area.[55]

48 On Lukashenka's consolidation of power through the 1996 referendum, see also Chapter 5 in Marples, *Belarus*.

49 Silitski, "Preempting Democracy," 86.

50 On the presidential takeover of judicial and legislative powers, see Zlotnikov, "Ètapy Transformacii," 33.

51 While the Presidential Administration was established by the March 1994 Constitution adopted before Lukashenka's coming to power, the office came into full operation once Lukashenka assumed the presidency in July of that year and, in particular, after the November 1996 referendum allowing the establishment of an undisclosed budget for the Presidential Administration. On decision-making in, and the growing power of, the Administration, see Romanchuk, "The Belarusian Republic," 11; and Karbalevich, *Aleksandr Lukashenko*, 358–359. On Lukashenka's growing monopolization of power see also ibid., 378–379.

52 See Romanchuk, "The Belarusian Republic," 11.

53 See Silitski, "The Tsar and his Boyars."

54 See Feduta, *Lukashenko*, 422.

55 See ibid.

Clans in a one-boss land?

But, what was the old *nomenklatura* system replaced with? Not a straightforward system of total personal control by Lukashenka, but a more complex mixture of personal control and clan politics. In terms of personal control, most crucial was the systematized power over associates and subordinates (the so-called presidential vertical) based largely on intimidation and blackmail.[56] Certainly, few in Belarus would deny the fact that most important political and economic decisions came to be controlled directly by President Lukashenka.

Yet, on the other hand, this system was also not simply one of total monolithic vertical control, as often portrayed in Western accounts. First, as discussed above, Lukashenka partially relied on contributions from "outside" businessmen (i.e., not part of the Presidential Administration) to carry out prestige projects highly beneficial to his popularity rating, such as the building of the National Library, and, most prominent at the local level, numerous ice-hockey stadiums built throughout the country (of which a flagship "ice palace" in Minsk was only the tip of the iceberg). Although these businessmen's access to rent-seeking opportunities was ultimately dependent on presidential favors, the importance of their financial contributions adds a small element of two-sidedness to a relationship normally seen only from the point of view of Lukashenka's unilateral power. Second, despite Lukashenka's overwhelming power, it was partially mediated by a number of "clans" existing within the system. From the case of Galina Zhurawkova and her initial difficulty in receiving an oil quota from Belneftekhim, we also know that good relations with Lukashenka did not always immediately trump other actors' networks involving the president.

The quiet reappearance of *nomenklatura* actors previously loudly fallen from grace, often into positions close to oil rent streams (such as in the cases of Aleksandr Borovsky, Nikolai Vorobei, and Viktar Sheiman) is a little-researched development which also prompts us to reassess Lukashenka's relationship with the *nomenklatura*.[57] It forces us to reassess the relationship as

56 During the period covered by this book, it was not uncommon for ministers to be harshly criticized by Lukashenka, accused of corruption, dismissed from their jobs, and arrested under accusations of corruption: all in one session and given TV coverage for broadcast in the nightly news. On Lukashenka's means of intimidation and control over his own nomenklatura, see Martynau, "The Non-Accidental President." See also Karbalevich *Aleksandr Lukashenko*, 375. As noted by Karbalevich, during this period, "being a high-level bureaucrat was the most dangerous profession" (ibid., 412).

57 After being sentenced in 2008 to five years in jail for abuse of power in the Belneftekhim corruption case that erupted in 2007, Aleksandr Borovsky was offered a presidential pardon, and in 2009 was named

it tells us that either many of the corruption trials were intended for public consumption and did not constitute a real battle against corruption, and/or that Lukashenka needed these individuals, each in turn with their own set of allies and partners, in order to maximize access to energy rents.

Indeed, what local observers describe with the word "clans" simply cannot be dismissed in the Belarusian case. This is so even when one takes into account the overwhelming power of President Lukashenka as compared to that of presidents in countries such as Ukraine, countries we most often associate with clans and powerful economic-political groupings as important organizing elements in political life.

But what did "clans" mean in the Belarusian case? There is some disagreement as to what has been the central principle of "clan" (in the sense of informal power network) differentiation in Belarus after 1994, with some arguing for a more territorial-based differentiation (supported by the importance of the "Mogilev group," from Lukashenka's home base[58]), others for a more economic/administrative sector-based division (emphasizing the role of agricultural, construction, former Soviet *nomenklatura*[59] and *siloviki* "security forces" groups) and still others for a generational/ideological differentiation (younger "pragmatic technocrats and reform-oriented managers" vs. conservative forces gathered around the security forces).[60] Of these various groups, perhaps the best known, and the one playing the most central role for much of the Lukashenka period, was the latter, centered around long-term Security Council head Viktar Sheiman, who occupied a number of high-level positions from 1994 to 2008.[61] In the course of those fourteen years, the Sheiman

general director of the tractor factory MAZ. Another major actor in the case, Nikolai Vorobei, was also freed in 2009, and later returned to the oil-related business through the oil-trading company Interservis. Viktor Sheiman became co-chairman of the joint Belarusian-Venezuelan commission and Lukashenka's special envoy to Latin America in 2009.

58 Upon reaching the presidency in 1994, Lukashenka brought to positions of power in Minsk a sizeable number of officials from Mogilev, who came to occupy important positions, including the heads of the country's largest commercial bank, the national TV and radio networks, and the Presidential Property Office. These individuals, like their region, had been largely overlooked by the more traditional *nomenklatura*. Silitski, "The Tsar and his Boyars."

59 See Eurasian Home Analytical Research, "Country Profile Belarus."

60 Andrei Liakhovich, "Belarusian Elites," 40.

61 Among Sheiman's duties and responsibilities were the following: Assistant to the President on Defense and Security issues (1994–1995); Head of the Presidential Administration (1994–1999); State Secretary of the Security Council (1994–2000 and 2006–2008); and General Prosecutor (2000–2004). By the time he was dismissed from his position as Secretary of the Security Council in July 2008, Sheiman was the only person from Lukashenka's original group still in power, overstaying early defectors such as Alieksandr Feduta (1995) and Ivan Tsitsiankow (1999). After his dismissal, he became aide to the President of Belarus on special matters, playing an especially significant role in the Belarusian-Venezuelan oil relationship.

"clan" had gone through confrontations most likely related to control over energy rents with at least two other important groups: Zhurawkova's group, discussed above, and the group around Lukashenka's son Viktar, with whom a confrontation that came to a climax in 2008 put an end to Sheiman's privileged position in the Lukashenka hierarchy. (We return to this issue in Chapter 5.) These various groups coexisted uneasily, largely on the basis of a set of informal "rules of the game" concerning the division of rent-seeking opportunities among them, which we discuss below.

The energy rent-seeking system as an instrument of elite cooptation and control: Informal "rules of the game"

How did energy rent-seeking, and rent-seeking in general, function as a *system*? How were these profits distributed and reincorporated into the political process, and what kinds of informal rules governed these?

It is unlikely that any energy-related rent-seeking, be it within or outside the Presidential Administration, could take place independently of the president. In the case of energy rent-seeking taking place within the Presidential Administration, those involved could be assumed to transfer a portion of the receipts for the needs of the Administration itself, and to respect a tacit division of rent-seeking "turf" between the main players involved. Belarusian observers agree in seeing Lukashenka as playing a central role in this division of rent-seeking areas as, in Belarus "it is possible to make good money only on the basis of one's closeness to the president."[62] This makes the "struggle between clans" for access to rent-seeking opportunities a struggle for access to the president.

In the case of large-scale businessmen working outside the Presidential Administration, their access to especially large rent-seeking opportunities seemed to take place in exchange for contributions to the president and the Presidential Administration. Among the "unspoken rules" that Belarus' richest businessmen needed to adhere to in order to survive and benefit from the system, a crucial one noted by Belarusian commentators such as Sukhovenko concerns Lukashenka's need to receive a "cut" from any deal, no matter how small.[63] In this view, it was transgression against this rule, not corruption itself,

62 Sukhovenko, "Oligarhi Lukašenko."

63 Analyst Andrei Suzdaltsev has gone further and argued that Lukashenka is "not a businessmen, but a '*dolshik*' owning a "share" or "cut" of the Belarusian economy. Suzdaltsev, interview in DW-World. Emphasis mine. See also Sukhovenko, "Oligarhi Lukašenko."

that was the main reason for prosecuting some cases of corruption and not others: "evidence that they stole not from the state, but from the main ruler."[64]

Other "rules of the game" included the need for favored businessmen (and, it could be argued, important rent-seeking players within the Presidential Administration as well) to stay "in the shadows" and away from public controversy and scandals or confrontations with other "oligarchs,"[65] instead dealing with any conflicts through Lukashenka's intervention, away from public attention. Similarly, not encroaching into other Presidential Administration actors' rent-seeking territory was a central unspoken rule.

In a context where the image of social equality and state control over the economy (as opposed to a state controlled by oligarchs, as Russia was portrayed to be) was crucial for Lukashenka's image, it was also necessary for major businessmen to keep a low profile and refrain from showing off their wealth too openly. Throughout this period, top businessmen largely stayed away from public attention.

Another crucial "rule of the game" concerned the need to prevent the rise of any alternative political or financial groups—including Russian ones—that could come to challenge Lukashenka's power.[66] This also meant that "oligarchs" should not participate directly in active politics.[67] While several of Belarus' wealthiest individuals during this period (such as Vladimir Konoplev and Juri Chyzh) were deputies in the National Assembly, given the largely non-confrontational nature of this parliament, this did not automatically amount to "active participation in politics."

A comparison with Ukraine under President Leonid Kuchma (1994–2004) highlights some of the specificities of the system.[68] While some observers have referred to Lukashenka's role in "balancing" between the various "clans" discussed here, any similarities with Kuchma's "balancing" of various important economic-political groups ("clans") in Ukraine are dwarfed by the reality that Lukashenka played a much more central role there than Kuchma ever did.[69] In particular, large-scale Belarusian businessmen did not have access to sources of income *independently of the president*, which meant

64 See comments by Anatol Labiedzka (Anatoly Lebedko), in "Pavinjen zastacca al"bo Shejman al"bo Viktar Lukashenka."

65 Although the term "oligarchs" is at times used by Belarusian commentators, I prefer to use the term "large-scale businessmen," as it does not convey the implication of political power that the term "oligarchs" does.

66 Sukhovenko, "Oligarhi Lukašenko."

67 On the need to stay away from active politics see also Oleg Manaev, cited in Daneiko, "Den'gi millionerov."

68 On the Kuchma period, see Balmaceda, *Energy Dependency, Politics and Corruption*.

69 See comments by Sheremet in "Barac"ba wladnyh klanaw."

much more limited freedom of action than in the Ukrainian case. But perhaps the largest difference between the Ukrainian and Belarusian cases has to do with the fact that, while in the case of Ukraine money made by various "clans" was funnelled into the financing of a variety of political groups, money made by such groups ("clans") in Belarus did not really finance alternative political groups. In reality, of course, their money often made it into politics, but to support *one* political force—President Lukashenka.

Energy rent-seeking as a means of managing the relationship with the *nomenklatura*

The energy rent-seeking system described above both supported the establishment of a new *nomenklatura* replacing the old Soviet one, and helped manage the relationship with the new one. It did so in a number of important ways.

First, the very significant rents associated with the oil refining and re-export business contributed to the building up of the Presidential Administration as an important center of economic power, which Lukashenka took advantage of as he gradually eased out the old Soviet *nomenklatura*. Second, energy rent-seeking helped Lukashenka manage the relationship with the *nomenklatura* through its role in helping shape the system of unwritten rules of the game discussed above. Third, by giving individual members (or groups) within the *nomenklatura* the approval (and, in many cases active support through changes in rules and regulations) to engage in profitable rent-seeking, the system worked as an important instrument of elite cooptation and reward.

Finally, the energy rent-seeking system helped with Lukashenka's management of his relationship with the *nomenklatura* by providing "sticks" in addition to "carrots." It did so through the opportunities it provided for extortion and blackmail, as the energy business—and the large number of administrative regulations affecting it—provided ample opportunities for corruption that could be brought up selectively as needed, to blackmail, prosecute, and/or jail individual officials.[70] More generally, the periodic "cleaning up" of corruption in the upper ranks of government tied in well with Lukashenka's populist strategy and his image as a "benevolent Tsar," prevented from carrying out virtuous policies only by the interference of self-interested officials.[71]

70 See also comments by Bjaljacki, in RFE/RL program for Belarus, and Karbalevich, *Aleksandr Lukashenko*, 367.

71 For example, in the case of Presidential Administration head Galina Zhurawkova's 2004 arrest, there seemed to be a direct rationale for her arrest above and beyond the merits of the case. The arrest was used by Lukashenka to promote his image as a fighter against corruption and to gain popularity for

Conclusion

The information unveiled in this chapter challenges us to reassess our understanding of the role of energy rents in the Belarusian political system, forcing us to move away from an exclusive focus on macro-level rents. It also forces us to reassess our understanding of power relationships in Lukashenka's Belarus, an understanding often based on the double assumptions of Lukashenka's tight control over the country's political system and of an overwhelming state control of the economy.[72] A deeper look into the Belarusian case, however, shows clearly that there is more to Belarusian politics than just Lukashenka's single-handed control. A realistic view of Belarus' "energy-political model," therefore, needs to take into account the role of a variety of local players above and beyond Lukashenka himself.

The evidence presented in this chapter also tells of the strong distributive effects of Belarus' "energy-political model" (and of energy rents in particular). Indeed, in the short term, this model provided agreeable short-term results for most Belarusian actors, from consumers of subsidized gas, to collective farms kept alive by cheap supplies of tractor fuel, to workers who saw their real incomes grow steadily, to newly enriched members of the *nomenklatura*. Due to good fortune or good design, during 1994–2004, the Belarusian government was able to manage the country's energy situation in a way that seemed to satisfy most actors involved. The particular combination of circumstances during this period made it possible for each and every actor involved in the Belarusian energy market to be reasonably satisfied. Russian oil producers were avoiding Russian taxes and increasing revenue. The Belarusian budget was reaping significant income from the refining and re-export of Russian oil. The Presidential Administration and key *nomenklatura* actors had additional resources at their disposal. Gazprom was on the way to making Belarus fully dependent on Russian gas. Last but not least, this model also allowed Lukashenka personally to strengthen his grip on power, while avoiding much-needed economic reforms.

---

the upcoming (2004) referendum on lifting presidential term limits. Moreover, it was a way to give the economic elites a disincentive for being disloyal to him. See Liakhovich, "Palitychny kantekst ," 16. On a previous wave of anti-corruption trials in 2001-2002 against the heads of important state companies such as Leonid Kalugin (Minsk refrigerator factory Atalant), Viktor Rachmankov (Belarusian Railways) and Mikhail Leontev (Minsk Tractor Factory, MTZ) as "show trials in order to silence any kind of opposition inside and outside the state apparatus," see Liakhovich, "Belarusian Elites," 39.

72 Indeed, as noted in Chapter 1, throughout the whole post-independence period up to 2010, the state share of GDP was no less than 70%, while in neighboring countries it had been reduced to no more than 35% already by the mid 2000s. Data from EBRD, *Transition Report.*

This systemic balance largely fuelled by the influx of external rents, however, was based not only on President Lukashenka's savvy manipulation of the situation and of the relationship with Russia, but also on a specific combination of external factors, including high world oil prices in comparison to those paid by Belarus and the business preferences of specific Russian actors. As these conditions started to change in 2004, new challenges began to face the Belarusian energy-political system. We turn to these in our next chapter.

5

The "Low Years": Energy and Russian-Belarusian Relations, 2004–2009

On February 18, 2004, something almost unthinkable happened: Gazprom completely suspended gas shipments to Belarus, citing broken agreements on the privatization of Beltransgaz and the stealing of gas from the pipeline. Although the cut-off lasted less than 24 hours,[1] it was unprecedented: not even during the worst accusations against Ukraine about gas theft had Gazprom fully stopped gas supplies, affecting not only domestic consumers but also Gazprom's consumers in Europe. In addition, effective gas prices paid by Belarus increased again in January 2005 as a result of a change in tax rules.[2]

From the Gas Stoppage of February 2004 to the "Last Ally" Revisited

The February 2004 gas cut-off marks a natural dividing line in Russian-Belarusian energy relations.[3] After this incident—the first time that Russia had completely cut off gas supplies to any state—the tone of energy interactions between Russia and Belarus changed. Regular threats of increasing gas prices to "world levels" started to be heard, as well as dire predictions by

1 Supplies were resumed a day later, after Beltransgaz signed a ten-day supply agreement with TransNafta and other independent gas suppliers.

2 Starting in January 2005, Russia started to apply VAT on a "country of destination" basis, which increased the effective price of Russian imports by 18%. With VAT income on imports now accruing to the Belarus side, income to the Belarusian budget increased significantly, while the competitiveness of Belarusian products fell due to the higher effective price of gas. See IPM, "Rost cen na gaz," 9-10, Footnote 10.

3 While oil had been cut off to Lithuania in the Spring of 1991, that event has a different significance, as it took place before the dissolution of the USSR.

Belarusian, Russian and Western observers that Belarus would not be able to withstand such increases and that, as a result, the regime would collapse or would, subject to energy blackmail, be forced to join a Russian-led Union on Russian terms, with a significant loss of sovereignty.[4]

Taking this event as a starting point, this chapter seeks to elucidate how Belarus dealt with the new conditions emerging after the 2004 cut-off, and how relationships with President Lukashenka's three main constituent groups were affected. It first analyzes Belarus' management of its energy dependency in the period 2004–2006, before looking at this management in 2007–2009 and at how the shrinking of the energy rents "pie" affected relations within groups in the ruling *nomenklatura*.

Gazprom's pivotal cut-off of gas deliveries in February 2004 took place in the context of gradually unfolding changes in the Belarusian-Russian relationship. Many of the changed energy dynamics and rhetoric we start to see around 2004 were delayed effects of the new tone in Belarusian-Russian relations following Vladimir Putin's election as president in 2000. It is also around this time that Russia begins to harden its position concerning a possible Belarusian-Russian Union, making it clear that, in order for monetary union to occur, Belarus would have to give up a significant degree of sovereignty.

Broader economic changes were also taking place in the relationship. If, throughout the 1990s and early 2000s, Belarus was heavily dependent on Russia as the main market for its exports, this situation started to change in the mid-2000s, when the relative weight of Belarus' exports to the EU started to grow significantly, and the EU replaced Russia as the main importer of Belarusian goods. (Although in 1999 49.6 percent of Belarusian exports went to Russia, by early 2009 this had been reduced to 37 percent;[5] during the same general period, exports to the EU had increased significantly, reaching 47.3 percent in 2007 and 44 percent in 2009.[6]) The large increase in exports to the EU was due to the increase in oil products exports and was therefore a direct result of the special trade relationship with Russia.[7] Yet these new trade balances reflected not only increased demand from Western Europe, but also

4 Analysts often referred to the worst-case possibility of Belarus being incorporated into the Russian Federation "as nine *gubernii*" districts, without a legal or institutional identity of its own.

5 Data for 1999 from Zaiko, "Russia and Belarus," 1.

6 2009 data from IPM, *BMER* 1/77, February 2009.

7 In 2003, 96.07% of Belarus' exports of oil products went to countries outside the CIS. See Alesin, "Za mesto pod solncem," based on statistics by Belarus' Ministry of Statistics and Ministry of Industry. In 2011, oil products accounted for around 66% of Belarusian exports to the EU. See "DyplJamatychnaJa vajna—nje pjerashkoda ekspartu naftapraduktaw."

declining Russian demand for the type of products Belarus traditionally exported to Russia, such as tractors, motors, and TVs, laying bare Belarus' rapidly declining competitiveness in the non-oil refining sectors.[8]

How did the Lukashenka regime adapt to this changed context? Up to which point were the strategies used similar to those used in the 1994–2004 period? Some of the tactics used in the pre-2004 period lost much of their effectiveness due to the changed Russian conditions discussed above: while Lukashenka continued to play the nostalgia-for-the-Soviet-empire card, by 2004 neither President Putin nor the Russian public were as receptive to such discourse as they had been before. Putin, a relative newcomer to the political stage, shared none of the "Belavezh guilt complex" of his predecessor Boris Yeltsyn, and was therefore less prone to Lukashenka's manipulations concerning any alleged responsibility for the dissolution of the USSR.[9] With the Russian economy flush with new energy-export revenues, presenting Belarus to the Russian public as—relative to Russia—an oasis of stability and prosperity was becoming increasingly difficult. Despite these limitations, Lukashenka continued to use politicization as a strategy after 2004, but now the emphasis was on the military and strategic value of Belarus as Russia's "last ally."

In this, Lukashenka had luck on his side: virtually every time the relationship with Russia threatened to go sour, a new international crisis would erupt that would reaffirm Belarus' continued value as an ally. Thus, for example, although it was also around this time that Russia began to harden its conditions for a possible Belarusian-Russian Union, as Russian relations with the US start to worsen around March 2003 in the run-up to the invasion of Iraq, Lukashenka was able to pressure Moscow to reassess his value and to support his bid to lift presidential term limits in the 2004 referendum.[10] Similarly, the coming to power of strongly anti-Russian Mikheil Saakashvili in the wake of Georgia's 2003 Rose Revolution, Ukraine's 2004's Orange Revolution, NATO's 2005 expansion to Russia's borders with the accession of Estonia, Latvia and Lithuania to the alliance, and Poland's 2008 announcement that it intended to set up a NATO radar station, all contributed to renewed Russian fears of Western encroachment in the immediate vicinity, and came to the help of Belarus. Easily presentable as threats, these events boosted

8 For a visual representation of the increasingly diverging fates of the oil and non-oil trade sectors after 2004, compare the graphs on "Oil Trade" and "Non-Oil Trade" in IMF Country Report No. 10/16 (Belarus), January 2010, 17.

9 See Drakokhrust and Furman, "Belarus and Russia," 255.

10 See for example Llakhovich, "Palitychny kantekst."

Lukashenka's value as an ally, given Putin's own worldview.[11] Indeed, a certain regularity could be observed: every time relations between Russia and the West worsened, the relative value of Belarus as an ally increased, and relations between Minsk and Moscow improved, at least in the short term. Lukashenka skillfully manipulated references to these events and reinforced Belarus' role as "last ally" by, on the one hand, offering increased military cooperation and modernizing its military,[12] and on the other, threatening to cut off military cooperation at times of crisis, such as the 2004 cut-off in gas supplies. At the same time, as will be discussed later in this chapter, during the few periods when relations with the West showed a positive tendency, Lukashenka also used this as a bargaining chip in the relationship with Russia.

How did Belarus adapt its policies to deal with this new situation? The following two sections approach this question from the perspective of gas and oil policies.

Dealing with New Energy Trade Conditions, 2004–2006: "Paying for Russian gas with Russian oil"

Gas: external and domestic management, 2004–2006

Especially in the gas area, Belarus sought—with varied success—to continue its previous strategy regarding the Yamal pipeline and the privatization of Beltransgaz as bargaining elements in its price negotiations with Gazprom and the Russian leadership.

Yamal and Belarus as a gatekeeper

If, in the late 1990s, Yamal was used mainly as a means to showcase Belarus as an indispensable transit gatekeeper, then by 2004 its role as a bargaining chip had changed. Now that the project was nearing completion, Lukash-

11 Writes Viktor Martinovich: "Putin the *chekist* understands the world as a dialectical war of 'ours' and 'those who are not ours'. In Putin's view, Lukashenka may be a complicated politician [...], but he is 'ours'." Martinovich, "Soûz po umolčaniû."

12 The 1999 Treaty on the Creation of a Union State included provisions for the establishment of a "single defense space." In July 2005, President Lukashenka announced a plan for the modernization of the Belarusian military involving the investment of nearly $500m a year.

enka used his power to block the final details of the pipeline from being completed as a means to pressure Russia to move the negotiations concerning Beltransgaz and gas prices in a manner agreeable to the Belarusian side. At stake were the speedy completion of the four compressor stations still needed for the pipeline, and Gazprom's desire to secure a long-term lease guaranteeing rights to the land under the pipeline.[13] Indeed, it is hard to avoid the impression that the Belarusian side purposefully created a number of hurdles to the completion of the pipeline (such as delays with land-rights approval and compressor-station construction) as a means to maintain leverage over Gazprom.

So, by 2004–2005 one additional reason for Gazprom's short-term accommodation with Lukashenka's demands had emerged: the need to complete Yamal's first line as soon as possible, despite its record of delays, in order to be able to fulfill its growing contractual obligations vis-à-vis its Western European clients.[14] With these goals in mind, Gazprom was willing, for the time being, to maintain low prices for Belarus, in exchange for progress towards the speedy completion of the pipeline. In April 2005, Gazprom and Beltransgaz agreed informally that gas prices for Belarus ($46.68/tcm) would remain unchanged throughout 2006 if these conditions were met.[15]

Yet Lukashenka's belief that "having control over the pipeline" would give him real leverage over Russia may have been overstated. Although using Yamal as an instrument of pressure was successful in the short term, the Russian leadership was becoming more savvy and less romantic in its relationship with Belarus. In any case, Belarus would never be able to achieve the pre-1999 Ukrainian position as virtual gatekeeper of Russian gas transit to Europe because after the completion of the Yamal pipeline there would no longer be a single, monopolistic gatekeeper, as Ukraine was until 1999. Rather, after 2004, the increased export capacities via Belarus and Ukraine (at 35 and 143 bcm/yr respectively in 2008) gave Russia some degree of flexibility in using these capacities as alternative routes.[16] (This flexibility was not absolute, however, as specific pipelines are tied to specific markets, and total flexibility presupposes free pipeline capacity, which is not always available.)

13 Mancnok, "Podarok s rasčetom."

14 Gazprom's exports to Western Europe required the use of Yamal's full 33 bcm/year capacity, but by early 2005 only 22 bcm were available.

15 Similarly, in informal conversations the top Gazprom management made clear that an additional 1.4 bcm of yearly gas deliveries (officially labeled "to be delivered according to technical possibilities") would only be available if Belarus demonstrated sufficient progress on completion of one of the compression stations. See Zhbanov, "Soûzniki optimistično 'gazanuli'."

16 Data on pipeline export capacity from East European Gas Analysis.

TABLE 5.1 TRANSIT OF RUSSIAN NATURAL GAS VIA BELARUS, IN BILLION CUBIC METERS, 2001–2011

Year	Volume
2001	24.6
2002	27.5
2003	33.1
2004	35.3
2005	40.8
2006	44.2
2007	49.5
2008	51.4
2009	44.6
2010	43.2
2011	44.3

Note: includes both the Northern Lights and Yamal-Europe pipelines systems.

Sources:
For 2001–2005: Yafimova, "Belarus: The Domestic Gas Market," 141; 2006–2009: Scherbo, "Tranzit: hlopotno"; 2010–2011: Interfax, various issues.

As Ukraine became a more reliable transit partner for Russia after 2000, Belarus' (and Lukashenka's) comparative advantage started to fade, and Lukashenka's unpredictability became more and more of a liability to Russia. Thus, it was only natural that, once the first line of Yamal was completed in 2006, Gazprom's attitude towards Lukashenka would change. Thus, despite the fact that the original agreement envisioned the building of two parallel Yamal lines by 2008,[17] this started to seem increasingly unlikely, a problem for Belarus, as transit income from a second line could potentially have covered nearly a fifth of Belarus' gas import costs.[18]

Gazprom's September 2005 agreement with Germany on the building of a gas pipeline from Russia to Germany (the Nord Stream project) avoiding transit through third countries in many ways represented the company's (and

17 Each with a capacity of 33 bcm per year. Agreement of January 5, 1994 between the governments of the Russian Federation and Belarus.

18 The estimated potential additional yearly income from transit via a second Yamal line, estimated at around $168m, was equivalent to 17.5% of Belarus' 2006 gas bill. See also Manenok, "Kto ostalsâ na trube?" By July 2005, Gazprom's chairman, Alexei Miller had made declarations to the effect that Gazprom was not interested in developing new gas transit lines through the territories of Latvia and Belarus. See Manenok, "Gazprom zaâvil."

the Kremlin's) realization that, in addition to Ukraine and Poland, it was desirable to do away with dependency on Belarus as a transit country. Indeed, it is clear that Gazprom's main reason for entering into the high-expense Nord Stream project[19] was not so much the need for additional export capacities, but the desire to have alternatives to transit through traditional partners Belarus and Ukraine. In November 2007, Russia officially backed away from the second Yamal line project.

Gazprom's interest in Nord Stream as an alternative to increased flows through a second Yamal line also represented the company's frustration about the slow pace of negotiations on the creation of a joint venture to control Belarus' gas transit system through Beltransgaz, which we discuss below.

Beltransgaz and Russian energy investments: delaying the moment of effective Russian control

In negotiations on the future of Beltransgaz, Belarus continued to use the same central tactic used from 1994 to 2004: promising a joint venture with Gazprom, but delaying the actual sale of shares. As in the pre-2004 period, the question of how Beltransgaz would be valued remained a crucial hurdle. It was only in July 2004 that both sides agreed on naming an independent auditor to assess the value of the company, but little happened between then and 2006.[20]

What changed, however, was the attitude on the Russian side. Not only did Gazprom feel justified in seeking additional transit routes bypassing Belarus, but, to the extent to which interest in transit through Belarus continued, the desirable forms of cooperation changed: from one based on informal agreements and a relationship of trust with Lukashenka to one based on the desirability of contractually grounded control of Beltransgaz.

Throughout 2005, Lukashenka found himself under strong behind-the-scenes pressure from the Kremlin, with Moscow demanding control over Beltransgaz in exchange for maintaining low gas prices. While similar demands had been heard before, changes in Belarus' international context were affecting the country's room for maneuver. Lukashenka's increasing iso-

19 The cost of building the pipeline was originally estimated at between EUR 7.4b (Gazprom's estimate) and 8.8b.

20 At one point, the sides even disagreed on what *office* of the International accounting firm PriceWaterhouse-Coopers would actually do the valuation: the Moscow office (favored by Russia) or the London one (favored by Belarus).

lation from Western institutions (the wave of peaceful revolutions in Georgia, Ukraine, and Kyrgystan made Belarus stick out even more as an exception to the democratizing trends observable in other post-Soviet states) was leaving Belarus one-on-one with Russia. The gas-supply contract signed on December 27, 2005 between Belarus and Gazprom stipulated that Gazprom would gain full ownership over the Belarus segment of the Yamal pipeline,[21] in exchange for maintaining current gas prices of 46.89/tcm throughout 2006 and a 10 percent increase in supplies.

A new attempt to acquire Beltransgaz came in 2006, when, using the threat of sharply increased prices, Gazprom once again sought to gain control of the company.[22] In December 2006 (in the midst of a separate gas supply crisis, discussed below), an agreement of principle (signed only in May 2007) was reached between Belarus and Gazprom covering both gas-price increases and ownership of Beltransgaz. On the basis of this agreement, from 2007 to 2010, Gazprom would each year acquire 12.5 percent of Beltransgaz's shares, up to 2010 when it would reach ownership of 50 percent of shares in the company, for a total price of $2.5b. Despite Belarus' long-drawn reticence to the deal, the actual agreement could be seen as favorable, as it was tied to a gradual timeline for gas price increases to Belarus, and as the purchase price would be paid in cash, as opposed to gas supplies.[23]

Politicization of the relationship and price negotiations

Lukashenka also continued to politicize the energy relationship as a means for managing Belarus' energy dependency on Russia, making sure that any gas price increases by Russia would create high costs for the Russian leadership: both high political costs vis-à-vis its own domestic electorate, and high reputational costs vis-à-vis Western European business partners and public opinion. An example of this manipulation was Lukashenka's response to the February 2004 gas cut-off, when he called the measures "terrorist" and stated that Belarusian-Russian relations "will be poisoned by gas for a long time to come;"[24] he also threatened to cut off military cooperation.

21 See Dempsey, "Gazprom Wins Belarus Victory," and "Gazprom and Beltransgaz," at www.gazprom.ru/eng/news/2005/12/18593.shtml.

22 Klishevich, "Istoriâ bor'ba."

23 IPM, *BMER* 1/52, January 2007, 2.

24 As quoted by the Associate Press Worldstream, February 19, 2004.

Although by now no longer able to reach the Russian electorate directly, Lukashenka was able to appeal indirectly to the population's enduring Soviet pride, allegedly affronted by Putin, through his passionate declarations that Belarus was being forced to get the money to pay for Russian gas "from the Chernobyl victims, from those who were rotting in the trenches," defending the Soviet Union in the Second World War.[25] In this way, Lukashenka was using the image of Russian disloyalty as a means of pressuring (some would say extorting) the Russian leadership. But the disloyalty in question was not simply a disloyalty to Belarus as an ally, or to the current Russian-Belarusian Union, but to a key normative belief underpinning Russia's sense of collective self-esteem and the legitimation for its Great Power role and special position in the post-Soviet area: the joint struggle in the Great Patriotic War. This was a discursive tactic Lukashenka continued to use throughout the following years and recurring instances of real or threatened worsening of energy trade conditions from Russia. Thus, journalist Viktor Martynovich's 2010 headline: "Buy a trench for $200m [or I will use it against you]."[26]

Such public relations gains were also intended to show Russia that Belarus still had significant weapons in its arsenal to respond to future instances of Russian energy pressure. Indeed, Belarusian observers such as Andrei Liakhovich have argued that, far from representing Belarus' "defeat," the 2004 cut-off and its aftermath represented a landmark of a very different kind: the Russian realization that its means for pressure on Belarus were limited, and that the threat of using the "ultimate weapon" (a gas supply cut-off) had only limited effects on Belarus although, objectively, Belarus had no means to replace this gas with other imports.[27] (Although in the past Belarus had been able to replace Gazprom gas with that purchased from other Russian suppliers, as noted in Chapter 4, most of these "independent suppliers" were closely tied to Gazprom, making them unlikely sources of real diversification.)

25 Aleksandr Lukashenka, on *Nashi Novosti*, ONT (TV news), February 19, 2004 quoted in Feduta, *Lukashenko*, 635.

26 In his article "Kupi okop" (in literal translation "Buy a trench"), Viktor Martynovich offers a general explanation of Lukashenka's behavior as blackmail vis-à-vis Russia. See Martinovich, "Kupi okop."

27 "After the gas cut off of January 24, 2004, Russia realized it could not 'do all it wanted' in Belarus." Author's interviews with independent political analyst, Minsk, November 17, 2008. Similarly, Danilovich talks of the confrontation ending with "a big embarrassment for the attacker" and a capitulation by Russia, as it was not able to immediately increase gas prices to Belarus. Danilovich, *Russian-Belarusian Integration*, 148.

The outcome of this "first gas war" of 2004 was, in fact, not the worst possible for Lukashenka. Following the Rose Revolution in Georgia, Belarus found it easy to continue presenting itself as Russia's "last ally" in the post-Soviet area.[28] After the gas cut-off, a pattern was established where Russia would increase prices but, at the same time, offer Belarus a number of other perks, in this case the provision of a $150 million credit—plus an additional $25 million to support trade—on favorable terms, extended as compensation for the 2004 increases. Similar concessions took place after subsequent gas price increases: after Belarus' complaints that changes in VAT legislation from January 2005 affected it negatively, in June 2005, Russia agreed to provide Belarus with an additional $146 million credit as compensation.[29]

Yet no less important than his ability to win palliative economic concessions was the political and public relations victory Lukashenka was able to score thanks to his crafty politicization of the issue, and a favorable combination of circumstances. In this and other similar situations, Lukashenka seemed to follow a dual-pronged approach: on the one hand, emphasizing his value as Russia's "last ally," while, on the other, accusing actors in Russia of relinquishing that very alliance, presented as nothing less than a continuation of the spirit of the Soviet Union.

A similar politicization took place following Russia's October 2006 announcement of its intention to significantly increase gas prices to Belarus, to up to $200/tcm. Lukashenka once again reacted by taking the offensive: "Such a price increase, in that amount, that is, unequivocally, the break-off of all relations."[30] Yet this politicization was not simply something that happened after the fact, as a reaction to Russian gas supply reductions, but a type of behavior used pre-emptively by Lukashenka and which actually helped shape the conflict itself and could, thus, be seen as a form of preventive management of the relationship. As noted by analyst and United Civic Party opposition politician Yaroslaw Romanchuk concerning the rapid escalation

28 Another version, circulated by Russian analyst Pavel Felgengauer, argues that the Russian agreement to maintain agreed gas prices throughout 2005 can be explained by a secret agreement between Lukashenka and Putin, by which the latter would "solve the problem" of how to maintain power after the expiration of his third term in 2008 by becoming the head of a Belarusian-Russian Union. See Martinovich, "Aleksandr Fadeev."

29 As noted in Footnote 2 above, the new rules prescribing the application of VAT on a "country of destination" as opposed to on a "country of production" basis, although increasing the Belarusian budget, also increased the prices paid by Belarusian consumers by 18%, which led the Belarusian government to request compensation, either in the form of reduced pre-VAT prices or other compensation. See IPM, "Rost cen na gaz," 9-10 (Footnote 10). See also Bruce, "Friction or fiction?" 18.

30 Aleksandr Lukashenka, in *Novaya Gazeta*.

of the conflict in December 2006: "The Belarusian side is not planning to sign the contract before New Year, because [it] needs a big scandal, a very big scandal. A scandal just about negotiations, that is not a scandal. But a scandal with a suspension of gas supplies, that is the kind of scandal that the Belarusian side is seeking to direct, among others, against Russia, presenting it as an unreliable partner" before new negotiations would start. "After that, an agreement will be signed in January."[31] In this interpretation, the Belarusian side was in fact provoking a high-visibility standoff in order to elicit concessions to soften the increase in gas prices.

Especially after the 2006 and 2009 Russian gas cut-offs to Ukraine that also affected EU consumers, Lukashenka's use of public relations as an arena for its energy confrontations with the Kremlin was acquiring a new and crucial audience: the EU leadership. Lukashenka was able to present the 2004 cut-off and other Gazprom ultimatums as a specifically Russian threat to its energy security. This was also an audience that, if needed, could magnify the message of Russia as an unreliable transit partner, increasing the reputational costs to Gazprom and Russia as well. In this sense, especially after 2006, Russian actors had to be aware that any gas sanctions against Belarus would be interpreted by the EU in this context, and could incur a high reputational price for Russia and Gazprom. As Belarus' relations with the EU started to improve in 2008, Belarus found in the EU an increasingly supportive audience for such messages.[32]

Domestic Management

In terms of domestic management, pre-2004 gas policies continued after 2004 with the attempt to recover import costs by passing them to most gas and electricity end users.[33] Thus, for example, while the price paid by Beltrangas for gas imports in 2006 did not increase, the prices charged to most industrial users increased by 4 percent.[34] However, the cross-subsidization

---

31 Yaroslav Romanchuk, quoted in DW program for Belarus. For a similar perspective see Manaev et al, "Povyšenie roli."

32 By 2008, a major thaw in relations with Belarus could be observed on the part of the EU, with a European Parliament resolution in November proposing restoring relations and a Council resolution of the same month suspending the travel ban on Lukashenka and 35 officials originally intended as a response to human rights abuses in the country.

33 As electricity is overwhelmingly gas-generated, electricity pricing can be considered an extension of gas pricing policies.

34 IPM, *MIB 2007*, 34

of key constituencies (mainly agricultural and residential users, but also a few hand-picked industrial users) continued, at the expense of higher prices charged to most industrial consumers. For most of the period between 2004 and 2007, the one group that consistently paid the lowest prices for (mainly gas-generated) electricity (from 17–34 percent less than its production cost) was the agricultural sector.[35] During that same period, industrial users consistently paid significantly higher prices (52.27–87.5 percent higher) than production costs.[36]

In the gas area as well, prices paid by residential users also remained lower (although less markedly so than in the case of electricity) than those paid by industrial users. Consistent with this trend, the prices of gas-generated residential heating increased more slowly than import prices for gas. A look at time-series data on cost-recovery levels for services provided by communal residential services (*Zhilichno-Kommunal'noe Khoziaistvo*, ZhKKh) for the 2001–2009 period (see Table 3.10 in Chapter 3) reveals two interesting trends. First, with both electricity and gas, the highest levels of cost-covering payments were seen between 2003 and 2007, with a sharp decrease in 2007, when subsidization of residential end users increased as gas prices charged by Gazprom went up. In residential heating, one of the most highly subsidized areas, there was not a single year where payments fully covered costs, instead covering only 17 to 50.8 percent of costs for most of the period.[37] In terms of Lukashenka's political strategy, this shows that he sought to maintain cost-covering prices domestically, but that for the agricultural sector and residential heating, end user prices remained largely unchanged. In addition, there were limits to this strategy (i.e., when import price increases would make this especially painful for the consumer, the cost-covering policy would be set aside).

35 Calculated by the author on the basis of Table 11 (based on data from the Ministry of Energy) in IPM, "Rost cen na gaz," 24.

36 Ibid.

37 2003 was an exception, when ZhKKh payments for heating covered 75.3% of expenses. For full data see Table 5.2 in Rakova, "Ènergetičeskij sektor," 23. Estimating actual levels of cost coverage in Belarus is made difficult by the lack of clear information, as different government entities (in this case the Ministry of Energy and the Economics Ministry) have provided different estimates of the level of "cost coverage" for households. For example, the January 2007 cost coverage for electricity used by households was 157% according to the Economics Ministry, but only 115% according to the Ministry of Energy. Centre for Social and Economic Research, *The economic aspects*, 145.

OIL: EXTERNAL AND DOMESTIC MANAGEMENT, 2004–2006

As noted in the previous section, between 2004 and 2006, energy pressure from Russia was seen mainly in the gas area. These years of toughening conditions in gas supplies, however, coincided with years of continued preferential trade conditions in the oil area and of nothing less than record profits for Belarus' refining and re-exports business. As seen from Tables 5.4 and 5.6, Belarus' income during this period from oil and oil-product exports allowed it not only to pay for Russian oil imports, but, for the first time in its history, to make significant additional profits. Belarus' growing arbitrage gains in oil trade resulted from, among other factors, growing world oil prices due to the disruption of supplies created by the Iraq war, while oil prices charged to Belarus by Russian companies grew at a much slower pace. Although, between 2004 and 2005, the unit price paid by Belarus for crude oil from Russia increased by 20 percent, the price for exported oil products increased by 42 percent.[38] The IMF estimated the additional yearly benefit resulting from these arbitrage gains as being in the order of 2–3 percent of GDP in the mid-2000s.[39]

By 2004, Belarus' oil-refining sector was becoming so significant that, despite the country being highly dependent on imported oil (producing less than 20 percent of its oil needs in the mid-2000s), in per capita terms it was exporting as much in oil products as oil-rich Russia.[40] As seen in Table 5.4, this growth was also exceptional in terms of the actual value of exports: from $3.6 b in 2004 to $7.4 b in 2006. The role of oil and oil products exports in Belarus' overall exports also increased sharply, going from 27.4 percent in 2004 to 38.8 percent in 2006, the highest level up to 2010.[41] These increased revenues were used to compensate for higher gas prices, allowing Belarus, in the words of a Russian analyst, to "pay for Russian gas with Russian oil."[42]

Oil refining, 2004–2006

These growing revenues also explain the state's eagerness to retain or regain control over the oil-refining sector, which we discuss below. This was especially clear in the case of the Mozyr refinery where, with 42.7 percent of

38 Source: calculated from data in Table 5.4 below.

39 IMF, "Rapid growth in Belarus," 9.

40 Zlotnikov, "Podcepili 'gollandskuû bolezn''."

41 See *Foreign trade of the Republic of Belarus* and *Rossia v tsifrakh 2008*.

42 Kirill Koktysh, interview in *Nashe Mnenie*.

shares, the Belarusian state held only a small advantage over Russian oil company Slavneft's 42.6 percent in 2004. As pressure from Slavneft to increase control over the company grew, the Belarusian state counteracted by, among other measures, trying to increase its share in the refinery by seeking to force the minority (12.2 percent) shareholder MNPZ Plus to turn over its shares to the state and, when this failed, by forcefully introducing a state controlling share in it.[43] There was little legal basis for applying 2004 regulations concerning a state "controlling share" in a private entity such as MNPZ Plus, however, and the measure was evidence of both the importance of the sector for top policy-makers, and of the weak state of property rights, corporate governance and rule of law in Belarus at the time. [44] (It has been argued that the main motivation for seeking state control of MNPZ Plus was to prevent Gazprom or other Russian companies such as LUKoil from controlling it, and, through it, the Mozyr refinery as a whole.)[45] Thus, despite Mozyr remaining formally private, the state was able to force important decisions upon it, such as the demand that it make a large ($100m) non-tax contribution to the budget.[46]

Oil rents as both a source of stability and challenge to the system

Oil rents provided both a source of stability and a challenge to the system. Taken together with the absence of painful economic reforms, oil-business revenues meant—at least in the short term—stability and rising living standards for the population. As acknowledged by the Belarusian opposition itself, 2006, the height of the oil-refining and re-export rents boom, was—or at least was largely perceived as being—"the best year ever for the Belarusian

43 See Manenok, "Mifičeskij dolg."

44 On the (lack of a) legal basis for introduction of a controlling share in MNPZ Plus, see declarations by Nikolai Yastremsbski, deputy director of the firm, in Manenok, "Mifičeskij dolg" and in "'Zolotaâ akciâ'."

45 Sekhovich, "1991–2006. Itogi. Neftânaâ i neftepererabatyvaûŝaâ otrasl'." It must be remembered that Gazprom was already playing a role in Mozyr, as in 2005 it had purchased 75% of Sibneft and, thus, indirectly gained control of Slavneft, which owned 42.6% of Mozyr's shares. (In November 2002, Belarus had sold to Sibneft its package of shares in Slavneft.)

46 Andrei Belousov, Deputy Minister for Economic Development of the Russian Federation, cited by Manenok, "Starye problemy." Economists such as Leonid Zlotnikov have argued that such informal powers held by the state render meaningless the difference in formal ownership between Naftan and Mozyr, as in all cases profits went ultimately to the state. I beg to disagree, as even small differences in corporate governance and in the mode of incorporation into value-added chains may lead to a different configuration of interests.

economy" (see Table 5.6).[47] That year, Belarus' GDP grew around 10 percent; exports grew 24.5 percent; inflation was the lowest since independence; personal income grew; and purchases of consumer goods—especially imported ones—increased significantly.[48] As seen in Table 5.3, by 2006, per-capita GDP at Purchase Power Parity prices had more than doubled from its near low point at the time of Lukashenka's election in 1994. Such results are crucial for explaining Lukashenka's relatively high popularity for much of this period, especially within the context of the long-standing connection between rising living standards and state legitimacy in Soviet and post-Soviet Belarus.[49]

To the stability-enhancing effects of the influx of oil-related rents we can add other, more problematic effects. Indeed, while the oil refining and exports strategy created massive profits, sectoral imbalances, already evident since the early 2000s, were becoming increasingly stark. With 25.4 percent of its export earnings coming from oil products in 2004, energy-poor Belarus was slowly catching its own "Dutch disease," as domestic manufacturing was becoming more expensive due to the strengthening of the local currency vis-à-vis the dollar;[50] non-oil-related trade balances moved to negative values from 2003.[51] The Belarusian government was not fully capable of controlling this situation because it had largely become hostage to an economic strategy based on oil refining and re-exporting. First, the country was becoming increasingly dependent on these exports as a means of managing its energy dependency, as the resulting profits helped pay for the gas bill, and as the role of refining center also provided a guarantee of stable and low-price Russian oil supplies.[52] Secondly, it had become dependent on this refining role as a means of assuring rising living standards and bolstering the value of the Belarusian rouble (BLR) vis-à-vis the US dollar, both important for domestic political legitimacy reasons. In particular, the decision to prop up the value of the BLR vis-à-vis the US dollar was related to a domestic political strategy evident from the very beginning of the Lukash-

47 The Pontis Foundation reports that, at the Congress of Democratic Forces in May 2007, opinions were expressed to the effect that "the Belarusian people have never lived as well as nowadays." See Pontis Foundation, "The Regime Change(s)."

48 Karbalevich, in *Pratskii Akzent.*

49 Praneviciute has argued that in the case of Belarus economic well-being (and ever-improving economic conditions) was so important as to became part of Soviet Belarus' (and Lukashenka's) "foundational myth." See Praneviciute, "Security and Identity in Belarus." See also the discussion of "performance legitimacy" in Huntington, *The Third Wave.*

50 Zlotnikov, "Podcepili 'gollandskuû bolezn'.'" Data for 2004 from Belarus' Ministry of Statistics and Analysis.

51 See graphs "Oil trade, 1992–2008" and "Non-oil trade, 1992–2008," IMF Country Report No. 10/16, 17.

52 Tatiana Manenok, "Valûtnye donory."

enka administration: to explicitly and demonstratively present wage increase promises and achievements specifically in US dollar terms. Moreover, a strong BLR made imported consumer goods (in particular automobiles) increasingly affordable, fostering popular perceptions of growing economic prosperity. Thus, Lukashenka's own rhetoric and sources of legitimation made the country dependent on a strong (and possibly over-valued) Belarusian rouble, pushing it further into the oil refining and re-exports business as a means of supporting its value despite its negative side effects. [53] However, such growth in living standards and the reliance on it for legitimation purposes was not without danger for the regime. As noted by Silitski, "the spread of consumerism encouraged by the regime [...] created expectations of higher levels of material well-being that [Belarus'] outdated Soviet system ultimately cannot meet."[54]

Energy Relations after the 2006–2007 "Gas-and-Oil War," 2007–2009: the shock that wasn't?

January 2007 brought Belarus into the international spotlight. If until then largely ignored and known to Western publics mainly thanks to its intriguing leader, by January 2007 Belarus entered world headlines with a big bang: following a dispute with Belarus, for the first time in history, Russian (or Soviet) oil supplies to several EU states were cut off. This was the first time Russian or Soviet oil supplies to the EU had been cut. After a short introduction to the "gas-and-oil-war" of December 2006–January 2007, this section analyses Belarus' dealing with the new gas and oil trade conditions emerging after this dispute.

The "gas and oil war" of December 2006–January 2007

At the end of 2006, in the negotiation of prices for 2007, Gazprom started to propose prices as high as $200/tcm, an almost four-fold increase. The confrontation came in the wake of a new wave of Russian restrictions on

53 Author's interviews, Minsk, November 19, 2008.

54 Vitali Silitski, "The State, Elections, and the Opposition," in Fischer (ed.), *Belarus*, 33–34. On the limits of a legitimacy based on material rewards, see also Gurr, *Why Men Rebel*.

Belarusian imports, such as those affecting sugar (February 2006), confectionery and candy products (November 2006), and alcohol (December 2006). (Although ostensibly related to technical and sanitary standards issues, each could also be interpreted as, at least partially, an attempt at putting pressure on Belarus on other issues.) After extremely tense negotiations, an interruption in supplies was narrowly avoided. According to a contract signed just a few minutes before midnight on December 31, 2006, prices for 2007 were more than doubled to $100/tcm, with further increases planned for the following years.

Even before the gas issue had been settled, a serious confrontation started to brew in the oil area in December 2006, when—effective from January 1, 2007—Russia announced its decision to eliminate most oil export duty preferences for Belarus, which had been in place since 1995. This was preceded, in the fall of 2006, by the Russian proposal that export duties levied on oil products exports refined from Russian oil in Belarus be shared according to the official stipulations of the 1995 Customs Union Agreement (i.e., with 85 percent going to Russia, and 15 percent to Belarus, instead of 100 percent to Belarus as had effectively been the case). At the same time, the threat was made that, should Belarus refuse the arrangement offered, Russia would introduce export duties (*poshlina*) on all oil exports to Belarus. Effective from January 1, 2007, supplies would have to pay the full duties of $180/t, instead of no duty, as had been the case since 1995.[55] As a response, on January 4 (retroactively effective from January 1) Belarus introduced a special transit tax of $45/t on Russian oil transiting through Belarus (in addition to previously agreed-to transit fees) intended to partially compensate for the new Russian duties. Russia declared Belarus' new special transit tax illegal, and refused to pay it. As a response, Belarus began siphoning Russian oil headed to Europe, allegedly in lieu of the payment owed by Russia. On January 8, in formal response to this siphoning, which it considered illegal, Russia's pipeline monopoly Transneft totally shut down supplies to Belarus through the Druzhba pipeline, briefly interrupting oil supplies to Poland and other points West: the first-ever interruption of Russian oil supplies to EU states. After a battle of wills lasting until January 10, the two countries agreed to transition gradually into a new division of oil export duties (discussed below); supplies via Druzhba were resumed a day later. Belarus also agreed to impose the same

55 As per the Customs Union agreements of May 12, 1995, Russian oil exports to Belarus were not subject to export taxes.

level of export duties on oil products as imposed by Russia, a provision which, as discussed in Chapter 3, had been on paper since 1995 but which had not been implemented by Belarus.

Despite the shock of these confrontations, in both the gas and the oil areas, Belarus and Russia found ways to soften and delay the shock until 2009–2010. We discuss these ways below.

Gas: External and domestic management, 2007–2009

Dealing with the gas shock of 2007

Despite the prediction of some analysts,[56] Belarus, at least in the short term, survived the over 100 percent increase in Russian gas prices effective from January 2007. Even after this increase, the politicization and special treatment of Belarus continued.

First of all, Belarus was offered a gradual, set in advance, transition to "European" gas prices.[57] According to an agreement reached in December 2006, in addition to continuing to receive gas free from Russian export duties,[58] 2008 gas prices paid by Belarus would be equivalent to 67 percent of European (Polish) prices (not counting transit costs),[59] in 2009, 80 percent, and in 2010 90 percent, before moving fully to European prices in 2011.[60] (Transit fees, however, were only minimally increased, with the effect that in 2009, in comparison to 2006, Belarus paid $1.61b more for gas imports, but received only $187.4m more in transit fees, a fraction of the increase in the gas bill.)[61]

Secondly, the actual prices charged to Belarus throughout October 2008 remained well below the values that would come up from such price formula,

56 See for example Yafimava, *Post-Soviet Russian-Belarussian Relationships.*

57 The agreement also included other clauses favorable to Belarus, for example a single contract covering gas prices and transit fees. This is significant because, when gas supplies and transit fees have been in separate contracts, this may open the door to a situation where gas prices may be increased unilaterally, but transit fees cannot (as was the case in the January 4, 2008 contracts between Ukraine and RosUkrEnergo), worsening the terms of trade for the gas importer. See Zhbanov, "Nazlo 'Gazpromu'."

58 Russian export duties (not to be confused with VAT taxes discussed above) comprised 30% of the sale price to other markets.

59 The difference in transportation costs corresponds to the cost of transit from Belarus to Poland. Calculated at $1.75/tcm per 100 km, a transit length of 600 km via Belarus costs around $10.50/tcm.

60 IPM, *BMER* 1/52, January 2007, 2.

61 For Belarus' expenditures on gas imports in 2006 and 2009, see Table 5.6. For income from transit fees, see Scherbo, "Tranzit."

for example reaching $127.9/tcm in the second quarter of 2008, when European (Polish) prices had reached $340 and thus a 67 percent share would amount to around $220.[62] Moreover, in June 2008, the Belarusian side suggested the agreement be changed to reflect the fact that—as a response to the sharp increase in world energy prices—Russia itself had decided to extend the timeline for the adaptation of domestic Russian gas prices to international levels.[63] In March 2009, Presidents Lukashenka and Medvedev reached a spoken agreement that the price of gas for 2009 would remain at $126/tcm, instead of the $210 foreseen by the December 2006 agreements.[64] These examples make clear the weak contractual basis of the gas relationship. In other words, the contract served a variety of purposes, but once it no longer fulfilled the political goals of the sides, its problematic elements were simply ignored.

Third, the "shock" value of the increase in gas prices can itself be qualified, since, given the faster rise in European prices compared with those charged to Belarus, gas subsidies actually increased between 2007 and 2008, and the average yearly gas subsidy for 2007–2009 was higher (at $3.5 b) than the average for 2004–2006 ($2.99 b).[65] Others calculated the full energy subsidy amount (including both oil and gas) at $5–6b per year in early 2008.[66]

Fourth, through its own management (and manipulation) of the issue, Belarus found ways to delay and soften the effects of these price increases: in 2007, for example, Belarus was successful in reaching an agreement by virtue of which, for the first half of the year it would only pay 55 percent of the new price of $100, with the rest put on credit to be paid by the end of the

62 Considering the transit cost of $10.50/tcm, the Polish price minus transit cost ($340 -10.50) would be $329.50, and 67% of it $220.76. Belarusian economist Leonid Zlotnikov confirmed: "In 2008 this price formula was not applied" and estimates the agreement-based price would have been c. $200-220/tcm. Zlotnikov in *Deutsche Welle program for Belarus*. See also IPM, *BMER*, 7/70, July 2008, 2, and 8/71, August 2009, 1.

63 The Belarus side argued, *post-facto*, that a basic (albeit unwritten) assumption of the 2006 agreements had been the expectation that gas prices for both countries would move simultaneously towards "European netback" levels. In November 2006, the Russian government had announced that domestic gas prices would gradually increase so as to reach "European netback" levels (i.e., the equal profitability [*ravnaya dokhodnost*] of foreign and domestic sales) by 2011. Due to the pressure of domestic groups concerned about the social and economic impact of such swift increase, in March 2010, it was announced that the target price parity date had been moved back to 2014.

64 Manenok, "Oplata v ramkah politsoglašenij." This oral agreement would create problems later on in 2010, as, to Belarus' total surprise, Gazprom demanded that by June 23, Belarus should pay $231 million in payment for the gas debt, and a suspension in supplies was narrowly averted.

65 Calculated from Table 3.1 in Rakova, "Ènergetičeskij sektor," 10. See also comments by Chubrik in *Ekspertiza Svabody*.

66 Zlotnikov, "Žestkaä posadka."

period.[67] A new $1.5 b stabilization loan, extended on favorable conditions, was secured from Russia in December 2007.[68]

In addition, the Belarusian side sought to make the best of the new agreements with Gazprom (the purchase of 50 percent of Beltransgaz's shares for yearly payments of US$ 625m during 2007–2010). The preferred scenario was to take advantage of the cash influx to soften the hit of increased prices, but without relinquishing—or at least, delaying the relinquishment—of control over the company. At issue seemed to be not only the desire to prevent any potentially powerful actors that could challenge Lukashenka's power from entering the scene, but also the issue of control over Beltransgaz's (and domestic distributor Beltopgaz's) policies, so that they could continue to be in line with Lukashenka's own political goals (including, as discussed above, softening the impact of increased gas prices on household users as a means to maintain popular support).

Indeed, although the May 2007 agreement on the sale of Beltransgaz shares included certain provisions protecting Gazprom,[69] it soon afterwards became clear that the Belarusian side had no intention of relinquishing real control of the company, nor of allowing Gazprom to reap significant profits. Two main measures pursued this goal. First, Beltransgaz was included in the list of profitable companies required to make non-tax contributions to the Ministry of Energy's Innovation Fund (*Innovatsionni Fond Minenergo*), to which it was made to contribute $70 million (19 percent of the value of its products and services) in 2007.[70]

Secondly, the mark-ups (*nadtsenki*) usually added to the price to be paid by final consumers were significantly reduced, thus also reducing Beltransgaz's profitability (which fell to an estimated one percent in 2007) and the profits the company would need to share with Gazprom.[71] Such profits were skimmed directly from the top and directed either to separate non-taxable budget funds

67 There was a small crisis in late July and early August 2007, as Belarus delayed paying back these amounts and Gazrom threatened to reduce gas supplies by 45% by August 3, 2007, should payments not be made by then. Payments were made at the last moment.

68 Favorable conditions included a 15-year re-payment schedule and a five-year grace period.

69 Concerning the inalienability of Gazprom's shares while the deal was completed, the commitment not to impose a "controlling share" in the company, as well as committing to an increase in the mark-up paid by Belarusian end users, see IPM, *BMER* 6/57, June 2007, 2.

70 IPM, *BMER* 4/67, April 2008, 2. See also Manenok, "Starye problemy."

71 The contract on the sale of Beltransgaz shares to Gazprom stated that the mark-up level would increase gradually and reach $11/tcm by 2011, but on the condition that the percentage of Gazprom's gas transit through Beltransgaz's pipelines (as opposed to through Yamal) would remain above a certain level. See IPM, *MIB 2008*, 33. On Beltransgaz profits see ibid., 35.

TABLE 5.2 GAS IMPORT PRICES AND PRICES PAID BY END USERS, IN US$/TCM, 2003–2011

	2003	2004	2005	2006	2007	2008	2009	2010	2011
Gas imports from Russia, in bcm	18.1	19.6	20.1	20.8	20.6	21.1	17.6	21.7	20
Price paid by Beltransgaz to Gazprom[a]	30	46.7	55	55	118	127	151	170	265
Price paid by industrial users	60-65	70	72.3[b]	75.6[b]	141.7[c]	171[c]	205.5[c]	261.3[c]	275.9
Price paid by residential consumers (for cooking)	N/A	N/A	82.7	84.4	101.7	N/A	174	159	143.8[d]

[a] Does not include additional supplies occasionally purchased from Gazprom or other suppliers at higher prices.
[b] Data from IPM, "Rost cen na gas," 12.
[c] Data from Stern et al., *The Russo-Ukrainian gas,* 7 (Table 1).
[d] Data from Interfax, "V Belarusi prompredpriâtiâ." 2011 tariffs for residential consumers are an average of winter and summer period tariffs, calculated at the official National Bank average exchange rate for 2011.

Sources:
Yafimava, *Post-Soviet Russian-Belarussian Relationships*, 58; Dashkevich, *Jenergeticheskaja zavisimost'*, 20 (Table 3); and (for 2009) IPM, *MIB 2010,* 39.

(the Energy Ministry's Innovation Fund discussed above), or shared with end consumers in the form of lower prices. This last point is especially significant, as until then, Beltransgaz had mainly passed price increases to end consumers and maintained relatively high mark-ups.[72] As shown in Table 5.2, in 2007, end-user gas prices failed to keep up with increases in gas import prices.

All of this points to the fact that the Belarusian government, even after the contract was signed, was not interested in providing Gazprom real (joint) control of Beltransgaz. As aptly stated by Elena Rakova, "the country's leadership does everything possible so that this part [Gazprom's package of shares]

72 See IPM, *MIB 2008*, 33. The period 2002–2004, when Beltransgaz and distributor company Beltopgaz reduced mark-ups, had been an exception in this regard. See Table 3 (based on data from the Ministry of Energy) in IPM, "Rost cen na gaz," 13.

would become a 'bone in the throat' of Russian capitalist 'sharks' interested in strengthening their positions in Belarus."[73] Chapter 6 discusses the situation after Gazprom reached 50 percent ownership of Beltransgaz in June 2010.

It must be noted, however, that despite the smaller margin of profitability, in 2007, Belatransgaz's tariffs, taken as a whole, continued to cover costs.[74] Concerning the related issue of (overwhelmingly gas-generated) electricity prices, after large price increases from July 1, 2007, the rate charged to industrial producers jumped to $0.103/kWh: "higher than in all other CIS states and comparable with prices in EU states."[75] However, although some of the price increases were passed on to end consumers,[76] the impact on these users was moderated by reserves especially earmarked for this purpose in the 2008 budget.[77]

Gas: domestic management, 2007–2009: conservation and energy efficiency

The year 2007, immediately following the "gas-and-oil war" with Russia, was especially rich in policy declarations in support of energy savings and energy diversification. The Concept of Energy Security approved by the president in September of 2007 presented the ambitious goals of increasing energy consumption by "only" 130 percent between 2005 and 2020, while increasing GDP by 320 percent during the same period.[78] The Energy Modernization Program,[79] approved in November of that year specifically spelled out the goal of reducing

73 Rakova, "Reformy administrativnymi metodami."

74 IPM, *MIB 2008*, 51.

75 Effective July 1, 2007, prices for industrial users and individual entrepreneurs increased by 12.1%; electricity prices for state organizations (*bjudzhetnye organizacii*) increased by 42.7%; and for agricultural producers by 20%. IPM, *BMER*, 8/59, August 2007, 1–2.

76 The steepest increase was in gas prices for enterprises and households, which increased significantly (from 20 to 60%) in January 2008. Electricity prices for most users were increased in July 2007, January 2008 and September 2008. Retail gasoline prices were increased in January, May and August 2007, each time by around 5%. The fact that the prices for (mainly gas-generated) electricity increased much less steeply than the import prices for gas meant that the brunt of the increase in gas prices fell on the electricity sector, which, not being able to compensate for its higher costs, "reduces its chances for investing in modernization and energy-saving." IPM, *BMER* 3/66, March 2008, 2. See also ibid., 8/59, August 2007, 1–2, and ibid., 3/66, March 2008, 2. Zlotnikov argues that these increases were actually less steep than may appear at first glance given the general over-valuation of the Belarusian rouble (at 7–10%) vis-à-vis the US dollar in 2006–2008. Zlotnikov, personal communication, December 13, 2008.

77 Manenok, "Izbiratel'nyj podhod."

78 See the official announcement, "Glava gosudarstva v celom."

79 Full title: *Gosudarstvennaâ kompleksnaâ programma modernizacii osnovnyh proizvodstvennyh fondov Belorusskoj ènergetičeskoj sistemy, ènergosbereženiâ i uveličeniâ doli ispol'zovaniâ v respublike sobstvennyh toplivno-ènergetičeskih resursov na period do 2011 goda.*

energy intensity by 25 percent from 2007 to 2010.[80] According to official statistics, 2010 goals on decreased energy intensity were reached. However, a number of independent Belarusian economists call attention to the fact that GDP levels reflected in these statistics may be inflated, thus conveying an artificially low level of energy intensity.[81] However, another important goal of the program, increasing the use of local energy resources in its energy balance to 28–30 percent, was not reached by 2010 as planned, and was postponed to 2015.[82]

In addition to investments in high-efficiency energy projects, measures aimed at domestic conservation included direct disincentives: for example, the September 2008 limitations on the amount of electricity that some factories and enterprises could use in the following year—prices charged to them would double should they overstep that limit.[83] However, two institutional factors related to the organization of the energy sector as a whole undermined the effectiveness of such measures. First, the total lack of transparency concerning electricity subsidies, and preferential pricing for some enterprises.[84] (As discussed in Chapter 3, some industrial enterprises received especially low electricity prices, but neither their names nor the criteria for their inclusion in the list were made public.) Some Belarusian commentators, such as Yaroslaw Ramanchuk, have argued that, given this lack of transparency, administrative measures to limit electricity use would most likely simply increase the "under-the-radar battle for electricity."[85]

A second limiting factor was the fact that the electricity sector had not been de-monopolized or "unbundled" (i.e., its electricity generation, transmission and sale activities had not been separated, a separation intended to make costs and tariffs more transparent, to promote Third Party Access to

80 Manenok. "Ènergobezopasnost' poka nedostižima."

81 Highly respected Belarusian economists such as Zlotnikov and Rakova have questioned official assessments of reduced energy intensity, pointing to possibly inflated GDP figures and to the disconnect between official energy intensity trends and the lack of any significant modernization outside the oil refining sector. Zlotnikov emphasizes the fact that these results are based on an artificially high value of the Belarusian rouble vis-á-vis the dollar, resulting from the large influx of dollars from record oil-product exports in the mid-2000s. Leonid Zlotnikov, in *Ekspertiza Svobody*. While they do not accuse the Belarusian government of intentionally making up economic data, they point to the possibility that, given pressure on state company managers to achieve annual growth goals set from above, these may be tempted to round up their results, leading to inflated country-level data as well. See also Rakova, in "Belorusskaâ èkonomičeskaâ model"; and Zlotnikov, "Leonid Zlotnikov."

82 See *Strategii razvitiâ ènergetičeskogo potenciala*.

83 The regulations applied to factories with an electrical power capacity of 750 kilovolt-amps and higher, organizationally depending on state organs, and to organizations in the housing sector with an electricity use of 1 million kWh and higher. Alekhnovich, "V Belarusi."

84 See Romanchuk, quoted in Alekhnovich, "V Belarusi."

85 See ibid.

transmission lines, and to decrease cross-subsidization), which meant that these measures could not work as market incentives, limiting their positive effects.[86] In addition, with the prices that factories were allowed to charge for their products still calculated on the basis of Soviet-school "cost-plus" principles (*zatratnoi printsip*), a reduction in electricity costs would mean the sale price of the produced goods would need to go down, providing no incentive for managers to increase efficiency. Thus, the new measures remained mainly administrative in nature, did not fully work with supply-and-demand incentives, and did not deal directly with the issue of energy inefficiency.[87] As a result, despite Belarus' achievements in decreasing energy intensity (see Table 5.3), the gap between its levels of energy intensity and those in EU and OECD countries actually increased in the 2000s.

Gas: domestic management, 2007–2009: energy-source diversification and the decision for nuclear power

To change without changing: the decision for nuclear power

In contrast with oil, where the transit infrastructure is much more flexible, gas presented Belarus with very limited geographic diversification possibilities. Thus, diversification was approached first and foremost from the perspective of energy source diversification. Presidential Directive No. 3, and the 2007 Concept of Energy Security presented the main means for reaching conservation and diversification goals: increasing investments in the energy sector, reducing dependency on gas by developing nuclear and coal-fired electricity generation plants, and increasing the use of renewable and local energy sources, especially peat and firewood.[88]

---

86 Although by 2003 the Ministry of Energy had already developed a concept of the electricity market that "included some careful steps towards introducing some market elements," even these modest reforms could not go forward, due to a lack of higher-level governmental support. Tatiana Manenok, "Litva namerena." Rakova goes further to argue that, as of the mid-2000s, not only was a reform of the electricity sector not being pursued, but it was not even discussed seriously by Belaruasian experts. Rakova, "Kakaâ ènergetičeskaâ bezopasnost'."

87 Argues Tatiana Manenok concerning the Concept of Energy Security approved in September 2007: it "includes everything, except a rethinking [*pereprofilovanie*] of the Belarusian economy." Manenok, "Ènergobezopasnost' v range prioriteta."

88 In addition, a plan was introduced to increase the use of brown coal through the creation of a "mining-chemical complex," a project that was subject to criticism in the independent press as there appeared to be a dubious Swiss-based intermediary company involved in project, a possible hint at the recycling of Belarusian *nomenklatura* capital and creeping "*nomenklatura* privatization." See Zhbanov, "Kak zaburel naš ugol';" Karbalevich in *Ekspertiza Svabody*; and "Novyj Invjestor prishjel."

Yet, very soon these conservation-based initiatives were largely replaced (although not necessarily at the declarative level) by one energy source diversification initiative much more compatible with continued top-down, state-controlled and non-transparent policies: nuclear power.[89] Nuclear power as an option had remained largely taboo since the 1986 Chernobyl accident, with previously existing plans for the building of a nuclear power plant quickly shelved at that time; in 1998, a Belarusian Academy of Sciences commission had concluded that nuclear energy should in principle be part of the Belarusian energy supply basket, but that, given the low price of Russian oil and gas at the time, there was little urgency to act. Instead, a seven-year moratorium was adopted.[90] By 2006, however, the discussion of energy-source diversification was gradually shifting emphasis and turning into a renewed discussion on the building of a nuclear power plant. By 2007, state interest in nuclear power had increased sharply, especially in the wake of 2007's Presidential Directive No. 3 calling for reduced dependency on gas. On January 2008 the final political decision to build a nuclear plant was taken.[91] The very way the decision was taken, the lack of real debate, and the way those who opposed the project were excluded from the debate, brought to the fore serious deficiencies in the energy policy-making process, deficiencies which would potentially affect European security in the sensitive area of nuclear power security.[92]

According to the January 2008 decision, a nuclear plant with a 2,000 MW capacity would be built in Ostrovets (Astravets), 20 kilometers from the Lithuanian border, by 2016. Although forcefully presented by the state-controlled media as the only viable solution to Belarus' problem of energy dependency, several factors made it unlikely that the nuclear plant, as planned, could help reduce this dependency. Instead, it was likely to create four new types of dependency on Russia: equipment and spare-parts dependency, as the necessary equipment would be purchased from Russia; fuel dependency, as nuclear fuel for the facility would need to be purchased from Russia; waste-disposal dependency, as Belarus would need to turn to Russia for storage of its nuclear

---

89 This section is based on Balmaceda, *The Politics of Energy Dependency*, Chapter 5. As argued by Karbalevich, "a number of programs [on renewable energy] were developed [in 2007], but in the final analysis the only ones that remained were the beginning of joint projects for oil production in Venezuela and Iran, and the political decision to build a new NPP." Karbalevich in *Belarusskie Novosti*, January 2008, cited in Mishin, "Luščee v Venezuele," 5.

90 Voitovich, in "Nakanunie âdernogo vozroždenâ."

91 Sovet Bezopasnosti Respubliki Belarus', *Postanovlenie Sovbeza No. 1*. See also Marples, "The Energy Dilemma of Belarus."

92 On the discussion of the issue in the Belarusian official and independent press, see Pilibaytite, *Nuclear Energy Discourses*, 88-105.

TABLE 5.3: GDP, ENERGY USE AND ENERGY INTENSITY IN BELARUS, 1990–2011

	1990	1991	1992	1993	1994	1995	1996	1997	1998	1999	2000
GDP in billion US$ at current prices	17.269	17.833	17.022	16.280	14.931	13.972	14.756	14.128	15.222	12.138	12.736
GDP in US$ at 2005 prices and purchasing power parities (PPP)	66.544	65.745	59.434	54.917	48.491	43.448	44.665	49.757	53.936	55.770	59.005
GDP at current PPP	48.051	49.158	45.494	42.959	38.726	35.418	37.106	42.07	46.119	48.386	52.3
GDP as percentage of 1990 GDP (PPP)	100	102.3	94.7	89.4	80.6	73.7	77.2	87.5	96	100.7	108.9
Energy use (in kilotons of oil equivalent)	42.3	40.7	38.3	31.4	26.8	24.7	25.4	25.3	24.8	24.1	24.6
Energy use as percentage of 1990 use	100	96.2	90.5	74.2	63.3	58.4	60	59.8	58.6	56.9	58.1
Energy intensity (unit of fuel (kg of oil equivalent) per $1000 of GDP) (@ 2005 PPP)	680	670	620	570	550	570	570	510	460	430	420

waste; and increased financial dependency, since, with few means of its own to finance the $9 b (2010 estimate) project, Belarus would need to obtain credit, most likely from Russia.[93],[94] Much of the argument for the building of the nuclear plant was based on the expectation that electricity consumption in Belarus would double between 2007 and 2017, something far from proven. Moreover, the expectation itself of a large generation capacity coming online would reduce the incentives to restructuring industry to make it more energy-efficient. The problem of over-supply (and of finding profitable sale markets for excess electricity produced) was complicated by the fact that, in a virtual proliferation battle, new nuclear plants were being planned simultaneously for Lithuania, Poland and Estonia, in addition to Russia's project for a Baltic plant in Kaliningrad.[95] The possibility of these four projects coming online between 2016 and 2020 opened the prospect of uncoordinated electricity overproduction in the region. In addition, independent commentators have raised the

93 The March 2011 agreement between Belarus and Russia on the building of the nuclear power plant makes it clear Belarus would need to purchase its nuclear fuel from Russia, and return the nuclear waste there.

94 On some of the tensions in negotiations with Russia on the nature and extent of Russian financing and ownership of the nuclear power plant, see Marples, "Surge in Nuclear Power Projects."

95 Despite much discussion concerning the joint building of a nuclear power plant with Lithuania by Poland, Latvia, and Estonia, by 2010 it was clear that Poland, Lithuania and Estonia were seeking to build their own individual nuclear power plants.

2001	2002	2003	2004	2005	2006	2007	2008	2009	2010	2011
12.354	14.594	17.825	23.141	30.210	36.961	45.275	60.763	49.271	55.220	55.136
61.793	64.911	69.482	77.438	83.491	92.259	101.344	110.006	110.186	118.670	124.960
56.014	59.795	65.387	74.939	83.491	95.260	108.226	119.431	120.898	131.708	142.476
116.6	124.4	136	156	173.7	198.2	225.2	248.5	251.6	274.1	296.5
24.7	25.2	26	26.8	26.8	28.6	28	28.1*	26.7	N/A	N/A
58.3	59.6	61.4	63.3	63.3	67.6	66.2	66.4	63.1	N/A	N/A
400	390	370	330	320	310	280	260	240	N/A	N/A

Sources:
World Bank World Development Indicators, available at www.databank.worldbank.org; and IEA *Key Energy Indicators* (energy use 2008 and energy intensity 2003–2008); and *www.worldenergy.org/documents/belarus.pdf*

possibility of the project being pursued by "lobbies" in both Belarus and Russia, more interested in gaining profitable contracts than on the actual completion of the project or its safe operation.[96] A corruption and misuse-of-funds scandal at Rosatom, Russia's nuclear-energy agency, involving some of its top managers, which came to light in summer of 2011, cast new doubts about the way in which the Belarus' nuclear-plant project would be carried out.[97]

Given the instability in relations with Russia in mid-2010, however, it was not immediately clear whether an agreement would be found between both sides to allow for the planned start to construction. In particular, Russia argued that it would only participate if a joint venture was created to sell the energy produced by the new nuclear plant, an option publicly rejected by Lukashenka.[98] (Such a joint venture, Interconnect, was eventually created in 2011, owned

96 On this issue, see "Začem Rosatom podogrevaet âdernye strasti v Belarusi?"

97 See Legina, "Rossiâ garantiruet."

98 Already by August 13, 2010 Lukashenka had declared publicly that Belarus needed to start thinking about a different (non-Russian) investor. See Krylovic, "Razdum'â o drugom investore." In September 2010, representatives of the Joint Institute of Power and Nuclear Research (Sosny) associated with the nuclear power plant project clarified that, while Belarus was against the creation of a joint venture devoted only to the sale of electricity from the new nuclear power plant, it would be in favor of a joint venture selling all electricity produced in Belarus. This is because electricity from the new nuclear power plant would be cheaper to produce than other types of electricity, and the Belarus side would want a marketing solution appropriate for the whole of its electricity system. See Krylovic, "Sbyt stoimosti."

in equal parts by Russia's Inter RAO and Belarus' state-run electricity company, Belenergo.) While there were some discussions with American and French firms in 2008, these did not progress far, due to tendering and financing issues. The fact that Belarus did not call for an open tender, nor separate the issue of construction from that of financing, severely limited the range of realistic options to Russia and, much less likely, China. (On March 14, 2011, two days after the explosion of the Fukushima nuclear plant in Japan, which forced major countries such as Germany to freeze and rethink their nuclear development strategy, Russia and Belarus signed an agreement on the building of the facility.)

Oil: External and Domestic Management: 2007–2009

Oil shock delayed: winners and losers of compensatory measures

In assessing the impact of the changed oil and gas trade conditions starting in 2007, an important circumstance should be kept in mind. First, some of the negative economic tendencies observable in 2007 were not (only) the direct result of the oil-and-gas shock, the effects of which were only beginning to be felt, but, as noted by some Belarusian economists, of broader negative tendencies accumulating since 2005, in particular Belarus' growing deficit in its trade with Russia.[99] Changes in energy trade conditions contributed to exacerbate these trends, which, to complicate any analysis, were also affected by broader trends in international markets above and beyond relations with Russia (discussed at the end of this chapter).

Without any "cushioning" measures, the change in oil trade modalities represented by the new division of export duties effective January 1, 2007, would have meant a yearly loss of $2b from the Belarusian budget, a significant shock to state income. In addition, Belarus started to apply similar (and higher than previous) oil-product export duties as Russia, reducing the country's attractiveness as a refining center. Belarus first responded to the new situation with a series of measures that, while compensating for some of the lost revenue, also put a significant burden on refineries. As the export of oil products became less profitable, a larger percentage of refined oil products also started to reach the domestic market, but this was less desirable for the state due to its high dependence on export duties. As a result, a number of corrective measures were

99 See Zlotnikov, "Igra v cejtnote."

introduced from March 1, 2007, intended to make oil refining on the basis of tolling arrangements in Belarus more attractive to Russian producers, providing compensation equivalent to (or, in some cases, exceeding) the Russian export duty paid.[100] With the refining sector providing tens of thousands of highly paid jobs directly and indirectly,[101] keeping those refineries working at or near capacity was an important political as well as economic goal. As a further incentive for the *export* of refined oil products (as opposed to domestic sales), the level of duties (*akcizy*) on oil products sold domestically was also increased.[102] Thus, income to the Belarusian budget grew as a result of the newly imposed export duty, but there were also significant new net expenses due to the compensations paid to oil products exporters.[103] (In 2007 for example, the money spent by the state in subsidies to tolling oil suppliers amounted to more than 50 percent of the budget revenues from export duties on oil products.)[104] In addition, oil transit fees through Belarus were increased (by about 30–50 percent in dollar terms) for the first time since 1995, nevertheless remaining about 50 percent lower than fees charged by Poland and Ukraine.[105]

The measures introduced by the Belarusian government to deal with the situation had differential effects on various domestic actors' profit and rents. Refineries were the main losers, affected in two negative ways: first, while compensation was paid to (mainly Russian) oil suppliers, it was not paid to individual refineries.[106] Secondly, because of a reduction in other duties (*akcizy*), the importing of refined-oil products from Russia became more profitable, creating competition for domestically refined oil products.[107] Thus, refineries saw their profits plummet from 20 percent to one percent after a 37.6 percent reduction in oil product exports in January 2007 as compared with Jan-

100 Manenok, "Nestabil'naâ neftânka." In addition to the monthly revision of the size of the export duty compensation, there were some changes in its applicability: while at first the compensation applied only to oil delivered by rail, it was later extended to all oil. Effective from May 1, this compensation amounted to 90% of the oil duty. Effective August 1, 2007, it amounted to 127% of the Russian oil duty for oil supplied by rail, and 110% of the duty for oil supplied by pipeline. It is interesting to note that these compensation procedures gave a higher compensation to oil supplied by rail, as opposed to by pipeline. While this is most directly related to the higher cost of transiting oil by rail as opposed to by pipeline, the fact that transit through rail is not directly controlled by Russian oil pipeline operator Transneft, and thus a somewhat feasible alternative to overcome a centralized stoppage in oil supplies, may have been a consideration as well. See ibid.

101 See Dashkevich, *Jenergeticheskaja zavisimost'*.

102 IPM, *BMER* 3/54, March 2007, 2.

103 IPM, *BMER* 2/53, February 2007, 2.

104 Data on subsidies to oil suppliers from IPM, *BMER* 3/66, March 2008, 2.

105 A first increase in oil transit fees took effect on February 15, 2007, a second on February 1, 2008.

106 Subsidies to Belneftekhim as a whole amounted to $1.08b in 2007, and $1.73 in 2008.

107 Indeed, the import of oil products from Russia to Belarus increased from 0.9 Mt in 2007 to 2.5 in 2008 and 3.78 in 2009. See Table 5.4 below.

TABLE 5.4 BELARUS: FOREIGN TRADE OF OIL AND OIL PRODUCTS, 2004–2011

	2004		2005		2006		2007	
	million tons	billion US$	million tons	billion US$	million tons	billion US$	million tons	billion US$
Export of oil products	12.96	3.3	13.46	4.84	14.8	6.7	15.1	7.6
Export of oil	1.55	0.31	1.75	0.6	1.72	0.73	1.25	0.68
Total export of oil and its products	14.51	3.61	15.21	5.44	16.52	7.43	16.35	8.28
Imports of oil from Russia	17.81	3.232	19.24	4.193	20.9	5.66	20.02	7.4
Imports of oil products from Russia	1.18	0.16	0.973	0.153	1.233	0.485	0.9	0.49
Total import of oil and its products	18.99	3.392	20.213	4.346	22.133	6.145	20.92	7.89
Import price of oil to Belarus from Russia US$/ton		181.5		218		270		366
Price of Russian oil exports to non-CIS states US$/ton		233		350		470		485
Belarus' income from oil and oil products' exports after paying for imports of oil and oil products (saldo)		0.218		1.094		1.285		0.39

uary 2006 (but profits partially rebounded to seven percent in 2008 and 5.3 percent in 2009).[108] Individual oil suppliers, on the other hand, were provided compensation for the higher duties paid, and the state continued to make a profit (albeit much lower than in the past) from export duties.

Shock softened and delayed: Russian 'cushioning' policies

But it was not only Belarusian domestic measures which allowed the effects of the January 2007 oil shock to be softened and delayed. Russia also took a more conciliatory position after the initial crisis. After originally insisting on accruing 100 percent of the oil export duties, on January 10, 2007, Russia agreed to a

108 Data on January 2007 refinery exports and profitability from IPM, *BMER* 4/55, April 2007, 2, and IPM, "Rost cen na gaz." Data for 2008 and 2009 refinery profitability from Rakova, "Ènergetičeskij sektor," 4.

	2008		2009		2010		2011	
	million tons	billion US$	million tons	billion US$	million tons	billion US$	million tons	billion US$
Export of oil products	15.52	10.73	15.83	7.1	11.3	6.75	15.6	12.84
Export of oil	1.46	0.99	1.72	0.788	0	0	1.7	1.39
Total export of oil and its products	16.98	11.73	17.548	7.89	11.3	6.75	17.3	14.23
Imports of oil from Russia	21.5	9.49	21.5	7.065	14.7	6.76	20.4	9.36
Imports of oil products from Russia	2.5	1.47	3.78	1.276	1.58	0.9	5.73	3.48
Total import of oil and its products	24	11.96	25.98	8.341	16.28	7.66	26.13	12.84
Import price of oil to Belarus from Russia US$/ton		441		329		460		459
Price of Russian oil exports to non-CIS states, US$/ton		626		420		801* (est)		820 (August)
Belarus' income from oil and oil-product exports after paying for imports of oil and oil products		-0.23		-0.45		-0.91		1.39

* 2010 price of Russian oil exports to non-CIS states estimated from statements by Russian Ministry of Finance concerning a 28% increased in the average price of Russian Urals oil from 2009 to 2010. See IFX-News, "Srednaya tsena nefti Urals v 2010 vyrosla na 28%," at www.finmarket.ru/z/nws/news.asp?id=1916102 (accessed May 9, 2011).

Sources:
Calculated on the basis of Ministry of Statistics and Analysis of the Republic of Belarus, *Foreign Trade of the Republic of Belarus. Statistical abstracts.* (Minsk, yearly); and *Rossiâ v cifrah. Oficial'noe izdanie. Federal'naâ služba gosudarstvennoj statistiki*, Moscow, 2008. Special thanks to Leonid Zlotnikov for his help in preparing this table.

gradual transition regarding the sharing of export duties for Russian oil refined in Belarus: in 2007, 70 percent for Russia and 30 percent for Belarus; in 2008, 80 percent and 20 percent; and in 2009, 85 percent and 15 percent; and 100 percent to Russia from 2010. In addition, duties on oil supplied to Belarus continued to be lower than those charged neighboring states: in 2007, 29.3 percent of the regular level, to be gradually increased to 33.5 percent in 2008 and 35.6 percent in

2009.[109] This coefficient was intended to reflect the fact that oil supplies intended for domestic Belarus use (around 6 Mt out of total imports of 21.5) would not be subject to export duties during this period; throughout this time, the possibility that the volume of crude oil supplies intended for domestic use in Belarus could be subject to export duties was never discussed. This reduced Belarus' additional expenses (stemming from the newly imposed Russian oil export duties) from $3b to $1b. There was also an agreement to limit oil-price increases;[110] in 2007–2009, Belarus was still receiving oil at prices at least $99–120 per ton lower than world prices. As seen from Table 5.4, the actual value of oil-related exports grew from $7.43b in 2006 to $8.28b in 2007, and $11.7b in 2008, before falling to its 2006 level (c. $7.89 b) in 2009. (It is important to note that while, for example, in 2008 the value of Belarus' oil products exports was much higher than in 2006, the size of the actual profits that could be shared by sector actors was much smaller, as the costs of imports and duties had increased even more significantly.) The role of oil and oil-product exports in Belarus as a portion of overall exports remained largely unchanged, and at its highest point in Belarus' history, went from 38.8 percent in 2006 to 38 percent in 2009 (see Table 5.4).[111]

Belarusian economists calculated that, even under the less favorable trade conditions in force after January 2007, the Russian subsidization of the Belarusian economy (through lower gas prices, sharing of export duties for refined oil products, and not charging export duties on a significant portion of crude oil) amounted to $6.4b in 2007, $9.9 b in 2008, and $4.15 b in 2009.[112]

Winners and Losers: Declining Rents and *Nomenklatura* Groups, Economic Actors and End Energy Users

In order to see the full effects of the new oil trade conditions, we need to keep in mind not only their effects in terms of reducing the size of the energy-related rents accrued by the state as a whole, but also their impact on

109 See Kostiugova, "Perspektivy učastiâ Belarusi," 11; and Manenok, "'Družbu' ne počinât." Thus, for example, in 2007, oil supplied to Belarus paid $53 per ton in Russian export duties, compared with $180 per ton for oil going to other markets.

110 Manenok, "Nevygodnyj èksport."

111 Even in 2008, after the conditions of oil trade with Russia had worsened for Belarus, Belarus continued to export nearly as many oil products per capita as Russia: 1.1 ton per year per capita, as compared with 1.2 tons for Russia. Source: calculated on the basis of *Statisticheskoe obozrenie*, No. 3 (2008), 116 and Table 6.1.

112 Calculated on the basis of Tables 3.1 and 3.2 in Rakova "Ènergetičeskij sektor," 10–11.

GRAPH 5.5 ESTIMATED PROFIT MARGINS FOR OIL REFINING AND EXPORT OPERATIONS IN BELARUS, AS PERCENTAGE OF THE EXPORT PRICE OF BELARUSIAN OIL PRODUCTS, 2005–2010

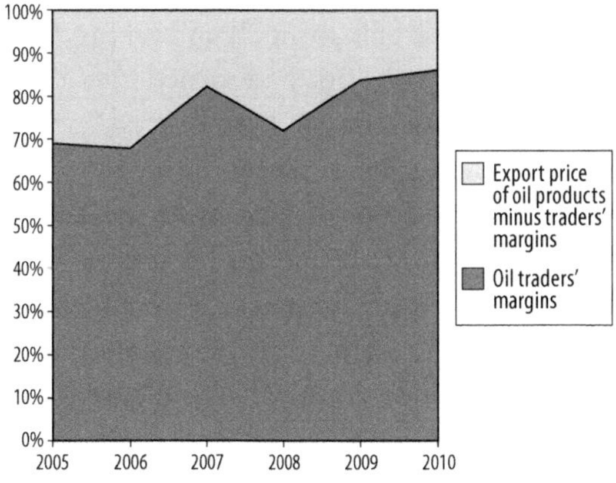

Year	Estimated potential profit margin
2005	30.28%
2006	32.01%
2007	17.50%
2008	28.22%
2009	16.52%
2010	13.68%

Sources:
Potential profit margins estimated on the basis of: prices of crude oil imports; export prices for oil products in Western European markets; dollar exchange rate; cost of refining services for tolling operations; and duties. Special thanks for Leonid Zlotnikov for help in the preparation of the data set, on the basis of which the potential profit margins reflected in this table were calculated.

the rents that could be accrued by specific groups. As can be seen from Graph 5.5, if throughout the mid-2000s there was much oil-products exports related potential rent that could be divided (between the state and various groups, or between various groups), starting in 2007 it started to decline steadily due to changed conditions of energy trade with Russia, dropping from 32 percent (2006) to less than 14 percent (2010) of the export price of oil products exports, and more than halving in dollar value. In dollar terms, given the oil and oil products export revenue noted in Table 5.4, this difference amounted to more than $1.2b in yearly revenue.[113]

Effects on economic policy

Although Belarus was able to largely soften the short-term shock of new oil trade rules imposed by Russia, some of the negative signs, although small, were clear: worsening trade balances (Belarus' trade deficit increased from 3.9

113 Dollar value of potential margins for oil export operations calculated as follows: for 2006, $6.7b x the margin rate of 32.01% ($2.14b); for 2010, $6.75b x the margin rate of 13.68% ($0.92b).

percent of GDP in 2006 to 11.3 percent in 2009, and 17.6 percent in 2010);[114] and the fact that many domestic companies had to increasingly rely on credits to compensate for the higher energy costs (see Table 5.6). As shown in Table 5.4, if in 2006 Belarus still had $1.285b in income from oil and oil products' exports after paying for similar imports, by 2010 this had turned into a deficit of $0.91b. As a response to the new stress on its economy by mid-2007, in particular the lack of investment capital, the Belarusian government put in motion a number of mild economic reforms. Some of these measures, such as the attempt to secure foreign-currency syndicated loans for the largest Belarusian banks,[115] and the modest beginnings of privatization,[116] were intended to bring more capital into the system. Others, such as the elimination of the state's right to a controlling share (the so-called golden share) in enterprises, and the reduction of bureaucratic red tape,[117] were intended to make the country more attractive to foreign investors. In addition, the tax burden on economic actors was reduced by some $480m in 2008, presumably to help them cope with the burden of increased energy prices.[118] An additional set of measures (such as the elimination of special aid for Chernobyl victims of and free use of public transportation for certain groups, effective from January 2008) was utterly surprising from the perspective of what could be expected from a populist regime such as Lukashenka's, and provided evidence of the increasing pressure on the budget.[119] Table 5.6 shows how decreases in energy trade balances affected overall trade balances and, in turn, budget deficits, which grew steadily after 2008.

114 Sokrat Research, *Belarus: country report 2008.* 2010 data from IPM, BMER, various issues.

115 The IPM called the bringing in of foreign resources to Belarusian banks "the main instrument currently used by the government to counteract the energy shock." IPM, *BMER* 8/59, August 2007, 4.

116 In addition to the privatization deals involving Motovelo and Velcom discussed in Chapter 3, a July 2008 state resolution confirmed a list of 519 state and 147 joint-stock companies which would be (at least theoretically) open for privatization between 2008 and 2011. IPM, *BMER* No. 8/71, August 2008, 2. The list included several energy objects, among them the Druzhba oil pipeline. Manenok, "Obstoâtel'stva prižali." However, the possibility should not be excluded that this privatization would be dominated by Belarusian (*nomenklatura*) capital abroad, as, given his distrust of Russian capital, opening the door for this capital to return to Belarus may be a good option from Lukashenka's perspective.

117 By instituting a simplified registration process, partial liberalization of land-sale regulations, and streamlining the process of registration of new businesses. Karbalevich, "Mâgkaâ adaptaciâ," 2.

118 Kalinovskaja, "Dlâ lataniâ dyr."

119 The elimination of these free services was agreed to in May 2007, theoretically to be replaced by targeted aid programs.

Table 5.6 Foreign trade operations in oil and gas (including oil products) and Belarus' trade balances in billion US$, 2004–2011

Year	Net income from foreign trade in oil and oil-product (exports–imports) (A)	Cost of gas imports (B)	Saldo of oil and gas trade operations (A–B)	Belarus' trade balance (Saldo)	Increase in foreign debt	Gross external debt as percentage of GDP (at end of year)	Budget surplus/ deficit (-) as % of GDP
2004	0.218	0.956	-0.738	-1.4	0.760	21.3	0.04
2005	1.094	0.956	0.138	0.3	0.193	17.0	-0.67
2006	1.285	0.956	0.329	-1.5	1.716	18.5	1.43
2007	0.039	2.100	-2.061	-2.9	5.650	27.6	0.43
2008	-0.023	2.663	-2.686	-4.6	2.660	24.9	1.43
2009	-0.045	2.570	-2.615	-5.5	6.900	44.8	-0.7
2010	-1.107	4.243	-5.349	-6.8	3.530	52.2	-2.59
2011	1.39	5.300	-4.91	N/A	N/A	66.8	2.10

Sources:
Ministry of Statistics and Analysis of the Republic of Belarus, *Foreign Trade of the Republic of Belarus. Statistical abstracts*; and (for foreign debt and budget surplus/deficit), IPM, *BMER* 4/103 April 2011, 5 and 4/127 April 2013, 5.

Attempts to take more direct control of the oil refining sector

This increased pressure on the budget helps us understand the government's return, in 2007, to an idea originally discussed in 1999: the creation of a centralized, state-controlled oil company on the model of the Belarusian Potash Company created two years earlier with the goal of concentrating in state hands income from the export of Belarus' second-most important export product, potash fertilizers. The Belarusian Oil Company (*Belorusskaya Neftenaya Kompania*, BNK) was created in May 2007. Officially, BNK was created with two main goals in mind. First, to reduce the number and role of private tolling operators[120] and thus, to keep in state hands the money spent by the state in subsidies to oil suppliers (which in 2007 amounted to more than 50 percent of the budget revenues from export duties on oil products).[121] Secondly, to centralize the export of oil products as a means to securing higher export prices, com-

120 As discussed in Chapter 3, the number of tolling operators had already been reduced in 2003 due to, among other things, restrictions on the ability of non-resident companies to conduct oil operations in Belarus.

121 IPM, *BMER* 8/59, August 2007, 4. Data on subsidies to oil suppliers from IPM, *BMER* 3/66, March 2008, 2.

pared with those that could be attained when there are many sellers offering competing prices. In reality, however, the extent to which these goals were actually fulfilled is unclear. The company seems to have taken a long time to get off the ground. Although, from early 2008, it was exporting 80 percent of the oil products produced by its founders (Naftan, Mozyr, Belarusneft, and the *Belorusskii Neftianoi Torgovii Dom*), it had failed to gain control over the marketing of oil refined by its original target group, tolling operators.[122] Thus, it has been argued that the company was less successful in fulfilling its official goals than in advancing unofficial agendas related to the reshuffling of rent-seeking opportunities: excluding certain actors from the oil refining and export market, and helping other actors solidify their position in it, even if this would take place behind the façade of increased state control.[123]

Energy rents, corruption, and the "low years"

The changes discussed above (changed trade conditions from Russia, as well as the measures introduced by the Belarusian government to deal with this situation) coincided with the height of the confrontation between old and new dominant *nomenklatura* groups. This confrontation was related first and foremost to the entrance, by 2006–2007, of a powerful new player in the person of Lukashenka's son, Viktor. Following his growing role in behind-the-scenes politics as a presumed heir-in-waiting,[124] by 2007 the confrontation between his group and others—in particular the *siloviki* (security services and KGB-related) elements associated with National Security Advisor Sheiman—gained momentum. The shrinking of the oil rents "pie" served as a push for a sharpening of this confrontation and a reorganization of the informal rent-seeking system to secure sufficient rents for Lukashenka Jr. and his group.[125]

122 Manenok, "Potoki s političeskoj logistikoj."

123 In an interview in the *Deutsche Welle* service for Belarus, Romanchuk argues that "the creation of [this] oil company amounts to, basically, the legalization of the status of lobbyist." Yaroslav Romanchuk in Alekhnovich, "Novaâ kompaniâ, starye problem." For a related interpretation of the relationship between the reduction in easy sources of energy rents and the establishment of the Belarusian Oil Company, see Chubrik, in RFE/RL program for Belarus, "JakiJa perspektyvy." See also Novozilova, "Fradkov podtolknet èkonomičeskie reformy v Belarusi?"

124 When asked publicly about a successor, however, Aleksander Lukashenka casually mentioned "the smallest one," a reference to his youngest son Nikolai, born 2004.

125 According to Kalinkina, for the emerging group of Viktor Lukashenka, it is very important to start controlling some important "streams" (*napriamki*) in politics and economics, "and here the oil business will always be in the first place." Kalinkina, in "Pavinjen zastacca al"bo Shejman al"bo Viktar Lukashenka."

A look at the most important oil-related corruption case brought to the courts during this period, related to Belneftekhim and the Naftan refinery, helps illustrate some of the dynamics at play here. In late May 2007, in the midst of the major confrontation between *nomenklatura* groups discussed above, another corruption scandal rocked the Belarusian oil sector with the arrest of Belneftekhim head Aleksandr Borovsky, accused of corruption.[126] More specifically, he was charged with creating a $1.6m loss for the state-owned Naftan refinery, by refusing to purchase a large amount of oil directly from one company in order to purchase it at a higher price from an intermediary. However, when Borovsky was sentenced in March 2008, he was acquitted of stealing, but was found guilty of misusing his position ("*zloupotreblenie služebnymi polnomočiâmi*") at the refinery,[127] providing grounds for further speculation as to the real reason behind the attack on him. Some argued that the arrest may have been a retribution for critical comments on Belarusian energy policy made by Borovsky in March 2007, when he allegedly criticized the stopping of oil transit through the Druzhba pipeline during the January 2007 conflict with Russia;[128] others saw it as a way for the government to "prepare the population for possible problems with gasoline supplies," by placing the blame on Borovsky and showing that he had been properly brought to justice.[129] Others noted his connection with privileged oil trader Juri Chyzh.[130]

Yet, two additionally important contexts of the arrest were, on the one hand, the growing desire on the part of the state to take increased control of the oil sector and ease out any remaining unaffiliated tolling operators and, on the other, the intensified battle for oil-related rents and change in the distribution of power at the top of the *nomenklatura*. A July 2007 incident of armed confrontation, where Zianon Lomats, head of the State Control Committee, was beaten up in Mogilev by KGB officials dressed as policemen,

---

126 Others were also arrested, but charges against them were subsequently dropped.

127 On this case, see Ankudo, "Èks-predsedatel' zloupotrebil," and Satsuk, "Ne ukral, no vse ravno vinoven." *Ezhednevnik*, 28 March 2008, 6. Borovsky was accused of buying a large (80,000 tons) party of light oil from an intermediary company at $350 per ton, instead of directly from another (TNK-BP Menedzhment) at $330 per ton. He was sentenced to five years in jail, but the decision overturned by President Lukashenka: in 2009, he was named general director of the flagship tractor factory MAZ. Another major actor in the case, Nikolai Vorobei, was also freed in 2009, and later returned to oil-related business through the oil trading company Interservis.

128 A tape with Borovsky's declarations could allegedly be found on the internet. Panchenko, "Podkovernye šagi ili bor'ba s korrupciej." See also Manenok in RFE/RL program for Belarus (Radio Svabody), *Ekspertiza Svabody*, "JakiJa perspektyvy."

129 See Zaiko, in Grigoreva, "V poiskah streločnika."

130 On the possible connection of the Borovskoi case with Yurii Chizh's privileged oil business, see "Rukovoditel' gruppy kompanij «Trajpl» Ûrij ČIŽ." See also Khartia 97, "Rossijskij jekspert."

brought many of these tensions out into the open, and strongly contributed to Sheiman's dismissal shortly thereafter. The incident also made clear how, in situations of flux and shrinking of the available rents "pie," the re-accommodation of relations between various *nomenklatura* groups could overstep the polite contours of Lukashenka's "rules of the game" discussed in Chapter 4, and acquire a much less orderly, and at times even violent character.

If, as discussed in the last chapter, staying away from public conflict with other "oligarchs" was a central principle of Belarus' unwritten "*nomenklatura* rules of the game," this principle was broken by the events of July 2007, which brought to the open the tension between these two groups, and solidified the growing power of Viktor Lukashenka's group. This was at the expense of Sheiman, who was first affected by Lukashenka's accusations that the KGB was providing illegal protection to corrupt business groups. Sheiman was dismissed from office in July 2008 in the wake of an unexplained explosion during National Independence Day celebrations, being accused by Lukashenka of negligence in preventing it. These events coincided with further "purges" in the top management of Beltransgaz and the new BNK in July of 2007.[131] In addition, other players informally involved in the oil business (such as, reportedly, Vladimir Konoplev, until 2007 head of the National Assembly) found it hard to continue with business as usual given Lukashenka Jr.'s interests in the sector. Konoplev's September 2007 resignation from high office has been repeatedly understood in this context,[132] which some have also related to the criminal investigations around Borovsky and the Naftan refinery that same year.[133] In fact, it could be argued that energy pressure from Russia (via a reduction of available rents, but also such mechanisms as forcing the Lukashenka regime to engage in a limited liberalization of the economy) fostered the transition from Sheiman's older *nomenklatura* clan to a younger, more "reformist" one associated with Viktor Lukashenka and his associates: "young wolves" head of the Presidential Administration Vladimir Makei and first deputy head Natalia Piatkevich.[134]

131 On these management changes, see Freedom House, "Belarus country report."

132 See comments by Kalinkina, in "Pavinjen zastacca al"bo Shejman al"bo Viktar Lukashenka." Many associate Konoplev with, until 2007, *neftetreider* Miraleks. See Sekhovich, "Skrytaâ storona neftânogo protivostoâniâ."

133 See Filin, "Cjen", vjedaj svajo mjesca!"

134 Referring to these events, some Belarusian analysts have argued such competition for "access to resources among elite groups" has been more significant for political change in the late 2000s than "activities of opposition parties or civil society actors." Liakhovich, "Belarusian Elites," 37.

OIL: EXTERNAL MANAGEMENT AND DIVERSIFICATION: 2007–2009

In addition to domestic measures to reduce the impact of new oil-trade conditions discussed above, the Belarusian side responded to this new situation by, first and foremost, seeking out new partners. In contrast with gas, oil presented Belarus with some limited but real geographic diversification possibilities once the decision to diversify was taken. Venezuela, where Hugo Chávez's regime appeared as a sympathetic partner of convenience for Lukashenka, and where an oil-producing joint venture was established already in 2007, became an important partner in this endeavor.

In addition, Belarusian delegations also visited the United Arab Emirates and Azerbaijan in 2007–2008, and agreements were reached with Azerbaijan on oil supplies to Belarusian refineries and on permission for Belarusneft to produce oil there.[135] Although the agreement with Azerbaijan was not immediately implemented, Azerbaijan proved a reliable ally in another respect: when $186m were urgently needed in June 2010 to deal with a Gazprom ultimatum on overdue gas payments, President Heydar Alyev promptly loaned the necessary funds (which were repaid 12 days later). Such a proactive search for new sources of oil imports was in sharp contrast with Belarus' policies and initiatives of the previous period, 1994 to 2004. In February 2011, the Mozyr refinery started to receive Azeri oil via the Odessa–Brody pipeline as a result of an oil swap with Venezuela; in the first ten months of 2011, nearly 1 Mt had been imported.[136]

In addition, in 2006, Belarus started to show increased interest in new oil transportation options, such as a participation in the Odessa–Brody oil pipeline system and its possible extension to Gdansk.[137] Immediately after the January 2007 oil crisis, Belarusian deputy PM Andrei Kabyakau (Andrei Kobyakov) declared that Belarus was considering supplying its refineries with non-Russian oil shipped by tanker to the Ventspils port in Latvia and, from there, transported through a reversed segment of the Novopolotsk-Ventspils pipeline.[138] The Belarusian energy security strategy document covering the period up to 2020,[139] approved in November 2007, envisaged that, by the end

135 IPM, *BMER* 4/55, April 2007, 1-2.

136 Between January and October 2011, Belarus imported 0.94 Mt of Azeri oil. Ivashkevich, "Belarus' i neft': po trope kontrabandistov," 1.

137 Manenok, "Podstegnet neftânoj stimul." Additional details in Kostiugova, "Perspektivy učastiâ Belarusi," 2.

138 Socor, "Belarus Warns It May Cancel Its Subsidies To Russia."

139 "Ènergetičeskaâ bezopasnost' Respubliki Belarus' na 2005-2010 gody i na period do 2020 goda," discussed in Manekok, "Deševogo gaza nužno vsë bol'še."

of 2010, 20 percent of Belarus' oil imports should come from non-Russian sources, shipped through ports on the Baltic and Black seas. Despite these declarations, however, the fact that Russia continued to offer Belarus favorable oil trade conditions (even if not as favorable as those in place in 2006) made it difficult for the Belarusian leadership to move quickly into implementing these initiatives, many of which would imply higher costs than current supplies from Russia.[140] In addition to price advantages, however, the political environment played a role as well. As will be discussed in the next chapter, in addition to prices, the political signals coming from Moscow also played a role in getting Minsk to pursue oil imports from Venezuela as a serious option.

Conclusion

After the announcement of the new, less favorable oil trade conditions and an increase in gas prices in early 2007, few expected the Lukashenka regime to be able to survive under these new conditions. Yet, due to a combination of large new foreign loans ($18.74 billion in 2007–2010 alone, see Table 5.6), income from privatization,[141] crafty bargaining, strong international demand for potash fertilizers (Belarus' other main export), continued politicization of the energy relationship, timely policies, and/or simply good fortune, Belarus was able to cushion the shock of worsened energy trade conditions during this period. In combination, these additional factors allowed Belarus to take some pressure off its balance of payments, and, domestically, continue expansionist wage and other monetary policies, intended to favorably dispose public opinion for the upcoming 2010 presidential elections.[142] Crucial in this mixture was the fact that, despite worsening relations and high-stakes public relations confrontations, significant levels of Russian subsidies and preferences in both the gas and oil areas continued. Thus, Russian assurances that the relationship with Belarus had been moved to an exclusively commercial basis are not supported by the actual record.

140 See Kostiugova, "Perspektivy učastiâ Belarusi," 2.

141 The $625m yearly payment from Gazprom was in addition to income from other major privatization sales during this period, such as $400m from the privatization of mobile operator Mobile Digital Communications ("Velcom") and others in 2007.

142 IPM, *BMER* 3/102, March 2011, 2.

The question thus inevitably arises: why did Russia continue to support Belarus at this moment, in light of Lukashenka's often aggressive declarations, when it seemed to have in its hands the key to force it into much more direct compliance with Moscow's views? In addition to some of the factors at play in the last decade (Belarus' real and psychological value as Russia's "last ally," and Lukashenka's instrumental politicization of the issue) there might have been some additional elements at play. A sudden and total collapse of the Belarusian economy, and a sudden stream of migrants to Russia, would bring destabilization to Russia as well. Here we can see an interesting parallel with the situation seen in Soviet East-European energy-trade relations in the 1970s and 1980s, where using energy subsidies as a means to maintain alliance loyalty faced clear limitations: there being no real energy "stick" to balance the "carrot" of subsidized supplies. The need to keep Eastern European regimes afloat after political crises reduced the possibility to use energy-based negative sanctions.[143] But there may have been another motivation for the Russian side as well: Russia's desire to use such softening measures (much in the same way it had been using subsidies) to delay the "moment of truth" for Belarus, and keep it dependent on the Russian economy until its transit counter-power in the relationship could be further diminished. This crucial shift was associated first and foremost with the progress of several Russian energy transit projects specifically avoiding Belarus, particularly the Nord Stream pipeline (also known as the North European Gas Pipeline)[144] and, in the oil area, the Baltic Pipeline System (BPS-1, commissioned in 2001, and BPS-2, completed in 2012), developing Russia's capacity to ship oil from Russian Baltic seaports. By 2010, as we will discuss in our next chapter, such a moment of truth seemed to be coming inexorably closer.

143 For a discussion of the issue in the context of Soviet-East European relations, see Reisinger, *Energy and the Soviet Bloc*, 70, 151.

144 Although Gazprom has repeatedly claimed that the volumes to be transited through Nord Stream constitute new volumes, this has often been disputed. Even assuming no actual diversion of existing gas volumes from Belarus would take place, with Gazprom's total export pipeline system to Western Europe expected to reach a capacity of 267 bcm in 2012, even without a reduction in transit through Belarus, the country's share of Russian gas exports could decline a few percentage points as a result. Moreover, the new capacities would increase Gazprom's options for re-routing volumes around Belarusian pipelines.

6

The Energy Prologue and Aftermath to the 2010 Elections: from Euphoria to Forced Concessions

The period between early 2010 and the end of 2011 was marked by a variety of, at times, seemingly contradictory events: attempts at energy diversification; the development of a new framework for a Customs Union with Russia; a bitter public relations campaign by Belarus and Russia against each other; the December 19 presidential elections and their aftermath of repression; and in 2011, a deep crisis of the Belarusian economy. In many ways, the 12 months between November 2010 and November 2011 represent the two extremes of a pendulum: on the one hand, relatively improved relations with the EU in the run-up to the elections, accompanied by a strong domestic, consumerist frenzy as a result of pre-electoral economic expansionism; and on the other, the reluctant sale to Gazprom of Belarus' closely guarded flagship energy company, Beltransgaz, amidst an unprecedented economic crisis. Belarus met the 20th anniversary of its independence in a state of deep crisis.

The road to the elections

A turning point in relations with Russia?

If, as discussed in the last chapter, Belarus had managed to soften the impact of the 2007-2009 changes in its energy relationship with Russia, and to avoid the "moment of truth" in the relationship, such a moment seemed to be approaching by 2010. Despite Lukashenka's continued politicization of the issue and attempts to make Belarus' joining of a previously agreed Russia-Belarus-Kazakhstan Customs Union (formally inaugurated in July 2010) conditional on Russia cancelling export duties on oil supplied to fellow member states, Russia's official position remained unchanged.

Russia's intransigency seemed to be related not only to economic interests, but to Lukashenka's perceived unreliability as an ally, manifested most clearly in his wavering stance concerning recognition of Abkhazia and South Ossetia after the August 2008 military conflict with Georgia. After a further worsening of relations in mid-2010, exemplified by a new threat of suspension of gas supplies due to unpaid gas debts by Belarus and unpaid transit services by Gazprom, a meeting between Lukashenka, and Moscow foe Georgian President Mikheil Saakashvili, and a Kremlin-supported smear campaign against Lukashenka, relations seemed to have reached a point of no return.

Tighter oil trade conditions from Russia in 2010

The new mood in relations with Russia was seen first and foremost in the oil area, where December 2009 brought a new period of tense negotiations on the issue of taxation of crude-oil exports to Belarus, related to Russia's declared intentions to tie the special duty regime to Belarus' openness to Russian energy investments. After weeks of tense negotiations and fears of a possible repetition of the January 2007 situation where Russian-Belarusian disagreements led to an interruption of supplies to the EU,[1] an agreement was reached and new trade rules entered into effect in January, 2010. Although a direct confrontation was avoided, the new trade regime clearly represented a worsening of trade conditions for Belarus. Among these, the most important was the replacement of the "special duty" on oil introduced in 2007, by full export duties on all oil not used domestically in Belarus. According to the new rules, nearly two-thirds of oil supplies would be subject to duties compared to only about one-third in 2009.[2] This change in Russian policy must be understood not only in terms of bilateral Russian-Belarusian relations (for

1 In early January 2010, the Reuters news agency reported supplies of Russian oil to Belarusian refineries had been suspended, but this was denied by both Belarusian and Russian sources. See Reuters, "Russia, Belarus oil supply talks."

2 According to the new rules, out of total supplies of around 21.5Mt, 15Mt would be dutied, compared to, *de facto* only 7.64Mt in 2009. Under the system in place in 2009 (payment of a special duty on all oil supplied, but at a reduced coefficient of 35.6%), Belarus received the equivalent of around 13.8 Mt of oil duty-free (21.5 Mt - 35.6%), while duty-free supplies would now be reduced to around 6.3Mt.

example, Kremlin pressure on Lukashenka to recognize Abkhazia and South Ossetia), but also in terms of the relationship between the Russian state and Russian oil producers, namely the Russian state's desire to limit Russian oil producers' use of refining-and-export oil operations in Belarus as a means of evading Russian export duties.[3] From the perspective of Russian oil-related actors with interests in Belarus, the situation was more complicated: while the new measures severely limited their ability to profit through tolling oil refining operations in Belarus, they also allowed them to put pressure on Belarus for the sale of the Naftan (since 2008 joined with the petrochemical company Polimir) and Mozyr refineries to interested Russian oil companies, first and foremost LUKoil.

The new policies represented a significant macroeconomic burden on Belarus, as the additional duties to be paid amounted to some $1.8b. At the level of specific economic actors, subjecting all oil intended for tolling (*davalcheskii*) operations to full Russian export duties meant such supplies would be, *de facto*, subjected to export duties twice – by both Russia (which levied an export duty on oil supplied to Belarus) and Belarus (which levied an export duty on the resulting oil products). Supplies would then become unprofitable, greatly reducing their attractiveness. As shown in Graph 5.5 in Chapter 5, potential margin profits from such operations went from an estimated 32 percent of export price per unit in 2006 to 13.68 percent in 2010.

The immediate results, in the first quarter of 2010, were a drastic fall in tolling oil supplies to Belarus, and an approximately 30 percent decline in the work of the country's two refineries. In an attempt to make refining in Belarus more attractive for Russian tolling oil suppliers, in March, Belarus cancelled export duties on oil products. While this reduced budget revenue,[4] Belarus was able to at least partially compensate for it with the additional foreign currency income accruing as a result of related exports.

Domestic manipulations with the duty-free portion of the oil received from Russia also played a role. The Belarusian government did not always fully separate the two categories of "dutied" (intended for refining and export) and "duty-free" (intended for domestic use in Belarus) oil, allowing some of the duty-free oil to be used in refining-for-export operations;[5] access to informal quotas of duty-free oil for refining and subsequent export became

3 Indeed, this factor was noted by the Russian side as justification for the change. See the declarations of Russia's first vice-PM Igor Sechin in Ermak, "Davajte bez daval'cev?"

4 IPM, *BMER*, 3/102, March 2011, 3.

5 Manenok, "NPZ balansiruût." See also Leonid Zlotnikov, personal communication, September 6, 2010.

Table 6.1 Main changes in the Russian–Belarusian oil trade system and their domestic effects, 1999–2011

Years	1999–2006	2007–2009	2010	2011
Basic framework of Russian–Belarusian oil trade	Belarus imports Russian crude oil duty-free (i.e., without export duties being levied on this oil). All income from the export of oil products stays in Belarus (de-facto).	Belarus imports Russian crude oil and pays a special duty (spetsposhlina) amounting to 29–35% of regular dues. This amounts to Belarus importing around 65% of its oil duty free, a significant amount above the approximately 35% consumed domestically. Export duties on oil products refined in Belarus are divided between both countries, with most of the income going to Russia. Gradual increase in the price of oil (and gas) paid by Belarus, bringing it closer to European prices.	Spetsposhlina replaced by Russia's application of export duties on all crude oil imported by Belarus, except that part used domestically. This amounts to Belarus importing only around 35% of its oil duty free. With the increase in duties, tolling operations become increasingly unprofitable.	Export duties on all oil exported to Belarus canceled. Strong increase in oil products exports ensues; for the first time since 2007, income from their export more than compensates cost of oil and products imports. But gains partially cancelled by higher prices charged by Russian suppliers, and export duties on oil products now accruing to Russia. Refineries see reduced profits. With Russian companies sharing into the export profits by charging higher prices, they lose interest in tolling operations compared to selling oil to Belarusian refineries.
Effects on Belarus' budget	Record income in the form of oil-product export duties and arbitrage gains.	Belarus loses income due to receiving a lower percentage of export duties on oil products while facing higher costs (spetsposhlina). But continues to receive record income due to price differentials and taxes paid by oil sector actors.	Belarus loses income due to a reduction in tolling operations (January-March), the cancellation of most oil export duties accrued by Belarus (starting in March), and a reduction in oil products exports. Price differentials continue, but at a lower level than in 2009.	Belarus saves c. $4b due to duty-free oil imports. C. $2b go back to Russia as Belarus turns over to Russia the export duties accrued on exported oil products.
Energy-sector specific palliative measures implemented by Belarus	(No need for palliative measures, as special energy trade conditions with Russia lead to record gains.)	Compensation paid to oil importers from Russia to offset Russian oil export duties (ended in early 2011).	(March) Belarus cancels export duties on oil products made from Russian oil as to remain attractive to tolling operators.	One-year (to June 2012) freeze in refineries' requirement to sell to state 30% of foreign currency income.
Other palliative measures implemented by Belarus	N/A	Foreign loans. Sale of some state assets via privatization. Attempts to improve Belarus' attractiveness for foreign investors.	Foreign loans. Short-term credits to bolster value of BLR. Improved relations with the EU, other international organizations (until December 19, 2010 elections).	Foreign loans (EurAsEC). Limits on domestic oil products prices. Export duties on second export item potash fertilizers increased 50%. Income from sale of Beltransgaz helps counter growing deficit.

a precious commodity available only to well-connected traders.[6],[7] Table 6.1 summarizes the main changes in the oil-trade system between Belarus and Russia in 1999–2011, and their effects on the main market players. (See Chapter 5 and Graph 5.5 for a discussion of the impact on the potential profits by oil traders.)

In addition, a favorable combination of factors in 2010 allowed Belarus to buffer the macro-economic impact of these changes. Among these was Belarus' increased income from other exports: in 2010, for example, the export of potash fertilizers (*kalijnye udobreniya*) grew by 132 percent relative to 2009, and brought more than $1.5 b in additional income, partially compensating for reduced oil products exports.[8]

The Belarusian government's attempts to soften the impact of the new Russian trade conditions, which had entered into force in January 2010, came in the context of other short-term changes in macroeconomic policy. If the initial Belarusian response to the shock of the 2008 world economic crisis was a rather tight monetary policy, by the second half of 2010, the upcoming elections had brought strong expansionist impulses. Some of its elements were significant increases in the minimum and state-sector wages, and high-cost domestic and external borrowing to support the value of the Belarusian rouble (BLR).[9] (Propping the value of the BLR was crucial for President Lukashenka's ability to keep a key campaign promise: to bring, by December 2010, the average monthly salary up to the equivalent of $500; a weaker BLR would have made this more difficult to achieve.) All in all, Belarus' ability to

6 Author's consultations, Minsk, November 2010 and January 2011. On quotas for duty-free oil to well-connected Tripl company, see Prime-TASS, "Belorusskoe OOO "Trajpl" planiruet."

7 In addition, it has been argued the Belarusian government turned a blind eye to the small-scale smuggling of oil products (gasoline and diesel intended for domestic consumption in Belarus and, thus, produced from duty-free oil) to Lithuania, as a means of creating additional demand for its refineries despite the official ban on the export of oil products refined from duty-free oil. In addition, as end prices of oil products were 33–43% higher in Lithuania than in Belarus, this increased the influx of hard currency to Belarus, even when such hard currency would avoid taxes and accrue directly to those engaged in smuggling, and not to the budget as in the case of official trade. This may explain the fact that the official domestic consumption of oil products in Belarus did not go back in the first half of 2010, despite the economic crisis and a significant increase in domestic end prices, but nearly doubled in comparison with the same period in the previous year: from 0.8 to 1.4 million tons. It has been argued that the Lithuanian government also had good reasons to close its eyes to this smuggling, as access to lower-priced Belarusian fuel made it possible for Lithuanian long-distance trucking companies to compete in the European market. Agenstvo Finansovikh Novostei, "Nepotopljaemyj belorusskij neftjanoj offshore."

8 *Social'no-èkonomičeskoe položenie Respubliki Belarus'*, various months, January–July 2010.

9 This especially affected state employees, an important Lukashenka constituency. According to one of Russia's major newspapers, the salaries of state-sector employees increased 50% in the year preceding the election. Ivanter and Aleksievich, "Ranennyj zubr."

not only buffer the impact of changed trade conditions, but even to increase wages during this period was due to a temporary combination of favorable circumstances and borrowing into future earnings, rather than to the Belarusian government having found a sustainable long-term solution to the matter. The bill for these expansionist policies, as will be discussed below, would become due in 2011.

The Russia-Kazakhstan-Belarus Customs Union and the Search for Continued Energy Advantages

If the attempt to maintain preferential energy conditions on the basis of the special bilateral relationship had *de facto* if not *de jure* failed by late 2009, the following year would provide new opportunities to continue (despite worsening relations with Russia) the game of "virtual integration," but now at another level and with additional players. Negotiations around the Russia-Kazakhstan-Belarus Customs Union that was to be inaugurated in July 2010, would provide ample opportunities for this.[10] If the Russian interest in the Union was related first and foremost to its desire to use it for political purposes, Lukashenka's interests were more direct: to use negotiations on possible membership as a means to exert pressure on Russia for a return to preferential energy trade conditions. Throughout 2009 and 2010, Belarus sought to use negotiations around the Customs Union and a Single Economic Space as a way to maintain or reinstitute preferential energy trade terms. This attempt was carried out on several fronts. On the one hand, in April 2010 Belarus sued Russia in the CIS Economic Court, arguing for the illegality of oil export duties on supplies between member states;[11] more generally, it insisted that oil supplies within the Customs Union should not be subject to export duties (in any case an instrument used by very few states besides Russia). In the gas area, Belarus continued its attempt to re-negotiate the 2007 agreements (calling for a move to European prices for Belarus by 2011) by continuing to insist that the move to netback pricing in Russia and Belarus should take place simulta-

10 A Eurasian Economic Union was created in 2000 with Russia, Belarus, Kazakhstan, Tadzhikistan and Kyrgyzstan. In 2006, three member states (Russia, Belarus and Kazakhstan) decided to start the process of developing a tighter Customs Union. On this basis, the Single Economic Space launched in January 2012 seeks to expand cooperation beyond trade issues to eventually create a single market. See Zagorski, "Russia's neighbourhood policy."

11 Belarus withdrew the suit in April 2011 on the assumption the issue would be regulated by Single Economic Space/Customs Union agreements regulating trade between Belarus, Kazakhstan and Russia.

neously (i.e., in 2014, so as to create "equal competitive conditions" for enterprises in all member states).[12] It also sought to include in Single Economic Space documents a point about the three member countries' simultaneous move to netback pricing.[13] Russia, however, remained reticent in its refusal to tie the Customs Union question to trade preferences in the energy area. At the same time, Russia sought to both assuage Belarus, and pressure her to join the Single Economic Space by arguing—without providing much detail on how—that the issue would take care of itself once the organization was fully in place. A similar approach was visible in the oil area, where in October 2010, Russia promised Belarus it would eliminate export duties on crude oil supplies as soon as Belarus would sign the Single Economic Space agreements.[14] Despite Belarusian attempts to use the Customs Union as a way to maintain or reinstitute preferential energy trade terms, there were inherent limitations to Belarus' ability to benefit from membership in the organization. At the very core of these limitations was the fact that, as the Union's sole energy-poor member state, Belarus faced very different challenges from those faced by Kazakhstan or Russia.

Belarus conducted its pre-accession negotiations as high-stake ones, implicitly threatening not to join the Union if its conditions were not met.[15] However, not joining would have put Belarus in a very difficult position, as it already had a separate Customs Union agreement with Russia (dating from 1995) which did not automatically translate into membership in the new organization. In defeat, Belarus joined the Union at the very last moment, (the official announcement came on July 3, three days after it was created), with the event receiving minimum coverage in the official media as a means to limit the domestic public relations loss-of-face that could be associated with such an awkward about-face.[16] Afterwards, Belarus continued to conduct negotiations within the Union—this time around the signing of the actual package of documents related to the creation of a Single Economic Space within the framework of the Customs Union—as a means to

12 Manenok, "Gazovye nedogovorennosti."

13 Zhbanov, "Ne v brov', a v gaz."

14 Manenok, "Gazovye nedogovorennosti."

15 As part of the high-profile treatment of the issue, as the Russian side declined to fulfill these conditions, Lukashenka cancelled an important visit to Moscow to discuss the issue, implying Belarus would not join the Union under such conditions. Russia and Kazakhstan answered by saying they would go ahead as planned (and that Belarus could join afterwards).

16 It is not fully clear when Belarus ratified the agreement. See Yafimava, "The June 2010 Russian-Belarusian," 12–13.

pressure for the continuation or re-establishment of preferential energy trade conditions. Thus, Belarus used the Customs Union as a means to continue longstanding debates with Russia, but now at the multilateral level provided by the organization. Russia, for its part, insisted in keeping gas and oil trade issues outside of the agreement. At the same time, the Customs Union agreements further reduced the policy instruments available to Belarus to compensate for changes in Russian trade policies (for example, being now bound to apply the same level of oil product export duties as Russia).

Attempts at Oil and Gas Diversification

Many of the exploratory discussions on diversification started around 2007 became a reality in 2010, when Belarus responded to its new oil trade situation by, first and foremost, seeking out new partners. Venezuela, with whom an oil-producing joint venture had been established in 2007, presented important opportunities. Between April and August 2010, four shipments of Venezuelan oil had been received, routed via terminals at Odessa and Muuga (Estonia). Although these first shipments, around 0.32 million tons in total, represented less than 1.6 percent of Belarus' yearly oil imports, the March 2010 agreement between Presidents Lukashenka and Chávez spoke of yearly supplies of four million tons, around 20 percent of Belarus' yearly imports. In the first ten months of 2011, Belarus imported 1.3 million tons of Venezuelan oil.[17]

Although the prices reportedly paid were nearly 20 percent higher than those paid to Russia at the time ($656/ton vs. $550/ton for Russian oil including duties),[18] the lighter Venezuelan oil allowed for easier processing into higher value-added, higher-profitability light oil products, partially compensating for the higher price. Most importantly, these imports provided Belarus with new—if limited—means of applying pressure on Moscow.

At the same time, the payment conditions for these imports remained murky, and the possibility of corruption could not be excluded.[19] In fact, as

17 See Ivashkevich, "Belarus' i neft': po trope kontrabandistov," 1.

18 See Manenok, "Aprobacija severnogo tranzita."

19 On non-transparent deals and possible corruption around Belarusian-Venezuelan oil operations and on weapons trade involving Belarus, Venezuela, and Colombian terrorist groups, see Rico, "Los papeles de las FARC," Nekrasevic, "Kto prodvigaet belorusskie interesy v Venesuèle?" and additional materials from *Belgazeta* and *Svobodnie Novosti-Ekspress*, November 2010. Having fallen off from the official hierarchy in 2008, Viktar Sheiman reappeared in the scene a year later as Lukashenka's personal representative in Venezuela.

found by Belarusian analysts, import operations involving Venezuelan oil and various swap operations around it occasionally served as a façade for corrupt operations involving the smuggling of Russian crude oil to Belarus under the guise of oil products, at the expense of the Russian budget which, it is alleged, in 2010 alone lost over $500 million in lost export duties.[20]

The Summer of 2010: Gazprom's warning and renewed propaganda battle

The summer of 2010 saw an unprecedented low in Russian-Belarusian relations. Russia's hardening positions on the energy issue, as well as the general worsening of relations, seemed to be related to Lukashenka's continued refusal to recognize Abkhazia and South Ossetia, his May 2009 refusal to take up his role as rotating chair of the Collective Security Treaty Organization, and general foot-dragging concerning Russian participation in the privatization of Belarusian refineries.

Exemplary of this new situation was a small-scale gas crisis in June 2010, where Gazprom threatened to suspend gas supplies should Belarus not pay its $187 million gas debt. The crisis came as a surprise, especially considering the fact that, by June 2010, Gazprom had reached 50 percent control of Beltransgaz, and in March 2010 a representative of the company had become head of the Beltransgaz's Supervisory Board. Given the fact that—as became clear during the course of the crisis—Gazprom ultimately owed Beltransgaz a similar amount in transit fees, it seems unclear why such a crisis should have emerged at all, forcing one to wonder whether it was not intended as a warning from Gazprom.[21] A mighty Kremlin-supported media campaign against Lukashenka followed, crowned by the showing on NTV (a Gazprom-friendly TV channel) of a four-part documentary, *Krestny Batka*, associating Lukashenka with a series of criminal offenses, including the disappearance (and presumed death) of four political opponents in the late 1990s. Lukashenka responded with a PR initiative of his own, placing a challenging open letter to the Russian leadership in Russia's Communist Party newspaper *Pravda*, holding a combative press conference with Russian journalists, meeting Moscow

20 See Ivashkevich, "Belarus' i neft': po trope kontrabandistov."

21 After a 30% reduction, regular supplies were restored after Belarus paid back its debt in full. It later became known that Azerbaijan's president Heydar Alyev had made the funds available to Lukashenka to pay this debt.

foe Georgian President Mikheil Saakashvili and, in October 2010 welcoming to Minsk the leader of Russia's Communist opposition, Gennadyi Ziuganov. By this point, relations seemed to have reached a point of no return.

Lukashenka, energy relations with Russia, and the Belarusian opposition's appeal to the electorate

The summer 2010 confrontation with Gazprom helped to highlight something already seen in previous energy crisis situations: Lukashenka's ability to successfully portray these confrontations to his own electorate not as a failure of his policies of integration with Russia, but as evidence of his own statesmanship in defense of Belarusian statehood. (Although the period of Lukashenka's rule was also a period of increased Russification, from the mid-2000s, he started to emphasize certain elements of Belarusian unique identity as separate from Russia's, and his role as guarantor of these, undoubtedly as a means to increasing his domestic appeal at times of worsening relations with Russia.) In doing so, Lukashenka was in fact continuing the type of politicization he had been conducting at the time of the 2007 crisis when, vis-à-vis the Belarusian electorate and even the opposition, he was able to present himself as a defender of Belarusian national interests in the face of Russia's encroachment and insult.[22] Indeed, in the immediate aftermath of the December 2006–January 2007 gas and oil conflict, 52.6 percent of those polled in Belarus agreed that Lukashenka had proved himself to be a "strong politician, capable of attaining his goals," in contrast with only 25.7 percent who believed he had acted as a "weak politician and made too many concessions."[23] Even opposition leader Stanislau Bohdankevich (Stanislav Bogdankevich), honorary head of the United Civic Party, felt compelled to comment: "Today, let's say, I personally share Lukashenka's position, as defender of the country's sovereignty and independence. But

22 One issue that was especially insulting for the Belarusian public was the constant reference in the Russian mass media to Belarus "not paying for gas," although Belarus' payment arrears during this period never reached levels comparable with Ukraine's. Moreover, as noted by Feduta (*Lukashenko*, 635), although the Belarusian *state* may have been in arrears vis-à-vis Gazprom, actual Belarusian end consumers had been paying their gas bills regularly, so Russian accusations sounded especially offensive to them. By 2003, cash collections by gas distributor Beltopgas had increased markedly and reached more than 85%. (See Figure 1.2 in World Bank, "Belarus: Addressing Challenges," 1.) The Belarusian failure to pay Gazprom in full, despite receiving payments from local consumers that more than covered the import price paid to Gazprom (see Table 3.9 in this book), seemed to be part of a larger strategy to take maximum advantage of the relationship with Gazprom, discussed in Chapter 3.

23 *Novosti NISEPI* 1/43, 2007, 15 (Table 20).

I do not share his impulsiveness, and aggressiveness, which turns into enemies not only the European Union, not only the USA, but ally [*soyuznaya*] Russia."[24]

At the same time, Russia's energy pressure on Belarus, and Lukashenka's proactive rhetorical explanation of it as an assault on Belarusian sovereignty affected the opposition by taking away from it two important "monopolies." First, as Belarus' improved relations with the EU in 2009-2010 were partially related to the Union's fear of Russian energy imperialism, the improved relationship with the EU meant the opposition's loss of its status as virtually its single interlocutor in Belarus, as Belarusian authorities "suddenly emerged as competitors for Western attention."[25] Second and most importantly, Lukashenka's sovereignity-based reading of the conflict took away from the opposition the monopoly on "pro-national" positions in Belarus. Openly decrying Russian pressure on Belarus, the regime took away from the opposition an important set of slogans.

The opposition started to decry Lukashenka's erratic behavior in the by now frequently recurring energy confrontations, and to call for more predictability in relations with Russia; they also criticized his growing friendship with authoritarian Third-World leaders such as Hugo Chávez, despite their possible role as source of energy diversification. Lukashenka was quick to strike back, accusing opposition leaders of betraying national interests to Moscow's advantage. A few weeks before the elections, Lukashenka publicly chastised presidential candidate Uladzimir Niakliaew for proposing to sell the Belarusian gas pipeline system to Gazprom.[26]

Yet, in December of that year, barely a week before the December 19 presidential elections, the Kremlin seemed to provide a renewed blessing for Lukashenka's electoral bid, in the form of concessions on increased duty-free crude oil supplies.[27] Many interpreted the meeting as a signal that Russia

24 Bogdankevich, in "Vremia gostei." For a discussion of poll data on how the January 2007 energy confrontation increased Lukashenka's rating even in close-to opposition sectors, see Rakova, "Rossijsko-belorusskie ènergetičeskie raznoglasiâ."

25 Silitski, "The State, Elections, and the Opposition."

26 See RFE/RL program for Belarus, *Ranishni ehyvy efir*, November 19, 2010. For Niaklajeu's declaration on the sale of oil and gas pipelines, see Andrei Dynko, "NJaklJajew hocha stac" bol"sh ruskim za Lukashenku," *Nasha Niva* 41 (687), November 3, 2010, 2, 7.

27 The announcement was made by Lukashenka after his meeting with Russian president Dmitry Medvedev on December 9, 2010, but no details of the deal were provided until early 2011. The agreement with Russia was preceded by a November 2 joint visit by Polish and German Foreign Ministers Guido Westerwelle and Radosław Sikorski, a visit interpreted by many as playing into Lukashenko's game of using any signs of support from the West to pressure Russia into providing Belarus additional advantages, lest Belarus be "lost" to the West.

would recognize the results of the election regardless of any manipulations, and as *carte blanche* for Lukashenka to use force against those opposing the results. On December 19, official results announced Lukashenka had been re-elected with nearly 80 percent of the votes; independent exit polls showed a much more modest result (51.1 percent).[28] Yet on the very night of the elections, after opposition protests against election fraud, a wave of mass repression quickly unfurled, including the jailing of five out of nine opposition candidates.

Did this mean the end of tensions with the Russian leadership? No—already on December 26 a program critical of Lukashenka's repressions was shown on one of Russia's most influential TV channels, NTV, undoubtedly with the blessing of the Kremlin, and Moscow's pressure for the freeing of Russian citizens detained in post-election protests continued. Indeed, there was a logic to this apparent chaos of constant ups and downs in the relationship: to the game of "virtual integration" was now added a game of "virtual divorce."[29] Mutual recriminations and make-ups continued, yet each time at a worsened level of real relations. If it could still be expected for the game of virtual integration to continue and that each "low" in the relationship would be followed by a new "high," both the high and the low points in the relationship became increasingly lower, decreasing the base value of the relationship.[30] In other words, as in the 1990s and 2000s, each low in the relationship was followed by a high, but with every passing year, both the lows and the highs would both be lower. The economic concessions made during each high point were also becoming increasingly less generous, and Belarus was further reducing its means of counter-power vis-à-vis Russia. In January 2010, Belarus agreed to set its oil transit fees in agreement with Russia, with the provision that, in the event of a lack of agreement, Belarus would only have the right to increase these fees by the rate of inflation in Russia,[31] thus losing one more instrument of counter-pressure (the power to set transit fees) within the relationship.

28 Source: *Novosti NISEPI*, Table 16 in the report of December 21-31, 2010 national poll, available at http://www.iiseps.org/data10-431.html (both accessed May 26, 2011).

29 Although not using the term "virtual divorce," Karbalevich, *Aleksandr Lukashenko*, 541, refers to closely related dynamics.

30 This is evident, for example, in the unprecedented (and, most likely, fully intentional) way Russian PM Putin referred to the relationship, at a time of relative calm in between the partners in January 2011, as one of subsidization: "We will strive to keep to keep the level of *subsidization* of the Belarusian economy" at the same level as in 2007–2008, "4.124 billion US dollars" (emphasis mine). Putin quotation from the official site of the Prime Minister of the Russian Federation.

31 Manekok, "Plata za komfortnyj zapusk EÈP."

The Lukashenka-Kremlin disputes in the context of the December 2010 elections

The sharp worsening of Russian-Belarusian relations in the year of presidential elections created new challenges for all the parties involved. (It may indeed be argued that the timing of the crisis was no coincidence, but a concerted attempt by Russia to create a crisis exactly in an election year.) For Russia, the elections brought to the fore the question of whether to support an opposition candidate, "create" its own candidate, or simply exert pressure on Lukashenka through the implicit threat of a possible non-recognition of the electoral results.

If navigating the landscape of uncertain Russian intentions was a challenge for Lukashenka, this was compensated for by his relative advantage in the home front. This advantage had to do not only with the bonus of being an incumbent president, but with his rhetorical abilities, for which the Summer 2010 confrontation with Russia provided a perfect stage. As in previous energy confrontations, Lukashenka was able to turn the tense situation with Russia in Summer 2010 to his advantage, by presenting himself as defender of a Belarusian-Russian Union and against "some elements" in Russia ("oligarchs") seeking to sabotage Belarus' independence. This was followed by much more aggressive statements in defense of Belarusian sovereignty in the face of Russian encroachment.

Although it was likely exactly the promise of Russian support which emboldened Lukashenka for a new wave of repression immediately following the December 19 vote, soon afterwards he was once again able to manipulate opposition declarations as means of presenting himself as a Belarusian patriot: the declarations of first Belarusian head of state Stanislau Shushkevich who declared, in shock at the wave of repression, that Russia, as part of its Union agreements with Belarus, should consider sending troops there to prevent further human rights violations,[32] were used by Lukashenka as an important means to discredit the opposition.

The development of an anti-Kremlin rhetoric for domestic consumption allowed Lukashenka to turn worsening relations with Russia into an asset in its own relationship with the Belarusian electorate. On the one side, this went hand-in-hand with the development of a "national ideology" starting in 2003, which, in turn, could be seen as a response to the failure of the inte-

32 See Stanislau Shushkevich, declarations in RFE/RL program for Belarus.

gration process with Russia, as the development of such a "national ideology" would be a natural way to justify the now undeniable reality of a more distant relationship.[33] At the same time, it is clear that the main purpose for Lukashenka in establishing a national ideology was the same as in his long battle against Russian energy investments in Belarus: not necessarily to defend Belarus' sovereignty, but to further strengthen his personal control over the country.

After the Elections: From Euphoria to Forced Concessions?

In the immediate aftermath of the elections and the ensuing wave of repression against the opposition, Lukashenka seemed once again to have outwitted everyone: the EU (which had believed his promises of freer elections); the Belarusian opposition (which had also taken Lukashenka's promise at face value and agreed to participate in the elections, and was now leaderless and impotent), and Russia itself (which once again found itself with no better choice but to support Lukashenka, at least in the short term). But the bubble of optimism that had accompanied the run-up to the elections would burst quickly after December 19.

By February 2011, one by one, each of the elements of the 2010 pre-election euphoria (improved relations with the West, a growing economy, and the maintenance of a preferred mode of relations with Russia) quickly started to come apart. Relations with the West, which had experienced a renaissance in 2010, quickly turned around in the wake of the post-election repression. Surprisingly, considering his previous attempts to balance relations between Russia and the EU, Lukashenka dangerously allowed this relationship to further deteriorate. Moreover, in exactly May 2011, as the domestic situation was worsening, Lukashenka allowed himself a series of unusually harsh statements vis-à-vis the EU and head of the European Commission José Manuel Barroso, which coincided with guilty verdicts and long sentences of five to six years for the former presidential candidates Andrei Sannikaw, Mikalai Statkevich, and Dzmitry Us.[34]

33 On the development of a Belarusian national ideology, see Goujon, *Révolutions politiques et identitaires en Ukraine et Biélorussie.*

34 Two additional candidates, Uladzimir Niaklajeu and Vital Rymasheuski, received two-year suspended sentences.

The economy quickly had to start compensating for the unsustainably expansionist policies of 2010. By February, the government had sharply restricted access to foreign currency and long queues had formed at exchange kiosks. By late March, Belarus' National Bank had reintroduced multiple exchange rates, a crude central-planning mechanism not used since the 1990s. On May 24, the Belarusian rouble was devaluated by an unprecedented 54.4 percent. As a result, average monthly wages, which had reached some $530 at the end of 2010, fell to around $317.[35] (Real wages also went down by about 24 percent during this period.) By April, the head of Belarus' statistical service had stated that an estimated 600,000 workers had been laid off or put on temporary unpaid leave as a result of the crisis,[36] a terrifying prospect for Minsk, as it meant not only a strong challenge to the Belarusian social contract model, but the prospect of thousands of new potential participants at opposition meetings.

Problems with access to foreign currency led to sharp increases in the price of some imported goods, and to the disappearance of others from store shelves. Restrictions on the use of credit and bank cards, and the sharp increase in the cost of gasoline, touched the middle classes especially hard. For the middle class, at issue was not so much economic survival per se, but the concrete content of the social contract tying them, however precariously, to the regime. This was seen clearly in the nature of protests that touched Belarus in 2011: not a continuation of traditional political protests, but so-called silent protests, and the non-politically motivated "Stop Benzin" campaign against increased gasoline prices. In a result unprecedented in the previous 17 years, some of the "Stop Benzin" protests had an immediate effect: after gasoline prices had increased 30 percent, on June 9, Lukashenka ordered them reduced by 20 percent. The protests and their success in limiting gasoline price increases also had distributional effects: unable to fully pass on to end consumers their higher (dollar-denominated) import costs, refineries, electricity generating companies and heat providers effectively became donors to other sectors of the economy and, with their own losses, helped limit the further depreciation of the BLR.[37]

In addition, one perverse coincidence also helped worsen the situation: with the February announcement that sharply higher duties on the import

35 Andrei Liakhovich, "Razvitie situacii v Belarusi."

36 Declarations of head of the National Statistics Committee Vladimir Zinovskyi.

37 IPM, *BMER* 8/107, August 2011, 2. Some electricity contracts with juridical persons adjust automatically to reflect changes in the US$/BLR exchange rate.

ing of used cars would enter into effect in July as a result of Belarus' joining the Customs Union, many citizens rushed to use their 2010 income gains to buy used cars abroad before the new duties (from four to ten times higher than existing ones) would come into effect, doubling the import of cars relative to previous periods, and creating an additional demand for foreign currency estimated at around $1.25 billion.[38] This came in the wake of a veritable consumer spending splurge in the last quarter of 2010.[39]

Most importantly from the point of view of our study, Lukashenka's preferred mode of relations with Russia, based on the idea of securing the maximum possible subsidies for Belarus, but without giving up control and ownership of important economic assets, entered a crisis phase.

On the one hand, the quick depletion of Belarus' currency reserves resulting from 2010's pre-election spending spree was made worse by the new oil trade conditions effective from 2011. In fact, despite the pledges offered by Moscow just before the elections that it would continue to support Belarus through even more generous trade terms, 2011 started poorly for Belarus' oil sector. At issue was the division of oil products export rents between various Belarusian and Russian market players, as Russian oil producers saw the new trade conditions as particularly beneficial to Belarus.[40] Under these new conditions, Russia would no longer charge oil export duties on any oil exported to Belarus (as compared to the previous year, where only oil intended for domestic use was supplied duty-free), in exchange for Belarus handing to Russia all export duties levied on the resulting oil products. As the latter duties were significantly lower per unit than those levied on crude oil, this meant significant savings for Belarus and, in particular, increased profits for non-tolling refining operations by Belarusian refineries. Wanting to share into this new source of rents, Russian oil producers insisted that a "price premium" of around $45 per ton be paid to the Russian companies above and beyond the base price, increasing Belarus' oil imports bill. While the discussion ensued, Belarus remained with no oil supply contract, and with no oil deliveries from Russia for almost all of January, which led to a significant reduction in oil product exports and related export revenue.

38 Estimated by the author from data in Alesin, "Konec ažiotaža." Although the document on increased duties on imported cars had been signed earlier, until July 1, 2011 Belarus was covered by a temporary exception. See also Ioffe and Yarashevich, "Debating Belarus," 751.

39 Zlotnikov, "The Foreign Exchange Crisis."

40 Other commentators have noted additional items straining the Belarusian-Russian oil relationship: Belarus' intention to increase oil transit fees effective from February 1, 2011, and Belarus' agreement with Ukraine to transit Venezuelan oil (swapped for Azeri) through the Odessa-Brody pipeline.

At the same time that oil-related revenues were diminishing, the amount spent by Belarus on the purchase of Russian gas was rising rapidly: from 2009 to 2010, it increased by 65 percent, to $4.24b; the estimate was $5.3b for 2011. (See Table 5.6). As a percentage of the country's GDP, the change for the worse was staggering: expenditures on gas imports increased from 2.8 percent of GDP in 2006 to 5.2 percent in 2009, and to around 8.9 percent in 2011.[41] Moreover, the lack of foreign currency was making it harder and harder for Belarus to pay back this bill. Given the sheer impact of these increases, negotiating a discount on these prices would have been the simplest way to achieve a short-term improvement in the current-account balance. After trying all possible means to slow the increase in gas prices, by June of 2011, under the pressure of sharply worsened current account balances (at a negative $4.8b),[42] and a sharp loss in value of the BLR, a sense of urgency was taking hold of President Lukashenka, who probably remembered how a similar gas crisis in 1993 had quickly deteriorated into hyper-inflation. Desperate to reduce expenditures on gas, and for an influx of foreign currency to help stop a dangerous trade deficit and inflationary process, Lukashenka was moving closer to an idea he had considered anathema for almost two decades: the sale of gas-transit company Beltransgaz to Gazprom.

Belarus had little choice but to acquiesce to the conditions proposed by Moscow: selling the remaining 50 percent of Beltransgaz in exchange for Russian approval of a $3 billion loan from the Stabilization Fund of the Eurasian Economic Community (EurAsEC)[43] and a reduction in the 2012 price of gas to $165/tcm, a yearly saving of $3b compared to the 2011 gas bill. Taken together, the injection of $2.5 billion for the purchase of Beltransgaz shares (transferred on December 3), and $1.24 billion for the first two installments of the EurAsEC loan meant a deep short-term respite for Lukashenka. Taken together with the savings implied in the 2012–2014 gas contracts, this new influx of money would allow the Belarusian economy to survive in the short term, despite its continued inefficiency and the burden of $12.3 billion in state

41 Calculated on the basis of gas imports expenditures data from Table 5.6 in this book, and nominal GDP in US$ from IPM, *BMER* 3/114, March 2012, 5.

42 IPM, *BMER* 6/105, June 2011, 5.

43 As a condition for the provision of $3b in loans (with $800m to be disbursed in June 2011, and the remaining $2.2b in five installments of $440m over three years), EurAsEC's stabilization fund stipulated Belarus should, between 2011 and 2013, privatize, via direct foreign investments, industrial and commercial actives in the value of $7.5b (i.e., $2.5b per year). See IPM, *BMER* 6/105, June 2011, 1, and Manenok, "Ne myt'em, tak katan'em." The $2.5b privatization due in 2011 corresponded exactly the sale price of the remaining shares of Beltransgaz.

and private loan payments becoming due in 2012.[44] The new, lower gas prices also meant a further delay in the reform of Belarus' economy, away from reliance on large energy-inefficient industries.

Conclusion

Through the fast-paced developments of 2010 and 2011, Belarus seemed to continue the pattern of cyclical highs and lows seen in its relationship with Russia since 1994. Yet now both the highs and the lows were becoming lower, and Belarus' base bargaining position was quickly worsening with Russia's ability to transit gas and oil through alternative routes. With higher base oil and gas prices, Russia was also much more able to exert economic pressure on Belarus.

Despite Lukashenka's success at negotiating lower gas prices in exchange for the selling of Beltransgaz, and better oil trade conditions as a result of joining the Customs Union, none of this promised a lasting solution to the question of Belarus' medium- and long-term development and incorporation into a globalized world economy. Indeed, the short-term economic respite of late 2011 promised to be exactly that: a short-term respite. Lukashenka's preference—selling the controlling package of shares in Beltransgaz, as long as this assured Belarus access to gas at domestic Russian prices[45]—was not fully achieved. Despite the new contract stipulating significantly lower gas prices (around $165/tcm as opposed to $265 in 2011) for the 2012–2014 period, the promise of receiving domestic Russian prices (in this case equivalent to these in the Yamal-Nenets Autonomous Area)[46] would only kick in by 2015. Yet, with many developments between 2012 and 2015 out of Belarus' control—in particular, changes in Belarus' and Russia's relative positions of power given Russia's growing ability to transit oil and gas to Western Europe by circumventing Belarus, and further delays in Russia's implementation of netback

44 In addition to $1.7b in state loans payments due in 2012, Zlotnikov estimated $10-11b in payments due from loans taken by Belarus' commercial banks and enterprises. Leanid Zlotnikau (Leonid Zlonikov), in Radio Svadova *Blic-analiz*, January 30, 2012, transcript available at www.svaboda.org/content/article/24468191.html (accessed March 10, 2012). Belarus' 2011 gross external debt was 66.8% of GDP, nearly three times higher than in 2008. See IPM, *BMER* 4/127, April 2013, 5.

45 Aleksander Lukashenka, declarations during visit to Mogilev, May 27, 2010, cited by Tatiana Manenok, "Derzhat' sosedej 'v tonuse.'"

46 Liakhovich, "Razvitie situacii v Belarusi vo vtoroj polovine Nojabrja 2011 goda: osnovnye sobytija i kommentarii."

pricing in its own domestic market—it remains open to question whether Lukashenka's dream of receiving energy at domestic Russian prices can be attained again. With renewed Russian pressure for monetary unification on Russia's terms appearing in 2011, Lukashenka's dream of having it all—Russian subsidies, but full control of economic policy in Belarus—seemed to be growing less and less realistic.

7

Conclusion

The repressive aftermath of the December 2010 presidential elections, together with the economic crisis of spring 2011, leave open many questions regarding Belarus' future political development.

Yet, regardless of how much longer Lukashenka will remain in power, a number of conclusions can be drawn about the role and long-term impact of the energy policies and discourses implemented by him during the 1994–2011 period. Analysis of these policies, discourses, and of Russian-Belarusian energy relations more generally allows us to draw broader conclusions about the nature of the Belarusian political system, Belarusian-Russian relations, and Russian energy behavior in the post-Soviet region. Last but not least, what we have learned in this book allows us to take a critical view at the impact of the Lukashenka legacy for Belarus and for Western policy towards the country.

Energy, power, and Lukashenka's constituencies

Lukashenka's adroit use of energy policies and discourses allowed him, in the short term, to maximize advantages vis-à-vis three important counterparts: Russian actors, the local *nomenklatura*, and the Belarusian electorate. At the same time, these strategies also carried within them important elements of instability and longer-term pressure for change.

What have we learned about Belarusian-Russian relations? Lukashenka, energy, and Russian constituencies

Lukashenka used energy policies and discourses craftily in relations with Russia, and in doing so, he perceptively followed distinct approaches to various Russian actors which included, in addition to the Kremlin, the military leadership, oil companies and traders, gas monopolist Gazprom, and provincial politicians. Towards each of these constituencies, distinct policies were pursued emphasizing Belarus' value in areas of their specific interest, be it in terms of the symbolic value of the relationship per se (vis-à-vis the top leadership) or of Belarus as a developmental alternative to Russia's high-social-cost post-communist transition (vis-à-vis provincial leaders and communist politicians), in terms of concrete military–strategic advantages (vis-à-vis the military and the top leadership), or of its role in the value-added chain and profit maximization by Russian energy producers (vis-à-vis the oil companies and Gazprom).

In relation to each of these groups, Lukashenka's Belarus was not only a recipient, but also a provider of both tangible and intangible goods. Within the realm of "intangible goods," we should not underestimate the value of psychological elements in the relationship in terms of helping individual Russian leaders deal with the trauma of the loss of empire and its domestic political consequences. Concerning the more tangible goods provided by Belarus as partner to each of the actors above, some of these were more straightforward in nature (use of military facilities), while others, such as those in the energy area, where mediated by the particular value-added chains of specific Russian actors.

While Lukashenka was able to carefully play the game of appealing specifically to various Russian constituencies in a way that enhanced his regime's stability, this strategy was not immune to pressure for change, including pressure from international markets (through changes in European prices for gas and oil, for example), which affected Russian energy actors' calculations concerning the value of their operations through (and preferential treatment of) Belarus.

What have we learned about the Belarusian political system? Lukashenka, energy, and the Belarusian *nomenklatura*

The patterns of energy rents discussed in this book also force us to reassess two central precepts about the way Lukashenka's Belarus worked during the period covered by this book..

The first belief has to do with the idea of Lukashenka's near-total control over Belarusian politics, prompting us to further examine the real power relationships within his "power vertical." In particular, struggles between various groups in the Lukashenka entourage for control of profitable rent-seeking monopolies emerge as especially important. In addition, the fact that Lukashenka partially relied on contributions from "outside" businessmen (i.e., businessmen not part of the Presidential Administration, even when their access to rent-seeking opportunities was ultimately dependent on the president's favor) to carry out politically prestigious projects adds a small element of reciprocity to a relationship normally approached only from the perspective of Lukashenka's unilateral power.

The real picture is a much more nuanced one, where both cooptation and control played a role. By giving individual members (or groups) of the *nomenklatura* the approval (and, in many cases, active support through changes in rules and regulations) to engage in profitable rent-seeking, the system worked as an important instrument of elite cooptation and reward. At the same time, the energy rent-seeking system helped Lukashenka exercise control over these elites. It did so by providing additional opportunities for pressure on and blackmail of his subordinates, and by helping shape a system of unwritten rules of the game regulating the relationship (with the caveat, however, that Lukashenka's impetuous decisions could never be totally excluded). Yet, these dynamics contained not only stabilizing elements, but also pressure for change, especially at times of shrinking energy rents, which created pressure for a re-accommodation of relations inside the *nomenklatura*.

Secondly, the evidence presented in this book forces us to reassess the role of the state in the economy. Despite Lukashenka's 1994 promise that the state and private sectors would be totally separate, many instances involving the use of official positions for private gain, or involving corruption, did exist. While official statistics (which show around 70 percent of GDP being generated by the state sector) and the official narrative of Belarus' path of development have emphasized the overwhelming role of the state in the economy, the evidence of energy rent-seeking and corruption, as well as personal interests in business operations related to the Presidential Administration force us to at least partially rethink this perspective. Many of the business operations conducted through the Presidential Administration could hardly be considered "state-owned," which, as discussed in Chapter 4, did not preclude them from receiving highly preferential treatment from the state, sometimes at the expense of actual state-owned businesses. In particular, the fact that regulations and rules of the game were often changed at the insistence of the Presidential Administration in order to give affiliated companies far-ranging privileges brings to the fore the question of state capture, bringing the Belarusian case closer to other post-Soviet cases (most notably Ukraine under Kuchma) than we would normally consider. This "capturing" does not necessarily need to be carried out by a business sector totally separate from the public sector, but may be carried out by state officials (effectively acting as semi-private businessmen), or organizations within the state. The amalgamation of presidential, "state" and "business" interests within organizations such as the Presidential Administration further muddled the picture.

The evidence presented in this book also forces us to rethink our assumptions about the differentiation of economic actors in Belarus. Behind the façade of state control of the economy, a real differentiation of economic interests was taking place during this period, which increased after new energy trade conditions were imposed by Russia in 2007. Going above and beyond the differing interests of various "clans" discussed in Chapter 4, this differentiation, including differentiation within the gas and oil sectors, encompassed actors such as tolling operators, managers of state-owned refineries, subsidiaries of Russian oil companies, and Presidential Administration bureaucrats-turned businessmen (see Figure 3.3, Table 3.4 and Table 6.1). Within this landscape, the extent to which crucial budget-contributing exporters such as the Naftan and Mozyr refineries (or others such as Grodno Azot, the largest producer of nitrogen fertilizers) and, alternatively, their managers, developed and retained separate corporate or personal interests independent of those of the state, is an area where further research is needed.

Given Lukashenka's record of intimidation and control over his own *nomenklatura*, it would be unrealistic to ascertain that these actors had any significant independent policy-making power during the period analyzed in this book. Yet, even taking into account the central role of the president, the differentiation of Belarusian economic interests—from each other but also from Russian ones—ultimately did start to take place during the Lukashenka period. If, indeed, the development of such interest-based actors is only at a very incipient stage and, in any case, remained largely underground, they will continue to develop and will increasingly come to the surface in a post-Lukashenka future. They are likely to play an important role in domestic policies and relations with both Russia and the West, and are likely to become the basis of support for important political actors. Thus, such actors will need to be reckoned with and taken into account in future policy-making vis-à-vis Belarus. It is time we started looking seriously at them.

What have we learned about Belarus' cycle of rents? Lukashenka's energy populism and the Belarusian electorate

As serious analyses of Belarus have shown, the Lukashenka regime has remained in power by much more than sheer repression, and its sources of popular support have been stronger than many would want to believe.[1] The trickling down of energy rents to support a populist agenda was crucial in this process, and the available evidence tells us of the tremendous impetus that energy rents provided to Lukashenka's project. The wide domestic distribution of these rents—through the keeping alive of an unreformed safety-net economy, through the general increase in wages, and through the targeted support of important constituencies such as the rural electorate—in turn guaranteed Lukashenka an important source of support.

Belarus' "energy-political model" not only helped keep afloat the economy as a whole, but also contributed directly to rising consumption levels as hard-currency earnings from the export of oil products to Western markets allowed the Belarusian government to maintain, until early 2011, a high value of the Belarusian rouble vis-à-vis the US dollar. This provided for increasing wages in dollar terms and made imported consumer goods increasingly accessible to the general population. Energy-related income also made possible the targeted support of specific social groups—such as the rural population—which also happened to be central sources of electoral support for Lukashenka. The new gas and oil agreements carved out by Lukashenka in

1 See Eke and Kuzio, "Sultanism"; Haiduk, "Social Contract"; Haiduk and Chubrik, "Specifikaciâ ponâtiâ"; Haiduk, Rakova and Silitski, *Social Contracts*; Ioffe, *Understanding Belarus*; Karbalevich, *Aleksandr Lukashenko*; Korosteleva, "Is Belarus"; Leshchenko, "The National Ideology"; Marples, "Color Revolutions"; and Pikulik, "Comparative Pathways."

late 2011—based on significantly reduced gas prices and the provision of oil on a 100 percent duty-free basis effective from January 1, 2012—once again provided the basis for keeping alive Belarus' unreformed safety-net economy, even if at a lower level than before.

However, this system was not free of internal contradictions, as the very policies and trickle-down effects of energy rents that allowed for the short-term rise in incomes and consumerism also solidified expectations of continued improvements in living standards. With the model clearly not sustainable in the long term, this increases the potential for social frustration should these expectations fail to be fulfilled.

The Belarus case and patterns of post-Soviet international relations

What have we learned about Russian energy behavior in the post-Soviet region?

Russia undeniably used energy to pursue foreign policy goals vis-à-vis Belarus. However, to look at the question solely in terms of "Russia's expansion" is not enough; it is no less important to look at the domestic conditions and cross-border ties of specific actors affecting Russia's ability to use energy as a foreign policy tool in specific countries such as Belarus. Similarly, focusing on Russia as a unitary actor has only limited explanatory power: as seen by the examples presented in this book, various actors within Russia exhibited distinct interests vis-à-vis Belarus. For example, part of the explanation for Russian acquiescence with Belarus' pre-2007 lack of compliance with existing agreements on the division of export duties had to do with the fact that such arrangements, while disadvantageous for the Russian budget, benefited Russian oil companies by allowing them to save on export duties that would otherwise go to the Russian budget. This tells us that, in order to understand Russian-Belarusian relations and Russian energy behavior in the post-Soviet area, we need to take into account that it was not simply some abstract "Russian side" that benefited from specific arrangements, but specific Russian actors with specific interests and distinct value-added chains, actors who, in turn, could affect Russian policy on related issues.

Above and beyond the specific case of Russian-Belarusian relations, the picture unveiled in this book tells us that, instead of focusing exclusively on energy relations as state-to-state relations, a more productive way of analyzing Russia's energy role in the region would pay special attention to the multiplicity of involved actors on the Russian side, and to their distinct interactions with the state on one hand and actors across borders on the other, and how these interactions are mediated by the distinct value chains prevalent in their specific industries.

Thus, for example, the unique value-added chains prevalent in the gas and oil sectors affected the distinct ways in which changes in international energy markets (and, in particular, price increases) would affect the preferences of various actors active in Belarus, and their relationship with Russian official state preferences. Growing European prices for gas, for example, increased Gazprom's opportunity costs in supplying gas to Belarus at preferential prices. Rising oil prices also had a variety of complex effects on various Russian actors: while they increased the gap between for-Belarus prices and those charged to Western European consumers and the opportunity cost of selling to Belarus instead of Western markets, they at times also increased the profits to be had from tolling oil operations via Belarus. In any case, the distributional effects of oil operations for a variety of Belarusian and Russian actors (oil companies with or without tolling operations, and the state) depended heavily on a variety of sectoral policy decisions including, among others: base prices charged to Belarus; any additional "premiums" paid to suppliers; how much oil Russian companies would be allowed to process in Belarus on a tolling basis (as opposed to through direct sales to Russian refineries); the cost of processing; the duty regime applied to crude oil supplies to Belarus; and the duty regime applied to the export of oil products from Belarus (including issues such as who would determine the level of these duties, what the level would be, and how they would be distributed between the Russian and Belarusian budgets). It is perhaps this complexity of policies and actors, which explains the constant change in policies between 2007 and 2011, and the constant bargaining about these.

As can be seen especially clearly in the case of oil and oil products trade, the rents accrued by Belarus as a result of its special relationship with Russia were effectively shared with Russian actors across the border. Interestingly, in the case of Belarus, this sharing of rents did not seem to take place so much at the expense of both states, as we saw in cases of energy corruption in Ukraine for example, but mostly at the expense of the *Russian* budget.[2] In fact, given

2 See Balmaceda, *Energy Dependency, Politics and Corruption*.

widely held assumptions about Belarus as a Russian client state, the Belarusian energy relationship with Russia turned out to be highly paradoxical. In the short term at least, President Lukashenka seemed to be able to push his interests—and perhaps the short-term interests of Belarus' population as well—more forcefully than less officially pro-Russian states such as Ukraine. This had to do, for example, with preferential trade agreements and with the broad sharing of energy trade rents throughout the population, as opposed to their concentration in the hands of a narrow group of "oligarchs" as seen in other cases such as Ukraine.[3]

Reassessing Belarusian-Russian relations and patterns of Russian behavior

If we look at the evolution of the Belarusian-Russian relationship through the prism of energy policy, several regularities and specificities can be discerned.

Partial institutionalization

First, a pattern where the value of official agreements was only limited. The politicization of the energy relationship discussed throughout this book was closely related to the weak contractual, corporate governance and property rights basis of the energy relationship between the partners. Despite the myriad agreements between both states concerning the creation of a single Union State, and energy relations more specifically, the actual behavior of the sides was only partially guided by these. Be it in the form of formulas for the division of oil products export duties in the early and mid-2000s (discussed in Chapter 3), or of blueprints for the gradual transition to European gas prices (discussed in Chapter 5), both of which were—to a lesser or greater degree—ignored, the weak contractual basis of the relationship could be seen. While contracts served a variety of purposes, once they no longer fulfilled one or both sides' goals, the problematic parts were often simply ignored.

This situation was part of a broader dynamic of weak institutionalization of the relationship, a dynamic that was manifested in a variety of ways: from the lack of a real, institutionalized union bringing together a core mass of post-

3 On the domestic distribution of energy rents in Ukraine, see ibid.

Soviet states (with Russia favoring bilateral relations), to the fact that many formal agreements were not followed, to the fact that the Belarusian-Russian Union remained for a long time a virtual good to be "cashed in" only at a some undetermined—and constantly deferred—future date. In fact, it could be argued that, even more than a lack of institutionalization per se, it was exactly the *partial institutionalization* of significant aspects of the relationship which, together with other factors, allowed Lukashenka to keep extracting energy rents and subsidies from Russia. Under a situation of full integration with Russia, Belarus would have been unable to, for example, maintain different oil product export duties than Russia, which lost billions of dollars of budget revenue in the process. Undoubtedly, this partial institutionalization benefitted many political and economic actors in both Belarus and Russia, allowing them to interpret various parts of existing agreements to their liking and, in general, to use these to advance their political goals, without having to engage in the much more problematic process of real integration.[4]

Russia's use of short-term preferential treatment for long-term advantage and Belarus' lost opportunities in the context of Russia's evolving energy strategies

A second regularity in the relationship was a cyclical pattern where energy pressure would be applied by the Russian side (in the form of higher gas prices or new oil trade conditions), with the implicit threat of reducing supplies and/or potential rents (a threat which on some occasions was carried through), but this was followed by other concessions on Russia's part which, if only partially, helped compensate for the new conditions. The examples of concrete Belarusian-Russian energy crises and their aftermath discussed in this book highlight how, after each crisis, the Russian side introduced a number of "softening" measures to prevent a collapse of the Belarusian economy. In many ways, these measures delayed the "moment of truth" for Belarus.

This "moment of truth," however, was looming closer as a result of two sets of developments. First, the gradual increase in energy prices charged Belarus to European ones, which—despite the short-term ups and downs related to yearly changes in regulations governing trade with Russia—would eventually lead to a decrease in the arbitrage gains and profits accruing to the coun-

4 On a related issue, see Danilovich, *Russian-Belarusian Integration*, 67

try.[5] This process is, in the final analysis, an unavoidable one, if only because it is related to deep changes underway in the domestic Russian energy political economy, such as the move towards higher "equal profitability" (*ravnaia dokhodnost'*) netback domestic energy prices.[6]

Second, the "moment of truth" was looming closer—and seemed to have a due date— with the commissioning of a number of Russian energy transit projects bypassing Belarus (first and foremost the Nord Stream gas pipeline). Looked at in this context, Russian energy policies vis-à-vis Belarus can be seen in a different light. Indeed, even those policies seemingly most advantageous to Belarus in the short term can be seen as a means of solidifying its dependency on Russia, not only in a general sense, but also very concretely to keep the country from looking for alternative energy sources until Russia's new pipeline projects would be completed and Belarus' counter power as a transit gateway would be greatly diminished. While some of the softening policies pursued by Russia, such as credits, contributed to increase Belarus' general dependency on Russia, others – such as agreements providing for low gas prices – had a more direct impact on the country's ability to diversify its energy supplies. In particular, some of the clauses attached to the 2011 agreement on the supply of oil duty-free were clear deterrents to diversification, as they stipulated that the premiums to be paid to Russian oil suppliers above and beyond the base price would increase if Belarusian imports would go below a certain threshold (21.7 Mt for 2011, i.e., 100 percent of the base consumption of oil), acting as a disincentive for both oil diversification and improved efficiency.

The agreements on the building of a new nuclear power plant, as discussed in Chapter 5, also add new types of energy dependency to those already tying Belarus to Russia. In this interpretation, once completion of the Nord Stream pipeline reduces Belarus' counter-power vis-à-vis Russia, Russia will be able to pressure Belarus much more effectively on issues of its interest, such as economic integration and control over Belarus' energy infrastructure – as was confirmed by Belarus' 2011 sale of Beltransgaz, a sale that deprived Belarus of one more element of counter-power vis-à-vis Russia.

The larger point is clear: as a result of a combination of factors, between 1995 and 2011 (especially 2003–2008), Belarus had access to an unprecedented windfall in energy profits, which until 2010 made possible robust increases in

5 On changing oil trade conditions, see Table 6.1.

6 On this issue see Balmaceda, *The Politics of Energy Dependency*, Chapter 3.

living standards and general economic well-being. Yet, Belarus did not use this windfall to engage in much-needed economic reforms and soften their blow. Neither did it use this windfall to prepare its economy for life after preferential trade conditions from Russia would come to an end. This is paradoxical, given the positive macroeconomic situation (and especially, the cushioning provided by high energy rents) present until at least 2006, which would have made such reforms much less painful than at a future point when such cushioning would no longer be available.

Lukashenka's energy legacy and the call of globalization: challenges for Belarus and the West

Even with Lukashenka still in power, we can already talk about a certain Lukashenka legacy in energy policy. Despite the significant changes in Belarusian energy policy in 2008–2010 in terms of searching for diversification alternatives, discussed in Chapters 5 and 6, the legacies of policies pursued since independence (and especially since 1994) will continue to matter, both in terms of the challenges the country will face, and of the technical and mental frameworks within which the country will have to deal with these.

This legacy is characterized by three main components.

First, that related to energy mixes. The Lukashenka regime, hostage to the euphoria that "Russia will supply us with cheap gas and only cheap gas,"[7] and seeking to reap maximum profits from highly preferential gas prices until 2006, made Belarus—a country with no domestic gas supplies, no alternative supply pipelines, and no port facilities to which a Liquified Natural Gas (LNG) terminal could be connected—one of the most gas-dependent countries in the world. Despite the initiative in the late 2000s to retro-fit a number of electricity-generation plants to make them run on fuels other than gas, the effects of a gas-based development model will continue to be seen for a long time.

A second long-term legacy concerns the role of Belarus as an oil refining center, and dependency on certain types of trade and trade arrangements with the major supplier, i.e., the inability of this sector—made into the main motor of Belarus' economic development under Lukashenka—to work prof-

7 Aleksandr Voitovich, quoted in Marina Mazurkevich, program "Drova, torf, veter i solnce," DW program for Belarus, February 4, 2007, available at: www.dw-world.de/dw/article/0,2144,2337240,00.html (accessed March 10, 2007).

itably under non-preferential trade conditions. The rapid increase in oil (and gas) prices is likely to lead to serious challenges to this mode of integration into the world economy. Once preferential price and trade conditions will no longer be available, this branch of the Belarusian economy (which for much of the 2000s accounted for over 35 percent of the country's exports) will cease to be competitive, forcing Belarus to rethink the character of its incorporation into the international division of labor. Lukashenka's Belarus has failed to develop an alternative model of how it could be sustainably incorporated into the international division of labor, a vision that could provide an alternative to a refining-and-exporting centered model, only sustainable under very special conditions of trade preferences and a favorable situation in international markets. If the particularities of the trade relationship with Russia provided significant oil refining and re-export rents in the short term, they also steered the country away from developing other economic sectors better suited for a small open economy such as Belarus.

A third legacy has to do with the role of Belarus' "energy-political model" in allowing the country to delay crucial economic reforms, and with the long-term impact of such a situation. For most of its first 20 years of independence, Belarus lived largely beyond its means.[8] This has manifested itself in increased wages and living standards, and has provided the basis for populist support of the president. Such an increase in living standards was made possible by a number of factors, of which energy subsidies from Russia was not the only one. Others included the delay of economic reform and its social costs, and a generally strong demand in world markets for Belarus' main exports outside the CIS (oil products, potash fertilizers and metals) for most of the period under study, which helped compensate the decreasing demand for Belarus' increasingly non-competitive traditional exports, mainly manufactured goods.

While providing for stability in the short and medium term, this arrangement was likely to backfire in the long term. Despite the income provided by Russian energy subsidies, the need for socially painful reforms has not magically withered away, but has simply been postponed; there is no doubt that such painful reforms will have to come one day. Yet once the (rents-supported) populist delaying of reforms will no longer be tenable, Belarus will

8 This was especially so during the oil import-and-refining-boom of the 2000s. According to calculations by economist Leonid Zlotnikov, between 2004 and 2009 Belarus consumed, in GDP terms, 19% more than it produced. Similarly, IMF calculations show how, from 2000 to 2009, increases in real wages significantly surpassed increases in productivity. See Graph "Labor Productivity and Wage Growth" in IMF Country Report No. 10/16 (2010), 17.

have to face serious economic costs – costs related, not only to a new type of relations with Russia, but to delayed reforms and to the need to finally pay for the living-beyond-one's means consumption of the 2000s.

Lukashenka's manipulation of energy relations with Russia throughout nearly two decades in power created difficult challenges for Western policy, torn between the perceived need for tougher policies and sanctions as a response to human rights abuses, and the fear that doing so may throw Belarus into a deeper embrace with Russia.

The legacies of this period will also create serious challenges for any post-Lukashenka government. Indeed, such challenges will eventually take place even if Lukashenka remains in power, but the challenge to the West will be especially high once a post-Lukashenka government takes power. When this happens, a serious confluence of circumstances is likely to come together: on the one hand, popular expectations will be high. Used to 15 years of rising living standards under Lukashenka, popular patience with any new regime that may attempt long-overdue but socially costly economic reforms is likely to be tested.

On the other hand, the objective conditions, in particular the burden of foreign debt re-payment, will make the situation especially difficult and will put any new regime under serious economic pressure.[9] On the part of the West, moreover, there will also be the temptation to turn attention away from Belarus once it no longer retains its unique and attention-grabbing role as the "last dictatorship in the middle of Europe." The challenges, however, will remain. With the Belarusian economy barely capable of functioning sustainably in a non-subsidized, no-preferences environment, the needed reforms and the closing of large energy-inefficient factories are likely to have huge social consequences for the country, with chain effects that could have politically destabilizing implications and send thousands of Belarusian economic refugees across the EU border.

The EU should be well-prepared to deal with such a scenario. It is exactly a post-Lukashenka government which, by having to carry out painful policies delayed during the Lukashenka period, will have to deal with a far-reaching pent-up economic crisis, a crisis which is closely connected to energy issues and which, should it fail to manage proactively, could lead to a quick return to authoritarian politics.

---

9 While relatively low, at below 25% of GDP for most of the 2000s, total foreign indebtedness grew sharply (to 52.2% of GDP in 2010 and 68.8% in 2011); payment of this debt will be especially difficult given worsening economic parameters in other areas. See Table 5.6.

Belarus in the Context of Russia's Major Oil and Gas Export Routes

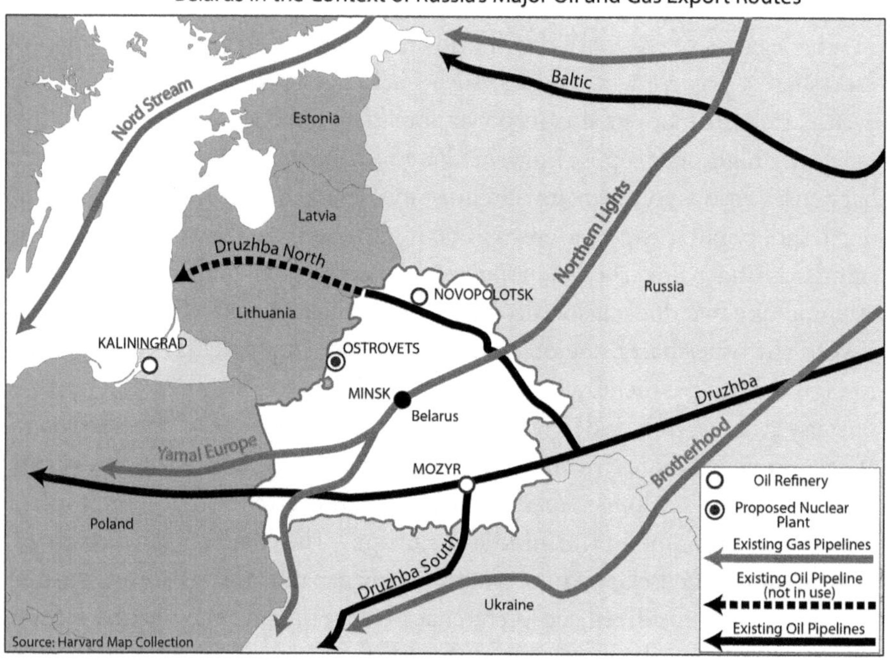

Bibliography

Abdelal, Rawi. "Interpreting Interdependence: Energy and Security in Ukraine and Belarus." PONARS Working Paper No. 20 (2002), available at: www.csis.org/ruseura/ponars/workingpapers/ (accessed October 10, 2006).

———. *National Purpose in the World Economy: Post Soviet States in Comparative Perspective.* Ithaca and London: Cornell University Press, 2001.

Agenstvo Finansovikh Novostei. "Nepotopljaemyj belorusskij neftjanoj offshore." (August 26, 2010), available at: http://afn.by/news/i/140372 (accessed April 4, 2011).

Agenstvo politicheskoi ekspertizi. "Segodnâ deševyj svet, a zavtra – ego otsutstvie? *Nashe Mnenie*, July 7, 2010. Available at http://nmnby.eu/news/analytics/2797.html (accessed February 2, 2011).

Akudovich, Velentin, Uladzimir Matskevitch and Hennadz Samusevich. In RFE/RL program for Belarus (Radio Svaboda), *Pratksii Akzent.* (August 14 2007), transcript available at: http://www.svaboda.org/textarticlesprograms/pragueaccent/2007/8/6C7AEF49-3584-4CD8-AE07-9AC0DA19D92A.html (accessed August 15, 2007).

Alekhnovich, Andrei. "Novaâ kompaniâ, starye problemy," March 20, 2007. Available at: www.dwworld.de/dw/article/0,2144,2397689,00.html (accessed August 7, 2011).

———. "V Belarusi ustanovleny limity na potreblenie èlektroènergii dlâ promyšlennyh predpriâtij." *Deutsche Welle* program for Belarus, *Belorusskaya Khronika*, September 17, 2008. Transcript available at: http://www.dw-world.de/dw/article/0,2144,3650767,00.html (accessed September 25, 2008).

Alesin, Aleksander. "Konec azhiotazha." *Belorusy i Rynok*, No. 25/960, July 4, 2011. Available at: http://belmarket.by/ru/132/30/10427 (accessed February 10, 2012).

———. "Ob iskrennosti družby kreditorov s dolžnikami," *Belorusskii Rynok* No. 37/417, September 17, 2000.

———. "Za mesto pod solncem nado platit'." *Belorusy i Rynok*, No. 41/625, October 18, 2004. Available at: www.br.minsk.by/index.php?id=397§ion=6361 (accessed March 14, 2012).

Ankudo, Elena. "Èks-predsedatel' zloupotrebil. Bez uŝerba." *Belgazeta*, No. 13/634, March 24, 2008. Available at: www.old.belgazeta.by/20080331.13/020040751 (accessed March 12, 2012).

———. "Triškin 'Naftan.'" *Belgazeta*, No. 2/521, January 16, 2006. Available at: http://old.belgazeta.by/20060116.2/020380751.

———. "'Vinovataâ â...' No tol'ko pered prezidentom." *Belorusskaya Gazeta*, No. 2/470, 17 January, 2005. Available at: http://dossier.bymedia.net/index.php?option=com_apressdb&view=publications&layout=entry&id=38706 (accessed March 12, 2012).

Aparina, Tatiana. "Trojnaâ udavka dlâ Belorussii." Levaya Rossiya, available at: www.left.ru/2004/3/aparina102.html (accessed May 9, 2011).

Associate Press Worldstream. (February 19, 2004).

Auty, Richard M. and Alan H. Gelb. "Political Economy of Resource-Abundant States." In *Resource Abundance and Economic Development*, ed. R. M. Auty, Oxford: Oxford University Press, 2001.

Azarov, Dmitrii. "Rossiâ i Belorussiâ podelât neftedollary po-bratski." *Kommersant*, January 20, 2011. Available at: http://kommersant.ru/doc/1570244 (accessed March 1, 2012).

Babanin, Olexander, Vladimir Dubrovskyi, and Olexyi Ivaschenko. *Ukraine: The Lost Decade and the Coming Boom*. Kyiv: CASE Ukraine 2002.

Balmaceda, Margarita M. "At a crossroads: the Belarusian-Russian energy-political model in crisis." In *Belarus and the EU—Ways Ahead*, edited by Sabine Fischer, 79–91. Chaillot Papers Series. Paris: Institute for Security Studies of the EU, 2009.

———. "Belarus as a transit route: domestic and foreign policy implications." In *Independent Belarus: Domestic Determinants, Regional Dynamics and Implications for the West*, edited by Margarita M. Balmaceda, James Clem and Lisbeth Tarlow, 162–196. Cambridge MA: HURI/Davis Center for Russian Studies, distributed by Harvard University Press, 2002.

———. *Belarus: oil, gas, transit pipelines and Russian foreign energy policy*. London: GMB Publishing, 2006.

———. *Energy Dependency, Politics and Corruption in the Former Soviet Union: Russia's Power, Oligarch's Profits and Ukraine's Missing Energy Policy, 1995–2006*. London and New York: Routledge, 2008.

———. "Myth and Reality in the Belarusian-Russian Relationship: What the West must Know." *Problems of Post-Communism* 46, No. 3 (1999): 3–14.

———. *The Politics of Energy Dependency: Ukraine, Belarus and Lithuania Between Domestic Oligarchs and Russian Pressure*. Toronto: University of Toronto Press, 2013.

———. "Russia's Central and Eastern European Energy Transit Corridor: Ukraine and Belarus" in *Russia's Energy Policies: National, Interregional and Global Dimensions*, edited by Pami Aalto, 136–155. Cheltenham: Edward Elgar, 2011.

———. "Some Thoughts on Rents of Energy Dependency, 'Rent-seeking Swamps,' and Political Development: the Ukrainian case in Comparative Perspective," circulated for discussion at the Workshop on Post-Communist Politics and Economics, Harvard University, March 13, 2006. Available at http://www.fas.harvard.edu/%7Epostcomm/papers/ 2005-06/Balmaceda.pdf

———. "Understanding Repression in Belarus." In *The Worst of the Worst: Rogue and Repressive States in the World Order*, edited by Robert Rotberg, 193–222. Washington DC: Brookings Institution, 2007.

Barnatovich, Aleksandr. "Biznes vlasti," *Belorusskaya Delovaya Gazeta* (October 26, 2004), available at http://bdg.press.net.by/2004/10/2004_10_26.1474/1474_7_1.shtml (accessed November 15, 2004).

Beblawy, Hazem and Giacomo Luciani, eds. *The Rentier State, Vol. 2, Nation State and Integration in the Arab World*. London: Croom Helm, 1987.

Beissinger, Michael. "Chernobyl and the Culture of Environmental Irresponsibility." In *Chernobyl: the Event and its Aftermath*, edited by Leonard Berkowitz, Norma Berkowitz, and Michael Patrick. Madison, WI: Goblin Fern Press, 2006.

Belapan, "Sankcii protiv," February 28, 2012 Belarus News. (February 28, 2007), available at: http://naviny.by/rubrics/inter/2007/02/28/ic_news_259_267457 (accessed on March 14, 2007).

Beltransgaz's official website. Available at: www.btg.by.

Bergasse, Emmanuel, Agata Loskot and Elena Rakova,"CIS Role for the EU Energy Supply." In Centre for Social and Economic Research, *The economic aspects of the energy sector in CIS countries*, 172- 207 (Economic Papers 327, June 2008). Brussels: European Commission, 2008.

Bergasse, Emmanuel, Agata Łoskot and Elena Rakova," Strategies and Policy Options for the Energy Sector Development in the CIS Region." In Centre for Social and Economic Research, *The economic aspects of the energy sector in CIS countries*, 208- 258. (Economic Papers 327, June 2008). Brussels: European Commission, 2008.

Berger, Ethan S. "Belarusian Weapons Exports: A Possible Source of Laundered Funds?" *Belarusian Review*, Vol. 15, No. 4 (2003) available at: www.belreview.cz/articles/2702.html (accessed May 19, 2011).

Berkowitz, Leonard, Norma Berkowitz, and Michael Patrick, eds. *Chernobyl: the Event and Its Aftermath*. Madison, WI: Goblin Fern Press, 2006.

"Bez iliuzii." *Belorusskii Rynok*, No. 35/619, September 6, 2004.

Bischof, Gunter. *Austria in the First Cold War, 1945–55: the leverage of the weak*. Basingstoke: Macmillan; New York: St. Martin's Press, 1999.

BISS Trends, No. 2 (January–March 2010).

Bjaljacki, Ales. In RFE/RL program for Belarus (Radio Svaboda), *Ekzpertiza Svabody* ["Ci z"Jawljajecca prysud Galinje Zhurawkovaj i jejnym suwdzjel"nikam pjeramogaj pravasudz"dzja?"] (February 9, 2005), available at: www.svaboda.org/content/Transcript/792257.html (accessed June 25, 2008).

Blokhin, A. In Tatiana Manenok, "Premeri ne dogovorilis." *Belorusskii Rynok*, No. 16/600, (April 28, 2004).

Bogdankevich, Stanislav. In RFE/RL program for Russia (Radio Svoboda), *Vremia Gostei* (January 9 2007), transcript available at: www.svobodanews.ru/Transcript/2007/01/09/20070109200031117.html (accessed October 8, 2007).

"Borovskij uhodit ot otveta." *Belorusskii Partizan*, February 14, 2008. Available at: www.belaruspartisan.org/bp-forte/?page=100&news=22220 (accessed December 10, 2010).

Brownlee, Jason. *Authoritarianism in an Age of Democracy*. Cambridge, UK: Cambridge University Press, 2007.

Bruce, Chloe. "Friction or fiction? The gas factor in Russian-Belarusian relations." *Chatham House Briefing Paper* REP BP 05/01 (May 2005). Available at: www.riia.org/pdf/research/rep/BP0501gas.pdf.

Carney, Christopher P. "International Patron-Client Relationships: A Conceptual Framework." *Studies in Comparative International Development*. Vol. 24, No. 2 (June 1989), 42–55.

Centr Palitynchaj Adukacyi. "Sostojanie i obozrimye perspektivy belorussko-rossijskih otnoshenij." In *Zbornik analitichikh dakladow*, 56–72. Minsk, 2007.

Centre for Social and Economic Research, *The economic aspects of the energy sector in CIS countries* (Economic Papers 327, June 2008). Brussels: European Commission, 2008.

Chaudhry, Kiren Aziz. *The Price of Wealth: Economies and Institutions in the Middle East*. Ithaca, NY: Cornell University Press, 1997.

Chelnok, Ivan. "Belarussiâ oplatit' staryj gaz cenami za novyj," Gazeta.ru, November 5, 2002.

Cherp, Aleh, Alexios Antypas, Vicken Cheterian and Mykhaylo Salnikov. *Environment and Security. Transforming Risks into Cooperation. The Case of Eastern Europe: Belarus-Moldova-Ukraine*. Belley, France: Nouvelle Gonnet 2007 for UNEP, 2007.

Chizh, Yurii. Interview in *Forbes* (Russian Edition, July 24, 2008). Cited and partial selections reproduced in: http://allminsk.biz/content/view/1772 (accessed August 12, 2008).

Chubrik, Aliaksandr. In RFE/RL program for Belarus (Radio Svaboda), *Ekspertiza Svabody*, "Jakija perspektyvy w bjelaruskaj naftavaj galiny?" (June 7, 2007) transcript available at: www.svaboda.org/content/Transcript/758628.html (accessed July 15, 2007).

———. In RFE/RL program for Belarus (Radio Svaboda), *Ekspertiza Svobody,* "Pryvatyzacyja Bjelarusi – usjo na prodazh rasjejcam?", May 20, 2008. Transcript available at: www.svaboda.org/content/Transcript/1116684.html.

Clement, Hermann. "Die Energiewirtschaft der GUS." *Arbeiten aus dem Osteropa-Institut Munchen,* No. 151, March 1992.

Cooper, Andrew F. and Timothy M. Shaw, eds. *The Diplomacies of Small States: Between Vulnerability and Resilience.* Houndmills, Basingstoke: Palgrave Macmillan, 2009.

Corrales, Javier. "Oil and Regime Change in Venezuela" (unpublished paper, Amherst College, 2007) (available at https://www.amherst.edu/media/view/48033/original/Polarization%2BDecember%2B2007.pdf (accessed December 8, 2010).

Dan, Georgij, and Sergej Sacuk. "Neftânye vojny: Osobye sčetyi." *BGD DSP,* July 3, 2002. Available at: http://who.bdg.by/data/docs/dsp-06-06.htm (accessed March 10, 2012).

Daneiko, Elena, "Den'gi millionerov dolžny ležat' v banke." Deustche Welle program for Belarus, available at: www.dw-world.de/dw/article/0,2144,2430697,00.html (accessed August 8, 2007).

Danilovich, Alex. *Russian-Belarusian Integration: Playing Games Behind the Kremlin Walls.* Aldershot, England: Ashgate, 2006.

———. "Understanding Politics in Belarus." *Demstar Research Report 3 (2001).* Available at: www.demstar.dk/papers/Belarus.pdf (accessed November 30, 2010).

Dashkevich, Valerii F. *Jenergeticheskaja zavisimost' Belarusi: posledstvija dlja jekonomiki i obshhestva.* Minsk: Lovginov/Fond imeni Fridrikha Eberta, 2005.

Dawson, Jane I. *Eco-nationalism: Anti-nuclear Activism and National Identity in Russia, Lithuania and Ukraine.* Durham: Duke University Press, 1996.

Dempsey, Judy. "Gazprom Wins Belarus Victory." *International Herald Tribune,* December 29, 2005.

Deyermond, Ruth. "The State of the Union: Military Success, Economic and Political Failure in the Russia-Belarus Union." *Europe-Asia Studies,* Vol. 56, No. 8 (2004): 1191–1205.

"Direktiva No. 3 Prezidenta Respubliki Belarus' ot 14 iulia 2007 g." Available at: www.government.by/index?page=rus_gdoc_prog21122007_5&mode=printable&lang=ru (accessed December 11, 2008).

"Dlja chago Raman Abramovich pryljataw u Mjensk?" *Nasha Niva,* No. 37/539, October 11 2007. Available at: http://nn.by/?c=ar&i=11982 (accessed March 12, 2012).

Doig, Alan and Stephanie McIvor. "Corruption and its control in the developmental context: an analysis and selective review of the literature." *Third World Quarterly,* Vol. 20, No. 3 (1999): 657–676.

Drakokhrust, Yurii, and Dmitri Furman. "Belarus and Russia: the Game of Virtual Integration." In *Independent Belarus: Domestic Determinants, Regional Dynamics and Implications for the West,* edited by Margarita M. Balmaceda, James Clem and Lisbeth Tarlow, 232–255. Cambridge MA: HURI/Davis Center for Russian Studies, distributed by Harvard University Press, 2002.

Dovnar, Vadim. "Glava "Belneftehima" postradal za rossijskuû neft," *Kommersant,* No. 93/3669, May 31, 2007. Available at: www.kommersant.ru/doc.aspx?DocsID=770151 (accessed August 14, 2008).

Dubnov, Vadim. In RFE/RL program for Belarus (Radio Svaboda), *Pratskii Akzent,* October 10, 2006 ("Klubok bjelaruskaj zamjezhnaj palityki: Rasjeja, Ewropa, "treci s"vjet,"), transcript available at: www.svaboda.org/PrintView.aspx?Id=774535.

Dubrovskiy, V. et al. "Reform Driving Forces in a Captured State." First draft. CASE Ukraine, 2004.

Dunning, Thad. *Crude Democracy: Natural Resource Wealth and Political Regimes.* Cambridge: Cambridge University Press, 2008.

———. "Endogenous Oil Rents." *Comparative Political Studies,* Vol. 43, No. 3 (2010): 379–410.

Dynko, Andrei. "Njakljajew hocha stac" bol"sh ruskim za Lukashenku." *Nasha Niva,* No. 41/687, November 3, 2010.

"Dypljamatychnaja vajna – nje pjerashkoda ekspartu naftapraduktaw," February 29, 2012, available at: www.svaboda.org/content/article/24500170.html (accessed March 12, 2012).

East European Gas Analysis, available at: www.eegas.com/fsu.htm#Tab (accessed May 15, 2011).

Econstats. "IMF Commodities." available at: www.econstats.com/commsp/commspaa1.htm (accessed December 1, 2010).

Eke, Steven and Taras Kuzio. "Sultanism in Eastern Europe: The Socio-Political Roots of Authoritarian Populism in Belarus." *Europe-Asia Studies*, Vol. 52, No. 3 (2000): 523–547.

Energosoft database. Available at: http://energosoft.info/news2004.html.

Energy Charter Secretariat. *Gas Transit Tariffs in Selected Energy Charter Countries.* Brussels: 2006. Available at: www.encharter.org/index.php?id=127 (accessed February 24, 2009).

Ermak, Dmitrij. "Davajte bez daval'cev?" *Naviny.by.* (January 30, 2010), available at: http://naviny.by/rubrics/economic/2010/01/30/ic_articles_113_166433 (accessed August 15, 2010).

Eurasian Home Analytical Research. "Country Profile Belarus." Available at: www.eurasianhome.org/xml/t/databases.xml?lang=en&nic=databases&country=24&pid=142 (accessed November 27, 2007).

Europa Publications, ed. *Eastern Europe, Russia and Central Asia 2004* . London: Routledge, 2003 .

European Bank of Reconstruction and Development. *Transition Report,* London: European Bank for Reconstruction and Development, various years.

Feduta, Aleksandr. *Lukashenko: Političeskaâ Biografiâ.* Moscow: Referendum, 2005.

———. "Skazka o zolotoj skumburii." *Belorusskaya Delovaya Gazeta.* (April 9, 1998), available at: www.bdg.press.net.by/1998/98_04_09/fish.htm (accessed July 15, 2008).

Filin, Valjery. "Cjen", vjedaj svajo mjesca!," *Svaboda*, September 21 2007, available at http://gazetaby.com/index.php?sn_nid=8718&sn_cat=37 (accessed August 13, 2008).

Fortescue, Stephen. *Russia's Oil Barons and Metal Magnates: Oligarchs and the State in Transition.* Basingstoke Hampshire: Palgrave MacMillan, 2007.

Freedom House. "Belarus country report." *Nations in Transit.* (2008), available at: www.freedomhouse.org/template.cfm?page=47&nit=446&year=2008 (accessed December 27, 2010).

Fritz, Verena. *State-building: a comparative study of Ukraine, Lithuania, Belarus and Russia.* Budapest and New York: Central European University Press, 2007.

Gaddy, Clifford C., and Barry W. Ickes. "Resource Rents and the Russian Economy." *Eurasian Geography and Economics,* Vol. 46, No. 8 (2005): 559–583.

———. Russia's Virtual Economy. Washington DC: Brookings Institution, 2002.

Gaz i neft'. Ėnergeticheskii biulleten', March 15, 2000. Accessed via the Internet Securities, Inc. portal, available at www.securities.com.

"Gazprom and Beltransgaz ink gas supply and transit contract for 2006." Available at Gazprom's website: http://www.gazprom.ru/eng/news/2005/12/18593.shtml.

"Gazprom Not Happy with Belarus." *RFE/RL*, (November 12, 2002).

Geddes, Barbara. "What Do We Know About Democratization after Twenty Years?" *Annual Review of Political Science.* Vol. 2 (1999), 115–144.

"Glava gosudarstva v celom odobril proekt Koncepcii ènergetičeskoj bezopasnosti Belarusi do 2020 goda," available at: www.president.gov.by/press34523.html#doc (accessed December 16, 2008).

Global Witness. "It's a Gas – Funny Business in Turkmen-Ukraine Gas Trade" (April 2006). Available at http://www.globalwitness.org/reports/show.php/en.00088.html.

"Gor`kij nefteklapan." *Oil Market Weekly (Nefterynok),* March 18, 2002. Accessed via the Internet Securities, Inc. portal, available at www.securities.com.

"Gosudarstvennaâ kompleksnaâ programma modernizacii osnovnyh proizvodstvennyh fondov Belorusskoj ènergetičeskoj sistemy, ènergosbereženiâ i uveličeniâ doli ispol'zovaniâ v respublike sobstvennyh toplivno-ènergetičeskih resursov na period do 2011 goda." *Ukas.* No. 575, (November 15, 2007). Available at: http://energosoft.info/news2007.html (accessed March 19, 2012).

Gotovskij, Aleksandr. "Ekonomičeskoe razvitie Belarusi v kontekste rosta cen na importiruemye energoresursy i mirovogo finansovogo krizisa" in *Èkonomiki ènergetičeskaâ i finansovo-ekonomičeskaâ situaciâ v Belarusi: Materialy kruglogo stola.* Minsk: Fond im. Fridrikha Eberta, 2009.

Goujon, Alexandra. *Révolutions politiques et identitaires en Ukraine et Bielorussie (1998–2008).* Paris: Belin, 2009.

Grib, Natalia. "Ivan Bambiza otkroet cello ... Prezidentu." *Belorusskaya Gazeta,* No. 21/438, (May 31, 2004).

Grivach, Aleksandr. "Minsk nachal platit'." *Vremia Novostei,* (November 11, 2002).

Guillet, Jerome. "Gazprom's Got West Europeans Over a Barrel." *The Wall Street Journal,* (November 8, 2002).

Gurr, Ted Robert. *Why Men Rebel.* Princeton: Princeton University Press, 1970.

Haiduk, Kiryl. "Social Contract: a Conceptual Framework." In *Social Contracts in Contemporary Belarus,* edited by Kiryl Haiduk, Elena Rakova and Vital Silitski. Sankt Petersburg: Nevskij Prostor, 2009.

Haiduk, Kiryl and Aleksandr Chubrik. "Specifikaciâ ponâtiâ 'social'nyj kontrakt' primenitel'no k Belarusi." Rabočij Material Issledovatel'skogo centra IPM WP/09/02 (2009).

Haiduk, Kiryl, Elena Rakova and Vital Silitski, eds. *Social Contracts in Contemporary Belarus.* Sankt Petersburg: Nevskij Prostor, 2009.

———. "Editor's Foreword." In *Social Contracts in Contemporary Belarus,* edited by Kiryl Haiduk, Elena Rakova and Vital Silitski. Sankt Petersburg: Nevskij Prostor, 2009.

Handel, Michael. *Weak States in the International System.* London: Frank Cass, 1981.

Harrison, Hope M. *Driving the Soviets up the Wall.* Princeton: Princeton University Press, 2003.

Hellman, Joel S. "Intervention, Corruption and Capture - the Nexus between Enterprises and the State." *Economics of Transition* 8, No. 3 (2000): 545–576.

———. "Winners Take all: The Politics of Partial Reform in Postcommunist Transitions." *World Politics* 50, No. 2 (1998): 203–234.

Hellman, Joel S. Geraint Jones and Daniel Kaufmann. "Seize the State, Seize the Day: State Capture, Corruption and Influence in Transition." World Bank Policy Research Working Paper No. 2,444 (September 2000), available at: www.colbud.hu/honesty-trust/hellman/pub01.PDF (accessed June 7, 2006).

Hermitage Capital Management. "How should Gazprom be managed in Russia's national interests and the interests of its shareholders?" Moscow: Hermitage Capital Management, 2005.

Human Rights Watch Report 1998: Belarus, available at: www.hrw.org/worldreport/Helsinki-04.htm (accessed March 14, 2007).

Huntington, Samuel. *The Third Wave: Democratization in the Late Twentieth Century.* Norman: University of Oklahoma Press, 1991.

Hutchcroft, Paul. "Booty Capitalism: Business-Government Relations in the Philippines." In *Business and Government in Industrializing Asia,* edited by Andrew McIntyre. Ithaca: Cornell University Press, 1994.

Interfax by. "Igry oligarhov: futbol," February 25, 2008. Available at: www.interfax.by/article/19322 (accessed May 20, 2011).

International Atomic Energy Agency. *Energy supply options for Lithuania: a detailed multi-sector integrated energy demand, supply and environmental analysis.* Vienna: IAEA, 2004.

International Monetary Fund (IMF). "Country Report Belarus." No. 06/316, Washington D.C: International Monetary Fund, 2006.

———. "Country Report Belarus." No. 07/311, Statistical Appendix. Washington D.C: International Monetary Fund, 2007. Available at: www.imf.org/external/country/blr/index.htm?type=9998.

———."Country Report Belarus." No. 10/16. Washington D.C: International Monetary Fund, 2011. Available at: www.imf.org/external/country/blr/index.htm?type=9998 (accessed February 5, 2011).

———. "Rapid growth in Belarus: puzzle or not?" (June 2005). Available at: www.imf.org/external/pubs/ft/scr/2005/cr05217.pdf.

———. "Republic of Belarus: Selected Issues." *Country Report,* No. 05/217, Washington D.C: International Monetary Fund, 2005.

Institut Privatizatsii i Menedzhmenta, *Belarus Macroeconomic Forecast,* various issues. Available at: www.research.by/eng/bmf.

———. *Belarus: Makroekonomicheskii Prognoz (BMF),* various issues. Available at: http://www.research.by/rus/bmf/.

———. *Ezhemesiachnii obzor ekonomiki Belarusi (BMER),* various issues. Available at: http://research.by/rus/bmer.

———. *Monitoring Infrastrukturi Belarusi,* various issues. Minsk: IPM, 2010. Available at: www.research.by/rus/bim.

———. "Rost cen na gaz: novye vyzovy dlâ belorusskoj èkonomiki." (Minsk, IPM, 2007, available at http://www.research.by/rus/wp/2007/) (Accessed January 30, 2008).

Interfax. "V Belarusi prompredpriâtiâ, ne vypolnâûŝie zadaniâ po ènergosbereženiû, budut bol'še platit' za èlektroenergiu i gaz." (June 23, 2011), available at: www.interfax.by/news/belarus/94515 (accessed March 19, 2012).

International Energy Agency, *Energeticheskaya Politika Rossii. Obzor 2002.* Paris: OECD/IEA, 2002.

———. *Energy Statistics of Non-OECD Countries.* Paris: OECD, various years.

———. *Russian Electricity Reform.* Paris: OECD/IEA, 2005.

———. *Russian Energy Survey 2002.* Paris: OECD/IEA, 2002.

———. *Ukraine Energy Policy Review 2006.* Paris: OECD/IEA, 2006.

Ioffe, Grigory. "Understanding Belarus: Belarusian Identity," *Europe-Asia Studies* 55, No. 8 (2003): 1241–1272.

———. "Understanding Belarus: Economy and Political Landscape." *Europe-Asia Studies* 56, No. 1 (2004): 85–118.

———. *Understanding Belarus and how Western Foreign Policy Misses the Mark.* Lanham, Md.: Rowman and Littlefield, 2008.

Ioffe, Grigory and Viachaslau Yarashevich. "Debating Belarus: An Economy in Comparative Perspective." *Eurasian Geography and Economics,* 52, No. 6 (2011): 750–779.

"Iskliuchenie iz pravila – Belarus." *Belorusskaya Gazeta,* No. 14/482 (April 11, 2005).

"Istochnik rosta i zavisimosti." *Belorusskii Rynok,* No. 12/647 (March 28, 2005).

Ivanter, Aleksandr and Mikhail Alekslevich. "Ranennyj zubr." *Ekspert,* No. 14 (April 11, 2011), available at: www.expert.ru.

Ivashkevich, Stas. "Belarus' i neft': po trope kontrabandistov." *Navyny,* December 22, 2011. Available at: http://naviny.by/rubrics/economic/2011/12/22/ic_articles_113_176255/ (accessed March 13, 2012).

Janeliunas, Tomas, and Arunas Molis. "Energy Security of Lithuania: Challenges and Perspectives," *Research Journal of International Studies* 5 (2006): 10–34.

Johnston, Michael. "The Political Consequences: a Reasessment," *Comparative Politics,* Vol. 18, No. 4 (1986): 459–477.

Jones Luong, Pauline, and Erika Weinthal. "Rethinking the Resource Curse: Ownership Structure, Institutional Capacity, and Domestic Constraints." *Annual Review of Political Science* 9 (2006): 241–263.

Kalinkina, Sveatlana. In RFE/RL program for Belarus (Radio Svaboda), *Ekzpertiza Svobody,* "Pavinjen zastacca al"bo Shejman al"bo Viktar Lukashenka" (September 12, 2007), available at: www.svaboda.org/content/Transcript/761925.html (accessed July 3, 2008).

Kalinovskaja, Tatiana. "Dlâ latanià dyr," *Belorusy i Rynok,* No. 49/784, December 24, 2007. Available at: www.br.minsk.by/index.php?article=31775&year=2007 (accessed March 12, 2012).

Karbalevich, Valer. *Aleksandr Lukashenko. Politicheskii Portret.* Moscow: Partizan, 2010.

———. "Belorusskie Novosti." January 2008. Cited in Aleksandr Mishin. "Luščee v Venezuele." *Ezhednevnik,* January 18, 2008.

———. "Mâgkaâ adaptaciâ." *Svobodnie Novosti Plus,* January 9, 2008.

———. RFE/RL program for Belarus (Radio Svaboda), *Ekspertiza Svabody* ("Chamu praces pryvatyzacyi njeprazrysty?") (October 8, 2007), available at: www.svaboda.org/content/Transcript/762906.html (accessed October 15, 2007).

———. RFE/RL program for Belarus (Radio Svaboda), *Pratskii Akzent,* "Jakija prychyny ekanamichnaga rostu?" (December 29, 2006), transcript available at: www.svaboda.org/content/Transcript/777228.html (accessed May 23, 2011).

Karl, Terry Lynn. *The Paradox of Plenty: Oil Booms and Petro-States.* Berkeley: University of California Press, 1997.

Karnej, Igor. "Rossijskij gaz-2007: Belorussia vzvolnovana." RFE/RL program for Russia (Radio Svoboda), December 31, 2007, available at http://www.svobodanews.ru/Article/2006/12/31/20061231134015550.html (accessed October 10, 2007).

Keohane, Robert O. "The Big Influence of Small Allies." *Foreign Policy* 2 (Spring 1971): 161–182.

Khartia 97. "Rossijskij jekspert nazval poimenno neftjanyh posrednikov v Belarusi." (January 8, 2010), available at: http://admin.charter97.org/ru/news/2010/1/9/25225 (accessed May 13, 2011).

Klishevich, Tikhon. "Gazovaâ vojna zaveršilas'?" *Deutsche Welle,* January 1, 2007. Available at www.dwworld. (accessed January 2, 2007).

———. "Istoriâ bor'ba za 'Beltransgaz'." (November 29, 2006), available at: www.dw-world.de (accessed August 5, 2007).

Koktysh, Kirill. Interview in *Nashe Mnenie* website, November 13, 2006. Available at: www.nmnby.org/pub/0612/13d.html (accessed August 10, 2007).

Korosteleva, Elena A. "Is Belarus a Demagogical Democracy?" *Cambridge Review of International Affairs,* XVI (2003): 527–535.

Kostiugova, Valeria. "Perspektivy uchastija Belarusi v jekspluatacii nefteprovoda Odessa-Brody." *Belarusian Institute for Strategic Studies,* BISS SA 4/2008-EG (2008). Available at: www.belinstitute.eu/images/stories/documents/odessabrody.pdf (accessed October 24, 2008).

Krukov, Valeriy and Arild Moe. "Russia's Oil Industry: Risk Aversion in a Risk-Prone Environment." *Eurasian Geography and Economics,* Vol. 47, No. 3 (2007): 341–357.

Krylovic, Irina. "Razdum'â o drugom investore." *Belorusy i Rynok*, No. 30/ 916, August 16, 2010. Available at: http://belmarket.by/ru/88/65/6887 (accessed March 10, 2012).

———. "Sbyt stoimosti." *Belorusy i Rynok*, No. 35/921, (September 20, 2010), available at: http://belmarket.by/ru/93/65/7312 (accessed September 10, 2010).

Latyshonak, Aleh and Yawhen Miranovich, *Historyia Belarusi ad siariadziny XVIII st. da pachatku XXI st.* Vilnius: Institute of Belarusian Studies, 2010.

Lebedko, Anatoly. "I v vozduh čepčiki brosali." *Narodnaya Volya*, 27 September 1997.

Legina, Polina. "Rossiia garantiruet." *Belorusy i Rynok*, No. 28/963, August 7, 2011. Available at: http://belmarket.by/ru/135/65/10647.

Lenzi, Mark. "Lost Civilization: The Thorough Repression of Civil Society in Belarus." *Demokratizatsia*, Vol. 10, No. 3 (2002): 401–424.

Leshchenko, Natalia. "The National Ideology and the Basis of the Lukashenka Regime in Belarus." *Europe-Asia Studies*, 60, No. 8 (2008): 1419–1433.

Levsina, Irina. "Belorusskuû verhušku vlasti lihoradit." (March 9, 2004), available at: http://charter97.org/bel/news/2004/03/09/beda (accessed June 23, 2008).

Liabiedzka, Anatol (Anatoly Lebedko). In RFE/RL program for Belarus (Radio Svaboda), *Ekzpertiza Svabody* ("Pavinjen zastacca al"bo Shejman al"bo Viktar Lukashenka") (September 12, 2007), www.svaboda.org/content/Transcript/761925.html (accessed July 3, 2008).

Liakhovich, Andrei. "Belarusian Elites – Change and Authoritarian Rule," in *Belarus and the EU—Ways Ahead*, edited by Sabine Fischer. Paris: Institute for Security Studies of the EU, Chaillot Papers Series, 2009.

———. "Palitychny kantekst napjaredadni parljamenckih vybaraw i referendumu." In *Najnowshaja gistoryja bjelaruskaga parljamentaryzmu*. Minsk: Analitychny Grudok, (2005), available at: http://kamunikat.fontel.net/www/knizki/palityka/parlamentaryzm/index.htm (accessed June 20, 2008).

———. "Razvitie situacii v Belarusi vo vtoroj polovine maja i nachale ijunja 2011 g.: osnovnye sobytija i kommentarii." Unpublished report distributed by electronic mail list, Center for Political Education, Minsk (June 2011).

———. "Razvitie situacii v Belarusi vo vtoroj polovine nojabrja 2011 goda: osnovnye sobytija i kommentarii." Unpublished report distributed by email, Center for Political Education, Minsk (December 2011).

Lindner, Rainer. "The Lukashenka Phenomenon." In *Independent Belarus: Domestic Determinants, Regional Dynamics and Implications for the West*, edited by Margarita M. Balmaceda, James Clem and Lisbeth Tarlow, 77–108. Cambridge MA: HURI/Davis Center for Russian Studies, distributed by Harvard University Press, 2002.

Lo, Shiu-hing. "Bureaucratic Corruption and its Control in Macao." *Asian Journal of Public Administration*, Vol. 15, No. 1 (1993): 32–58.

Lukashenko, Aleksandr. In Irina Khalip, "Lukašenko prigrozil Rossii razryvom otnošenii." *Novaya Gazeta*, October 2, 2006. Available at: www.novayagazeta.ru/data/2006/75/09.html (accessed October 1, 2009).

Magaloni, Beatriz. "Credible Power-Sharing and the Longevity of Authoritarian Rule." *Comparative Political Studies* 41 (2008): 715–742.

Makarov, Igor, interview in *Gas Matters,* (November 2002), 12–16.

Manaev, O, A. Sosnov, V. Dorokhov, and I. Burina. "Povyšenie roli nezavisimyh social"nyh issledovanij i `ekspertnyh setej v Belarusi." *Novosti NISEPI*, No. 1/31, (March 2004) 11, available at: www.iiseps.org/bullet04-1.html (accessed May 24, 2011)

Manenok, Tatiana. "Aprobacija severnogo tranzita." *Belorusy i Rynok*, No. 28/914, July 26, 2010. Available at: http://belmarket.by/ru/86/65/6680 (accessed July 28, 2010).

———. "Benzinovyj signal." *Belorusskii Rynok*, No. 43/678, November 8, 2005. Available at: www.br.minsk.by/index.php?article=25999&year=2005 (accessed March 12, 2012).

———. "Derzhat' sosedej 'v tonuse,'" *Belorusy i Rynok*, No. 15/950, April 18, 2011. Available at: http://belmarket.by/ru/122/65/9564 (accessed May 1, 2011).

———. "Deševogo gaza nužno vse bol'še." *Belorusy i Rynok*, No. 51/635, December 27, 2004. Available at: www.br.minsk.by/index.php?article=23797 (accessed February 7, 2009).

———. "'Družbu ne počinât." *Belorusy i Rynok*, No. 46/781, December 3, 2007. Available at: www.br.minsk.by/index.php?article=31605 (accessed March 12, 2012).

———. "Ènergobezopasnost' poka nedostižima." *Belorusskii Rynok*, No. 34/669, September 5, 2005. Available at: www.br.minsk.by/index.php?article=25542&year=2005 (accessed March 12, 2012).

———. "Ènergobezopasnost' v range prioriteta." *Belorusy i Rynok*, No. 34/769, September 10 2007. Available at: www.br.minsk.by/index.php?article=30965&year=2007 (accessed March 12, 2012).

———. "Gaz kak instrument nesocialističeskogo realizma," *Belorusskii Rynok*, No. 1/534, January 13, 2003, available at: http://www.br.minsk.by/index.php?article=11476 (accessed May 21, 2011).

———. "Gazovye nedogovorennosti." *Belorusskii Rynok*, No. 40/926, October 25, 2010. Available at: www.belmarket.by/ru/98/65/7730 (accessed March 12, 2012).

———. "Gazprom" zaâvil o neželanii sozdavat' novye tranzitnye mošnosti na territorii Belarusi." *Belorusskii Rynok*, No. 26/661, July 11, 2005. Available at: www.br.minsk.by/index.php?article=25205 (accessed May 20, 2011).

———. "Izbiratel'nyj podhod." *Belorusy i Rynok*, No. 4/788, January 28, 2008. Available at http://www.br.minsk.by/index.php?article=31998&year=2008 (March 12, 2012).

———. "Kto ostalsa na trube?" *Belorusy i Rynok*, No. 36/671, September 19, 2005. Available at: www.br.minsk.by/index.php?article=25626 (accessed March 12, 2012).

———."Litva namerena ostat'sâ c atomnoj ènergiej." *Belorusskii Rynok*, No. 42/677, October 31, 2005. Available at: www.br.minsk.by/index.php?article=25987&year=2005 (accessed March 12, 2012).

———. "Mifičeskij dolg." *Belorusskii Rynok*, No. 15/650, April 18, 2005. Available at: www.br.minsk.by/index.php?article=24609 (accessed March 12, 2012).

———. "Načinaem s podorožania." *Belorusy i Rynok*, No. 1/936, January 10, 2011. Available at: http://belmarket.by/ru/108/65/8458 (accessed March 10, 2011).

———. "Ne myt'em, tak katan'em." *Belorusy i Rynok*, No. 20/955, May 30 2011. Available at: http://belmarket.by/ru/127/60/9983 (accessed March 1, 2012).

———. "Nestabil'naâ neftânka." *Belorusy i Rynok*, 30/765, (August 13, 2007), www.br.minsk.by/index.php?article=30803 (accessed August 29, 2007).

———. "Nevygodnyj èksport." *Belorusy i Rynok*, No. 8/743, February 26, 2007. Available at: www.br.minsk.by/index.php?article=29634&year=2007 (accessed May 15, 2007).

———. "NPZ balansiruût," *Belorusy i Rynok*, No. 33/919, September 6, 2010. Available at http://belmarket.by/ru/91/65/7142 (accessed September 15, 2010).

———. "Obstoâtel'stva prižali." *Belorusy i Rynok*, No. 36/820, 8 September, 2008. Available at: www.br.minsk.by/index.php?article=33527&year=2008 (accessed March 12, 2012).

———. "Oplata v ramkah politsoglašenij." *Belorusy i Rynok*, No. 13/848, March 30, 2009. Available at: www.belmarket.by/ru/20/65/1342/# (accessed May 26, 2011).

———. "Plata za komfortnyj zapusk EEP." *Belorusskii Rynok*, No. 48/985, December 19, 2011. Available at: http://www.belmarket.by/ru/155/65/12371/Плата-за-комфортный-запуск-ЕЭП.htm?tpl=93 (accessed August 4, 2013).

———. "Podarok s rasčetom." *Belorusskii Rynok*, No. 15/650, April 18, 2005. Available at: www.br.minsk.by/print.php?article=24602 (accessed March 12, 2012).

———. "Podstegnet neftânoj stimul." *Belorusy i Rynok*, No. 20/804, May 19, 2008. Available at: www.br.minsk.by/index.php?article=32808.

———. "Političeskij barter." *Belorusskii Rynok*, No. 20/655, May 23, 2005.

———. "Po ŝadâŝej stavke." *Belorusskii Rynok*, No. 3/787, January 21, 2008. Available at: www.br.minsk.by/index.php?article=31941 (accessed March 12, 2012).

———. "Poslednij argument." *Belorusskii Rynok*, No. 7/591, February 23, 2004.

———. "Potoki s političeskoj logistikoj." *Belorusy i Rynok*, No. 15/799, April 14, 2008. Available at: www.br.minsk.by/index.php?article=32589 (accessed June 16, 2008).

———. "Prem'ery ne dogovorilis'." *Belorusskii Rynok,* No. 16/600, April 28, 2004. Available at: http://br.minsk.by/index.php?article=21701.

———. RFE/RL program for Belarus (Radio Svaboda), *Ekzpertiza Svabody*, ("Kryzys z pastawkami rasjejskaga gazu w Bjelarus"), (November 4, 2002), transcript available at: http://archive.svaboda.org/programs/bel-rus/2002/11/20021104175816.asp (accessed April 25, 2008).

———. RFE/RL program for Belarus (Radio Svaboda), *Ekspertiza Svabody*, ("Jakija perspektyvy w bjelaruskaj naftavaj galiny?"), (June 7, 2007), transcript available at: www.svaboda.org/content/Transcript/758628.html (accessed July 15, 2007).

———. "Sozdaetsâ valûtnyj goseksporter." *Belorusskii Rynok*, No. 20/655, 23 May, 2005. Available at: http://www.br.minsk.by/index.php?article=24867&year=2005 (accessed March 12, 2012).

———. "Spor isčerpan." *Belorusskii Rynok*, No. 42/626, October 25, 2004.

———. "Stavka na povyšenie," *Belorusskii Rynok*, No. 34/669, September 5, 2005.

———. "Starye problemy dlâ novogo pravitel'stva." *Belorusy i Rynok*, No. 12/796, March 24, 2008. Available at: http://www.br.minsk.by/index.php?article=32430 (accessed March 14, 2012).

———. "Tol'ko po rinočnoi stojmosti." *Belorusskii Rynok*, No. 5/690, February 6, 2006.

———. "Torg za lgoty." *Belorusy i Rynok*, No. 4/890, January 25, 2010. Available at: http://belmarket.by/ru/62/65/4780 (accessed January 28, 2010).

———. "Valjutnaja blagodat'." *Belorusy i Rynok*, No. 13/197, March 31, 2008. Available at: www.belmarket.by/index.php?article=32499.

———. "Valûtnye donory slabeût." *Nashe Mnenie*, November 27, 2008. Available at http://www.nmnby.org/pub/0811/27j.html (accessed December 11, 2008).

———."Valutnyj ručej." *Belorusy i Rynok*, No. 1/785, January 8, 2008. Available at: www.br.minsk.by/index.php?article=31801 (accessed March 12, 2012).

———. "Vse resursy v odnih rukah." *Belorusy i Rynok*, No. 13/698, April 3, 2006. Available at: www.br.minsk.by/index.php?article=27180 (accessed May 20, 2011).

———. "Vtoraâ otklûčka.' *Belorusskii Rynok*, No. 6/590, February 16, 2004. Available at: www.br.minsk.by/index.php?article=20999&year=2004.

———. "'Zolotaâ akciâ vvedena na častnom predpriâtii." *Belorusskii Rynok*, No. 19/654, May 16, 2005. Available at: www.br.minsk.by/index.php?article=24836.

Marples, David R. *Belorus. A Denationalized Nation*. Amsterdam: Harwood Academic Publishers, 1999.

———. "Color Revolutions: The Belarus case." *Communist and Post-Communist Studies*, 39, No. 3 (2006): 351–364

———. "The Energy Dilemma of Belarus: The Nuclear Power Option." *Eurasian Geography and Economics* 49, No. 2 (2008): 215–227.

———. "Lukashenka removes KGB Chief." *Eurasia Daily Monitor*, 4, No. 140 (July 19, 2007). Available at: www.jamestown.org/edm/article.php?article_id=2372302. (accessed August 9, 2007).

———. "The Political Consequences of the Chernobyl Disaster in Belarus and Ukraine." In *Chernobyl: the Event and Its Aftermath*, edited by Leonard Berkowitz, Norma Berkowitz, and Michael Patrick, 53–67. Madison, WI: Goblin Fern Press, 2006.

———. "Surge in Nuclear Power Projects Imperils Belarusian Program." *Eurasia Daily Monitor* 7, No. 150, (August 4, 2010).

Marples, David R. and Uladzimir Padhol. "The Opposition in Belarus: History, Potential and Perspectives." In *Independent Belarus: Domestic Determinants, Regional Dynamics and Implications for the West*, edited by Margarita M. Balmaceda, James Clem and Lisbeth Tarlow, 55–76. Cambridge MA: HURI/Davis Center for Russian Studies, distributed by Harvard University Press, 2002.

Marples, David R. and Marilyn J. Young, eds. *Nuclear Energy and Security in the Former Soviet Union*. Boulder, Colorado: Westview, 1997.

Martin, Terry. *The Affirmative Action Empire: Nations and Nationalism in the Soviet Union, 1923–1939*. Ithaca, NY: Cornell University Press, 2001.

Martinovich, Viktor. "Aleksandr Fadeev: Ne budet nikakogo akta." *Belorusskaya Gazeta*, No. 24/492, June 20, 2005. Available at: http://old.belgazeta.by/20050620.24/340190142 (accessed March 14, 2012).

———. "Kupi okop. Cena – 200 mln USD." *Belorusskaya Gazeta*, No. 24/747, June 21, 2010. Available at: www.belgazeta.by/20100621.24/010030141 (accessed May 20, 2011).

———. "Souz po umolčaniû." *Belorusskaya Gazeta*, No. 29/497, July 25 2005. Available at: http://old.belgazeta.by/20050725.29/010280142 (accessed March 12, 2012).

Martynau, Alexander. "The Non-Accidental President." *Transitions Online* (December 2, 2010), available at: www.tol.org/client/article/21998-the-non-accidental-president.html (accessed December 20, 2010).

Matyas, Aleksandr. "Analiz osobennostei, faktorov i istochnikov ekonomicheskogo rosta v Respublike Belarus." In *Nashe Mnenie* (2005), available at: www.nmnorg.by (accessed June 13, 2008).

Mazeikiu Nafta. Available at: www.nafta.lt (accessed May 9, 2009).

Mazurkevich, Marina. "Drova, torf, veter i solnce" (February 4, 2007). Available at: www.dw-world.de/dw/article/0,2144,2337240,00.html (accessed March 10, 2007).

Milov, Vladimir and Boris Nemtsov. *Nezavisimyj èkspertnyj doklad. Putin i Gazprom*. Moscow: Novaya Gazeta, 2008.

Mishin, Aleksandr. "Luščee v Venezuele." *Ezhednevnik*, January 18, 2008.

Mitrova, Tatiana. "Natural Gas in Transition: systemic reform issues." In *Russian and CIS Gas Markets and their Impact on Europe*, edited by Simon Pirani. Oxford and New York: Oxford University Press for the Oxford Energy Institute, 2009.

Moravcsik, Andrew. "Introduction: Integrating International and Domestic Theories of International Bargaining." In *Double-Edged Diplomacy: International Bargaining and Domestic Politics*, edited by Peter B. Evans, Harold K. Jacobson, and Robert D. Putnam, 3–42. Berkeley: University of California Press, 1993.

Morrison, Kevin. "Oil, Nontax Revenue, and Regime Stability." *International Organization*, Vol. 63, No. 1 (2009): 107-138.

"Mozyrskij NPZ ocenili v 1,1 mlrd. dollarov." *Belorusy i Rynok*, No. 36/671, September 19, 2005. Available at: www.br.minsk.by/index.php?article=25645 (accessed March 12, 2012).

Muntean, Ion. "The first consequences of the third energy package for the Republic of Moldova." Eastern Partnership Community, available at: www.easternpartnership.org/publication/economy/2011-12-21/first-consequences-third-energy-package-republic-moldova (accessed March 15, 2011).

Nekrasevic, Nikolai. "Kto prodvigaet belorusskie interesy v Venesuele?" In *Narodnaya Volya,* March 24, 2010. Available at: www.nv-online.info/by/58/10/11091 (accessed May 21, 2011).

Nemtsov, Boris. "Rossiâ stroit narodnyj kapitalizm v soûze s nami, no bez nas." *Belorusskaya Delovaya Gazeta,* September 25, 1997.

Nezavisimyj institut social'no-èkonomičeskih i političeskih issledovanij (NISEPI). *Novosti NISEPI,* various issues, 2004–2011. Available at: http://www.iiseps.org.

———. Report of December 21–31, 2010 national poll, available at: www.iiseps.org/data10-431.html (accessed May 5, 2011).

Novozhilova, Elena, "Fradkov podtolknet èkonomičeskie reformy v Belarusi?," *Narodnaya Volya,* No. 103–104, June 29, 2007. Reprinted in http://naviny.by/rubrics/economic/2007/06/20/ic_articles_113_151527/ (accessed July 15, 2007).

Novozhilova, Elena, and Vadim Sekhovich. "Gazavat' po-gazpromovskii," *Belorusskaya Delovaya Gazeta,* November 6, 2002.

"Novyj Invjestor prishjel v Bjelarus" Javno nje za ugljem." (September 21, 2007), available at: http://expertby.org/article/investor-ne-za-uglem/ru/ (accessed November 25, 2007). Also reprinted in http://kurt-bielarus.livejournal.com/531016.html (accessed May 26, 2011).

Omonbude, Ekpen J. "The Transit Oil and Gas Pipeline and the Role of Bargaining: A Non-Technical Discussion." *Energy Policy,* Vol. 35, No. 12 (2007): 6188–6194.

Panchenko, Sergei. "Podkovernye šagi ili bor'ba s korrupciej." Deutsche Welle program for Belarus, (May 30, 2007) available at: www.dw.de/dw/article/1/0,,2569596,00.html (accessed March 12, 2012).

Panjushkin, Valerij and Mihail Zygar'. *Gazprom: Novoe russkoe oruzhie.* Moscow: Zakharov, 2008.

Pavel, F. and A. Chukhai. *Ukrainian Gas Imports: Towards secure and economically reasonable transactions.* IER Policy Paper 12, Kiev (2006), available at: http://ier.org.ua/papers en/ v12 en.pdf as cited in *Ukraine Analyse,* No. 50 (2009).

Pavel, F. and E. Rakova. "Improving Energy Efficiency in the Belarusian Economy – an Economic Agenda," GET Policy Paper (Minsk, 2005).

Pikulik, Alexei. "Comparative Pathways of Belarus and Ukraine (1991–2007)." PhD. Dissertation, Political Science, European University Institute, 2010.

Pilibaytite, Vaida. *Nuclear Energy Discourses in Lithuania and Belarus.* MSc thesis. Budapest: Central European University, 2010.

Pilloni, John R. "The Belarusian-Russian Joint Defense Agreement." *The Journal of Slavic Military Studies,* Vol. 22, No. 4 (2009): 543–548.

Pirani, Simon. *Ukraine's Gas Sector.* Oxford: Oxford Institute for Energy Studies, 2007. Available at: http://209-20-84-91.slicehost.net/assets/2009/2/3/Ukraine_s_Gas_Sector.pdf (accessed March 20, 2012).

Pontis Foundation. "The Regime Change(s): Survey of Current Trends and Development in Belarus. Summer 2007." Available at: www.nadaciapontis.sk/tmp/asset_cache/link/0000017223/Pontis%20Survey%20The%20Regime%20Change(s).pdf (accessed October 15, 2008).

Portnikov, Vitalii. "Krasnaja metka." *Belgazeta,* No. 43/766, November 1, 2010. Available at: http://belgazeta.by/20101101.43/010032841 (accessed March 18, 2012)

Postanovlenie Soveta Ministrov Respubliki Belarus' No. 1680, December 2004. Available at: http://pravo.by/webnpa/text_txt.asp?RN=c20401680 (accessed November 9, 2008).

Praneviciute, Jovita. "Security and Identity in Belarus: How Securitization of National Identity Defines Foreign Influence." Paper presented at the 2008 *Convention of the Association for the Study of Nationalities*, Columbia University, New York, April 10–12, 2008.

Prime-TASS. "Belorusskoe OOO 'Trajpl' planiruet v avguste pererabotat' po 29,4 tys t pošlinnoj i bespošlinnoj rossijskoj nefti" (August 2, 2010), available at: www.advis.ru/cgi-bin/new.pl?6329AF4C-AD2F-254D-9CCD-AC86C83F3584 (accessed May 20, 2011).

Projekt Budgeta Respubliki Belarus'. Minsk, various years.

Przeworski, Adam and Fernando Limong. "Modernization: Theories and Facts." *World Politics*, Vol. 49, No. 2 (1997): 155–183.

Puglisi, Rosaria, "Clashing Agendas? Economic Interests, Elite Coalitions, and Prospects or Co-operation between Russia and Ukraine," *Europe-Asia Studies*, Vol. 55, No. 6 (2003): 827–845.

Putman, Robert D. "Diplomacy and Domestic Politics: The Logic of Two-Level Games." *International Organization*, 42 (1988): 427–460.

Radnitz, Scott. "The Color of Money: Privatization, Economic Dispersion, and the Post-Soviet Revolutions." *Comparative Politics*, Vol. 42, No. 2 (2010): 127–146.

Rakova, Elena. "Analiz ènergetičeskoj i èkologičeskoj situacii v Belarusi s točki zreniâ perspektiv èkonomičeskoj celesoobraznosti i èkologičeskoj bezopasnosti," available at http://research.by/pdf/wp2010r10.pdf (accessed May 19, 2011).

———. "Ènergetičeskij sektor Belarusi: povyšaâ èffektivnost'." Working Paper WP/10/04, Institut Privatizatsii i Menedzhmenta, Minsk, 2010, available at: www.research.by (accessed September 9, 2010).

———. "Energetičeskij sektor: sokraŝenie renty." In *Belorusskij Ežegodnik 2009*, 282–290. Minsk: BISS, 2010.

———. "Kakaâ ènergetičeskaâ bezopasnost' nužna Belarusi?" *Nashe Mnenie*, July 6, 2005. Available at: http://nmnby.eu/news/analytics/367.html (accessed March 14, 2012).

———. Participation in round table on "Belorusskaâ èkonomičeskaâ model." (July 6, 2005), *Nashe Mnenie*, available at: http://nmnby.eu/news/discussions/2280.html (accessed March 12, 2012).

———. "Reformy administrativnymi metodami." *Nashe Mnenie*, March 14, 2007. Available at: http://nmnby.eu/news/analytics/892.html (accessed March 19, 2011).

———. "Rossijsko-belorusskie ènergetičeskie raznoglasiâ glazami predprinimatelej," *Nashe Mnenie*, March 21, 2007. Available at: http://nmnby.eu/news/analytics/900.html (accessed May 21, 2011).

———. "Tarifi i lgoti: kto pobedit?," (June 1, 2007), published in *Nashe Mnenie*, available at www.nmnby.by.

"Ravnenie na Belarus." *Oil Market Weekly* (September 9, 2002). Accesed via the Internet Securities, Inc., portal, available at: www.securities.com.

Reisinger, William M. *Energy and the Soviet Bloc: Alliance Politics After Stalin*. Ithaca: Cornell University Press, 1992.

Reppert, John C. "The Security Dimension in the Future of Belarus." In *Independent Belarus: Domestic Determinants, Regional Dynamics and Implications for the West*, edited by Margarita M. Balmaceda, James Clem and Lisbeth Tarlow, 256–269. Cambridge MA: HURI/Davis Center for Russian Studies, distributed by Harvard University Press, 2002.

Republic of Belarus. Ministry of Statistics and Analysis Database, available at: http://belstat.gov.by.

———. Ministry of Statistics and Analysis. *Foreign trade of the Republic of Belarus. Statistical abstracts* (Minsk: yearly).

———. Presidential ukase 291 of July 7, 2003 in "O dopolnitel'nyh merah gosudarstvennoj podderžki futbol'nyh klubov."

———. Ministry of Statistics and Analysis. *Foreign trade of the Republic of Belarus'. Statistical abstracts* (Minsk: yearly).

———. *Social'no-ekonomicheskoe polozhenie Respubliki Belarus'* (monthly statistical survey) various months, January–July 2010.

———. Sovet Bezopasnosti Respubliki Belarus', *Postanovlenie Sovbeza No. 1 "O razvitii atomnoj ènergetiki v Respublike Belarus'"* (January 31, 2008), available at: http://law.sb.by/647 (accessed March 12, 2012).

———. Strategii razvitiâ ènergetičeskogo potenciala Respubliki Belarus'. Postanovlenie Soveta Ministrov Respubliki Belarus', available at: http://www.pravo.by/webnpa/text.asp?start=1&RN=C21001180.

Republic of Moldova, National Agency for Energy Regulation (ANRE). "Monitoring rynka." Available at: www.anre.md (accessed July 15, 2010).

Reuters. "Russia, Belarus oil supply talks breakdown-agency" (January 6, 2010), available at: www.reuters.com/article/2010/01/06/russia-belarus-oil-talks (accessed March 12, 2012).

RFE/RL Newsline, September 21, 1998.

RFE/RL program for Belarus (Radio Svaboda), *Ranishni zhyvy efir,* heard live on November 19, 2010, available at http://www.svaboda.org.

Richer, Thomas. "The Political Economy of Regime Maintenance in Egypt: Linking External Resources and Domestic Legitimation." In *Debating Arab authoritarianism: dynamics and durability in non-democratic regimes*, edited by Oliver Schlumberger, 177–194. Stanford, CA: Stanford University Press, 2007.

Rico, Maite. "Los papeles de las FARC acusan a Chávez." *El Pais* (May 10, 2008), available at: www.elpais.com/articulo/internacional/papeles/FARC/acusan/Chavez/elpepuint/20080510elpepiint_6/Tes (accessed May 21, 2011).

Romanchuk, Yaroslav. "The Belarusian Republic. Genesis, Results and Perspectives of the Neo-Planned Economy." Unpublished manuscript (October 2007).

———. "Belarus: perestrojka ili perezagruzka?," *Evrazijskij Dom*, July 25, 2007. Available at: www.eurasianhome.org/xml/t/expert.xml?lang=ru&nic=expert&pid=1181&s=00x020fxtaznt53qngmjxe45 (accessed August 13, 2008).

———. "Degradaciâ monopolista. Kak »Belneftehim« tanet na dno belorusskuu èkonomiku."(April 7, 2002), available at http://liberty-belarus.info/content/view/449/46 (accessed July 15, 2008).

———. "Do gazovogo armageddona poka daleko." *Belorusskaya Gazeta,* No. 28/496, July 18, 2005. Available at: www.belgazeta.by/20050718.28/040260240 (accessed March 18, 2012).

———. Deutsche Welle program for Belarus, December 26, 2006. Heard live on www.dw-world.de (accessed December 26, 2006).

———. "Kormiaschie Belarusi." *Belgazeta* No. 39/609, October 1, 2007. Available at: www.belgazeta.by/20071001.39/040150241 (accessed November 15, 2007).

———. "MVF rasskrivaet sekret." *Belorusskaya Gazeta*, No. 17/497 (July 11, 2005).

———. "Nado chasche vstrechat'sia: Putina i Lukashenka vnov potianula drug k druga." *Belorusskaya Gazeta,* No. 2/369 (January 20, 2003).

———. RFE/RL Program for Belarus (Radio Svaboda), *Ekspertiza Svobody* (February 13, 2008). Transcript available at: http://www.svaboda.org/content/Transcript/977620.html (accessed July 8, 2008).

———. "V strane slučilsa bum." *Belorusskaya Gazeta*, No. 8/486, May 9, 2005. Available at: http://old.belgazeta.by/20050509.18/010160212/ (accessed March 12, 2012)

Rublev, Andrei. "Naš benzin zadeševo ne prodaetsia." *Svobodnie novosti plius,* No. 42/282, October 22, 2008.

Rublevic, Roman. "V 'liderah' po korrupcionnosti - upravdelami prezidenta." *Belorusskii Partizan,* October 25, 2008. Available at: www.belaruspartisan.org/bp-forte/?page=100&backPage=6&news=6159&newsPage=0 (accessed August 18, 2008).

"Rukovoditel' gruppy kompanij 'Trajpl' Urij ČIŽ: Zaderžaniâ ne bylo! Menâi prosto priglašali v prokuraturu!" *Konsomolskaya Pravda,* June 1, 2007. Available at: http://kp.by/daily/23911.4/144804 (accessed October 15, 2010).

Russian Federation. Office of the Prime Minister. Official website of the Prime Minister of the Russian Federation, available at: http://premier.gov.ru/premier/press/ru/5347/print/ (accessed May 21, 2011).

———. *Rossiâ v cifrah. Oficial'noe izdanie. Federal'naâ služba gosudarstvennoj statistiki.* Moscow, 2008.

Sabonis-Chafee, Theresa. "Power Politics: National Energy Policies and the Nuclear Newly Independent States of Armenia, Lithuania and Ukraine." Ph.D. dissertation, Political Science, Emory University, 1999.

Sahm, Astrid. *Transformation im Schatten von Tschernobyl. Umwelt- und Energiepolitik im gesellschaftlichen Wandel von Belarus und der Ukraine.* Munster: Lit Verlag, 1999.

Sahm, Astrid, and Kirsten Westphal. "Power and the Yamal Pipeline." In *Independent Belarus: Domestic Determinants, Regional Dynamics and Implications for the West,* edited by Margarita M. Balmaceda, James Clem and Lisbeth Tarlow, 270–301. Cambridge MA: HURI/Davis Center for Russian Studies, distributed by Harvard University Press, 2002.

Satsuk, Sergei. "Ne ukral, no vsë ravno vinoven," *Ezhednevnik,* March 28, 2008.

Savelev, Vitalii. *RFE/RL* program for Belarus (Radio Svaboda), "'Gazpram' zajawljaje, shto, pastawljajuchy gaz u Bjelarus," zajmajecca dabrachynnas"cju," September 14, 2002. Transcript reprinted at http://www.ucpb.org/?lang=bel&open=206.

Sawyer, John E. "Natural gas prices impact nitrogen fertilizer costs," available at: http://www.ipm.iastate.edu/ipm/icm/2003/4-14- 2003/natgasn.html (accessed October 23, 2008).

Scherbo, Ivan. "Tranzit: hlopotno, no očen' vygodno." *Ekonomika Belarusi* 4 (2010). Available at www.belarus-economy.by (accessed March 1, 2012).

Sekhovich, Vadim. "'Belorusskaya promyshlennost': v novyi god s novymi khvorami." *Belorusskaya Delovaya Gazeta,* December 29, 1997.

———. "1991–2006. Itogi. Gazovaya otrasl'." October 30, 2006. Available at: www.gazetaby.com/index.php?&sn_nid=3380&sn_cat=34 (accessed August 15, 2008).

———. "1991–2006. Itogi. Neftânaâ i neftepererabatyvaûŝaâ otrasl'." October 30, 2006. Available at: www.gazetaby.com/index.php?&sn_nid=3380&sn_cat=34) (accessed August 15, 2008).

———. "Skrytaâ storona neftânogo protivostoâniâ," *Ezhednevnik,* January 10, 2010. Available at: www.ej.by/news/companies/2010/01/10/skrytaya_storona_neftyanogo_protivostoyaniya.html (accessed March 10, 2012).

———. "200 samyh uspešnyh i vliâtel'nyh biznesmenov Belarusi-2011," *Ezhednevnik* (February 13, 2012), available at: www.ej.by/news/companies/2012/02/13/200_samyh_uspeshnyh_i_vliyatel_nyh_biznesmenov_belarusi-2011___.html (accessed March 6, 2012).

———. "Zalozhniki truby," *Belorusskaya Delovaya Gazeta,* March 29, 1999.

Selivanova, Irina. "Èkonomičeskaâ integraciâ Rossii i Belorussii i ee vliânie na razvitie narodnogo hozâjstva Belorussii." In *Belorusiâ i Rossiâ: Obšestva i Gosudarstva,* edited by D. E. Furman. Moscow: Prava Cheloveka, 1998.

Sheremet, Pavel. RFE/RL program for Belarus (Radio Svaboda), *Ekzpertiza Svobody* ("Barac"bawladnyh klanaw i adstawki w KDB"), (July 18, 2007), transcript available at: www.svaboda.org/content/Transcript/760013.html (accessed July 10, 2008).

———. RFE/RL program for Belarus (Radio Svaboda), *Pratskii akzent*, (November 11, 2011), audio file available at www.svaboda.org (heard live on November 11, 2010).

Shiells, Clinton R. "VAT Design and Energy Trade: The Case of Russia and Ukraine." *IMF Staff Papers*,Vol. 52, No. 1 (2005): 103–119.

Shoemaker, Christopher C. and John Spanier. *Patron-client Relationships*. New York: Praeger, 1984.

Shushkevich, Stanislau. Declarations in RFE/RL program for Belarus (Radio Svaboda) (December 22, 2010), transcript available at: www.svaboda.org/content/article/2256316.html (accessed December 22, 2010).

Silitski, Vital. "From Social Contract to Social Dialogue: Some Observations on the Nature and Dynamics of Social Contracting in Modern Belarus." In *Social Contracts in Contemporary Belarus*, edited by Kiryl Haiduk, Elena Rakova and Vital Silitski, 157–159. Sankt Petersburg: Nevskij Prostor, 2009.

Silitski, Vitali. "The Tsar and his Boyars," *Transitions Online* (June 7, 2004), available at: www.tol.org/client/article/12212-the-tsar-and-his-boyars.html?print (accessed March 18, 2012).

———. "Preempting Democracy: The Case of Belarus," *Journal of Democracy*, Vol. 16, No. 4 (2005): 83–97.

———. "The State, Elections, and the Opposition." In *Belarus and the EU—Ways Ahead*, edited by Sabine Fischer, 25–36. Chaillot Papers Series. Paris: Institute for Security Studies of the EU, 2009.

Siriprachai, Somboom. "Rent-Seeking Activities in Developing Countries: A Survey of Recent Issues." (1994) Available at: ftp://econ.tu.ac.th/class/archan/SOMBOON/my%20discussion%20Papers (accessed March 1, 2006).

Smith, Benjamin. "Life of the Party: Origins of Regime Breakdown and Persistence Under Single-Party Rule," *World Politics*, 57, No. 3 (2005): 421–451.

———. *Hard Times in the Lands of Plenty: Oil Politics in Iran and Indonesia*. Ithaca NY: Cornell University Press, 2007.

Snyder, Timothy. *Bloodlands: Europe Between Hitler and Stalin*. New York: Basic Books, 2010.

Social'no-èkonomičeskoe položenie Rossii. Moscow, various issues.

Socor, Vladimir. "Belarus Warns It May Cancel Its Subsidies to Russia." *Eurasia Daily Monitor*, 4, No. 17, (January 24, 2007). Available at: www.jamestown.org/edm/article.php?article_id=2371830 (accessed July 13, 2007).

Sokrat Research. *Belarus: country report 2008*. Available at: http://investory.com.ua/community/diary/1208/sokrat_daily__december_11__2008/ (accessed December 11, 2008).

"Sredneevropejskaâ cena za gaz," available at: www.terra.md/ru/news/moldova/gaz.cena.moldova.filat/default.aspx (accessed August 26, 2010).

Statisticheskoe obozrenie, No. 3 (2008).

Stein, Janice Gross. "The Political Economy of Security Agreements: The Linked Costs of Failure at Camp David." In *Double-Edged Diplomacy: International Bargaining and Domestic Politics*, edited by Peter B. Evans, Harold K. Jacobson, and Robert D. Putnam, 77–103. Berkeley: University of California Press, 1993.

Stern, Jonathan, Simon Pirani, and Katja Yafimava. *The Russo-Ukrainian gas dispute of January 2009: a comprehensive assessment. NG27*. Oxford: Oxford Institute for Energy Studies, 2009. Available at: www.oxfordenergy.org/pdfs/NG27.pdf (accessed June 1, 2010).

———. *The April 2010 Russo-Ukrainian gas agreement and its implications for Europe. NG42*. Oxford: Oxford Institute for Energy Studies, 2010. Available at: www.oxfordenergy.org/pdfs/NG42.pdf (accessed July 1, 2010)

Sukhovenko, Stephan. "Oligarhi Lukašenko. Ili na čem zarabatyvaût samye bogatye lûdi Belarusi?" Kompromatby. Last modified March 12, 2012. http://kompromatby.com/node?page=13.

Suzdaltsev, Andrei. Interview in DW-world, available at: www.dw-world.de (January 1, 2007), transcript available at: www.dw-world.org/dw/article/0,2144,2296562,00.html (accessed February 1, 2007).

Šyrokaŭ, Jaŭhen. "Mit dem Wind: Energiewirtschaft und nachhaltige Entwicklung." *Osteuropa* Vol. 54, No. 2 (2004): 84–95.

Teplov, Leonid. "Obesslavlennaja SLAVNEFT." *Infobank Oil and Gas Monitor,* June 13, 2002.

Titenkov, Ivan (Ivan Tsitsiankow). "Lukašenko nužno projti čerez nezavisimuû èkspertnuû komissiu." *Belorusski Chas,* May 25, 2001. Reprinted in: www.charter97.org/bel/news/2001/05/25/16 (accessed August 21, 2008).

Tomashevskaya, Olga. "Lëgkaâ pobeda," *Belorusskaya Delovaya Gazeta,* November 13 2002.

Transparency International Corruption Perceptions Index 2004. Available at: www.transparency.md/Docs/2004_indicele_perceperii_cor_en.pdf. (accessed March 25, 2008).

Transparency International Corruption Perceptions Index 2006. Available at: www.transparency.lt/new/images/tils_cpi_2006.pdf (accessed March 25, 2008).

"UCP Urges V. Sheiman to Confess Illicit Arms Sales" (March 12, 2002), available at: http://charter97.org/eng/news/2002/03/12/07, (accessed May 19, 2011).

Urban, Aleksei, and Aleksei Nikolskii. "Bez pridannogo. Gotovit'sia Belarus otdat' 'Beltransgaz." *Vedomosti,* (November 25, 2002).

U.S. Census Bureau. Database for Trade in Goods, Belarus. Census.gov. Last modified March 13, 2013. www.census.gov/foreign-trade/balance/c4622.html#2010.

Vandewalle, Dirk. *Libya Since Independence: Oil and State-Building.* Ithaca, NY: Cornell University Press, 1998.

Vernon, Raymond, *Sovereignty at Bay: the Multinational Spread of US Enterprises.* New York: Basic Books, 1971.

Voitovich, Aleksandr. Quoted in Marina Mazurkevich, "Drova, torf, veter i solnce." Deutsche Welle program for Belarus (February 4, 2007), available at: www.dw-world.de/dw/article/0,2144,2337240,00.html (accessed March 10, 2007).

———. In round table "Nakanunie âdernogo vozroždenâ." Debate organized by the Belarusian Institute for Strategic Studies, Minsk (February 29, 2008), available at: www.eurasianhome.org/doc/BISSROUNDTABLENUCLEAR.pdf (accessed March 12, 2012).

von Hirschausen, K. and I. Rumiantseva. "Èkonomičeskye aspekty razvytiâ âdernoj ènergetiki v Belarusi." In *Ènergetika Belarusi: puti razvitiâ,* 85–122. Minsk: IPM, 2006.

Vydrin, Dmytro. Quoted in "Gazovyi kontsortsium. Otsenki ėkspertov," *Gaz i neft'. Ėnergeticheskii biulleten',* July 16, 2002.

Way, Lucan. "Authoritarian State Building and the Sources of Regime Competitiveness in the Fourth Wave: The Cases of Belarus, Moldova, Russia, and Ukraine," *World Politics,* 57 (2005): 231–61.

———. "Deer in Headlights." Paper presented at the Danyliv Seminar in Ukrainian Studies, University of Ottawa, October 2008. Available at: www.ukrainianstudies.uottawa.ca/pdf/P_Danyliw08_Way.pdf (accessed May 21, 2011).

Wendt, Alexander. *Social Theory of International Politics.* Cambridge, UK: Cambridge University Press, 1999.

Wilson, Andrew. *Belarus: The Last Dictatorship in Europe.* New Heaven and London: Yale University Press, 2011.

World Bank, "Belarus: Addressing Challenges Facing the Energy Sector" (June 2006), available at: http://siteresources.worldbank.org/BELARUSEXTN/Resources/BelarusEnergyReview_July 2006- full.pdf (accessed May 26, 2011).

———. "Belarus Energy Sector 1995." Report No. 12804-BY, available at http://www-wds.worldbank.org/external/default/WDSContentServer/WDSP/IB/1995/04/21/000009265_3961008003331/Rendered/INDEX/multi_page.txt (accessed November 8, 2008).

———. "Belarus: window of opportunity to enhance competitiveness and sustain economic growth." *Country economic memorandum on Belarus*, World Bank Report No. 32346-BY, (May 2005) available at: http://siteresources.worldbank.org/INTBELARUS/Resources/328178-1120132035392/1365350-1120132328436/cem_by06_full.pdf (accessed March 15, 2012).

World Development Index Online. Available at http://ddp-ext.worldbank.org/ext/DDPQQ/report.do?method=showReport.

Yafimava, Katja. "Belarus: the domestic gas market and relations with Russia." In *Russian and CIS Gas Markets and their Impact on Europe*, edited by Simon Pirani, 133–169. Oxford and New York: Oxford University Press for the Oxford Energy Institute, 2009.

———. *The June 2010 Russian-Belarusian Gas Transit Dispute: a surprise that was to be expected. NG43.* Oxford: Oxford Institute for Energy Studies, 2010. Available at: www.oxfordenergy.org/wpcms/wp-content/uploads/2010/11/NG43-TheJune2010RussianBelarusianGasTransitDisputeASurpriseThatWasToBeExpected-KatjaYafimava-2010.pdf (accessed March 19, 2012).

———. *Post-Soviet Russian-Belarussian Relationships: The Role of Gas Transit Pipelines*. Stuttgart: Ibidem-Verlag, 2007.

"Začem Rosatom podogrevaet âdernye strasti v Belarusi?" In *Proekt Belorusskoj AES*, available at: http://www.bellona.ru/articles_ru/articles_2010/belarus-aes-rosatom (accessed March 26, 2011).

Zagorskaya, Marina, Vadim Sekhovich and Aleksandr Starikevich. *Belarus. 1991-2006. Itogi*. Minsk: Avtorskii kollektiv, 2008.

Zagorski, Andrei. "Russia's neighbourhood policy." European Union Institute for Security Studies, February 14, 2012, available at: www.iss.europa.eu/publications/detail/article/russias-neighbourhood-policy (accessed March 19, 2012).

Zaiko, Leonid. In Natalia Grigoreva, "V poiskah streločnika," Deutsche Welle program for Belarus (June 1, 2007), www.dw-world.de/dw/article/0,2144,2572385,00.html (accessed July 11, 2007).

———. "Leonid Zaiko: Putin nakazyvaet Lukašenko za tretij srok," *Belorusskii Partizan*, November 14, 2006. Available at: www.belaruspartisan.org/bp-forte/?page=100&backPage=13&news=6704&newsPage=0 (accessed May 13, 2011).

———. "Russia and Belarus: Between Wishing and Reality," *Russia in Global Affairs*, 1, (2006). Available at http://eng.globalaffairs.ru/numbers/14/1003.html (accessed December 4, 2008).

Zaiko, Leonid and Yaroslav Romanchuk. *Belarus' na razlome*. Belgorod, Russia: Belgorodskaya poligrafiya, 2008.

Zhbanov, Sergei. "Bačili voči, šo kupovaly." *Belgazeta*, No. 13/634, March 31, 2008. Available at: http://old.belgazeta.by/20080331.13/040080421 (accessed March 12, 2012).

———. "Kak zaburel naš ugol'." *Belgazeta*, No. 38/608, September 24, 2007. Available at: www.old.belgazeta.by/20070924.38/020470421 (accessed March 14, 2012)

———. "Komu – gaz, komu – pedigree." *Belorusskaya Gazeta*, No. 14/482, April 11, 2005. Available at: http://old.belgazeta.by/20050411.14/020260422 (accessed March 12, 2012).

———. "Nazlo 'Gazpromu.'" *Belgazeta*, No. 39/609, October 1, 2007. Available at: www.old.belgazeta.by/20071001.39/040120421 (accessed March 12, 2012).

———. "S novym gazom," *Belorusskaya Gazeta*, No. 2/470, January 17, 2005. Available at:http://old.belgazeta.by/20050117.2/040050420/ (accessed March 12, 2012).

———. "Souzniki optimistično 'gazanuli'." *Belorusskaya Gazeta*, No. 26/494, July 4, 2005. Available at: http://old.belgazeta.by/20050704.26/040110420/ (accessed March 12, 2012).

———. "'Zolotuû akciû spisali v util'." *Belgazeta*, No. 10/631, March 10, 2008. Available at: http:// http://old.belgazeta.by/20080310.10/010020421 (accessed March 12, 2012).

———. "Ne v brov', a v gaz" *Belorusskaya Gazeta*, No. 41/764, October 18, 2010. Available at: http:// old.belgazeta.by/20101018.41/040090421 (accessed March 12, 2012).

Zinovskyi, Vladimir. In http://www.interfax.by/news/belarus/91626, (April 28, 2011) (accessed March 4, 2012).

Zlotnikov, Leonid. Deutsche Welle program for Belarus, *Belorusskaya Khronika*, December 17, 2007. Heard on www.dw-world.de (accessed December 17, 2008).

———. "Ètapy Transformacii Èkonomiki Belarusi: Problemy i dostiženii." In L. K. Zlotnikov, T. A. Bykova, G. P. Badei and Zh. K. Badei, *Predprinimatelstvo. BSPN. Biznes-sreda*. Minsk: BSPN, 2005.

———. "Faktor nomer 1-Rosssia," *Belorusskii Rynok* No. 16/600, (April 28, 2004).

———. "The Foreign Exchange Crisis in Belarus: its causes and effects." Center for European PolicyAnalysis, (August 1, 2011), available at: www.cepa.org/ced/view.aspx?record_id=315 (accessed March 4, 2012).

———. "Igra v cejtnote." *Belorusy i Rynok*, No. 39/774, October 15–22, 2007. Available at: www.br.minsk.by/index.php?article=31260&year=2007 (accessed March 12, 2012).

———. "Leonid Zlotnikov: Real'no – VVP u nas ne vyros, a upal na 10%." (June 5, 2009), available at www.belaruspartisan.org/bp-forte/?page=102&news=41578 (accessed May 21, 2011).

———. "Podcepili "gollandskuû bolezn'." *Belorusskii Rynok*, No. 17/652, May 2, 2005. Available at: www.br.minsk.by/index.php?year=2005&id=424§ion=7071 (accessed March 20, 2012).

———. "Possibilities for the Development of a Private Economic Sector and a Middle Class as a Source of Political Change in Belarus." In *Independent Belarus: Domestic Determinants, Regional Dynamics and Implications for the West*, edited by Margarita M. Balmaceda, James Clem and Lisbeth Tarlow, 122–161. Cambridge MA: HURI/Davis Center for Russian Studies, distributed by Harvard University Press, 2002.

———. RFE/RL program for Belarus (Radio Svaboda), *Blic-analiz* (January 30, 2012), transcript available at: www.svaboda.org/content/article/24468191.html. Belarus'2011 (accessed March 10, 2012).

———. RFE/RL program for Belarus (Radio Svaboda), *Ekzpertiza Svobody* ("Ci vyratuje dyrektyva #3 bjelaruskuju ekanomiku?"), June 18, 2007. Transcript available at: www.svaboda.org/content/Transcript/758987.html (accessed July 15, 2007).

———. "Vyzhivanie ili integracija?" *Pro et Contra*, Vol. 3, No. 2 (Spring 1998): 81–94.

———. "Žestkaâ posadka," *Belorusy i Rynok*, No. 46/830, November 17, 2008. Available at: www.belmarket. by/ru/2/10/51 (accessed March 14, 2012).

Zygar', Mihail and Urij Svirko. "Člena "sem'i" sdali organam." *Kommersant*, February 13, 2004. Available at: www.kommersant.ru/doc.aspx?fromsearch=02166f53-83e8-4205-b1c5-f31f6ccc266f&docsid=449515 (accessed November 8, 2011).

Index

For Product Safety Concerns and Information please contact our EU representative GPSR@taylorandfrancis.com Taylor & Francis Verlag GmbH, Kaufingerstraße 24, 80331 München, Germany

Batch number: 10370533

Printed by Printforce, the Netherlands